Ford MUSTANG
HOW TO BUILD AND MODIFY

1964 ½ - 1973

Frank Bohanan

MW00785001

CarTech®

CarTech®

CarTech®, Inc.
39966 Grand Avenue
North Branch, MN 55056
Phone: 651-277-1200 or 800-551-4754
Fax: 651-277-1203
www.cartechbooks.com

© 2014 by Frank Bohanan

All rights reserved. No part of this publication may be reproduced or utilized in any form or by any means, electronic or mechanical, including photocopying, recording, or by any information storage and retrieval system, without prior permission from the Publisher. All text, photographs, and artwork are the property of the Author unless otherwise noted or credited.

The information in this work is true and complete to the best of our knowledge. However, all information is presented without any guarantee on the part of the Author or Publisher, who also disclaim any liability incurred in connection with the use of the information and any implied warranties of merchantability or fitness for a particular purpose. Readers are responsible for taking suitable and appropriate safety measures when performing any of the operations or activities described in this work.

All trademarks, trade names, model names and numbers, and other product designations referred to herein are the property of their respective owners and are used solely for identification purposes. This work is a publication of CarTech, Inc., and has not been licensed, approved, sponsored, or endorsed by any other person or entity. The Publisher is not associated with any product, service, or vendor mentioned in this book, and does not endorse the products or services of any vendor mentioned in this book.

Layout by Connie DeFlorin

ISBN 978-1-61325-430-1
Item No. SA212P

Library of Congress Cataloging-in-Publication Data

Bohanan, Frank.
 Ford Mustang performance projects 1964-1/2-1973 / by Frank
Bohanan.
   pages cm
 ISBN 978-1-934709-60-3
 1. Mustang automobile–Motors–Modification. 2. Mustang automobile–Performance. I. Title.

 TL215.M8B63 2014
 629.28'722–dc23

               2013038101

Printed in U.S.A.
10 9 8 7 6 5 4 3 2 1

Title Page: *Upgrading the forward lighting is simple, yet tremendously effective. Much higher output headlamps with vastly improved optics/lenses that are direct replacements for the original sealed-beam units are readily available. Units such as these from Hella look like the original lamps yet function much better.*

Back Cover Photos

Top Left: *One carb per cylinder provides a calibrated fuel charge for each bore but synchronizing the carbs can difficult. The short intake path and direct-acting throttles can provide very good throttle response because there are enough fuel enrichment streams to minimize any bog/hesitation if they are tuned properly. A proper and slow throttle linkage that allows the throttle blades to open more gradually is usually best.*

Top Right: *When rebuilding the Ford 9-inch differential, I use one of the strongest combinations of the center section casting (note the reinforced inner pinion support) and bearing caps (thicker caps with ribs and the side-locking strap/bolt). There's no need to remove the grease on the gear.*

Middle Left: *An aftermarket four-piston caliper is a much better choice compared to original/OEM offerings. This SSBC product also has a quick-change pad feature, which uses simple clips instead of bolts, thus eliminating the need for a tool. It is also much easier to find pads in a variety of compounds compared to older/ OEM parts. A system such as this is clearly a superior choice for both regular street use as well as being able to handle frequent, yet moderate, track use.*

Middle Right: *This front suspension uses reinforced stock-type control arms and strut rods plus upgraded bushings. The springs and shocks have been replaced with more performance-oriented parts and the spring perches were replaced with polyurethane parts. Even though more radical (and costly) options are available, this simple level of upgrading still makes a dramatic improvement in vehicle performance.*

Bottom Left: *This high-performance dash panel provides essential information on the health and running condition of the engine.*

Bottom Right: *A main cap girdle, such as this one from CHP, is a good way to add strength to a stock-type two-bolt main cap block. These girdles strengthen the whole bottom end by tying the main caps together so they reinforce each other. This stabilizes the block and crankshaft, thus allowing higher power levels with far less concern for bearing or part failure.*

CONTENTS

ACKNOWLEDGMENTS

I'd like to thank my family and friends for supporting me during this book project. Due to several other challenges while writing it, they really helped me see it through. I'd also like to thank the many companies that provided information and essential support. Without this support, I would not have been able to write a book that is so comprehensive and valuable.

I'd especially like to thank Ron Bramlett of Mustangs Plus for his vision and efforts to promote the "restomodding" of first-generation Mustangs. They're as close as it gets to being a one-stop shop for this type of car.

Finally, I'd like to dedicate this book to my dad. Even though he was too busy to get heavily involved in hot rodding, his love of cars surely rubbed off on me from a very young age. He didn't live to see this book get finished but he had a lot to do with it getting done.

INTRODUCTION

The purpose of this book is to show you a spectrum of options for improving the performance of each component group in your classic 1964½–1973 Mustang. I specifically show you how to upgrade your Mustang to three distinct levels: the daily driver, the high-performance street car, and the streetable track-day car. By utilizing three specific vehicle types as examples I am able to better tailor the recommended modifications to the intended use of the vehicle. This not only saves time and money for the projects you choose, but it also explains why a particular modification or upgrade was chosen.

In addition, I also show how the job is accomplished when the installation process differs significantly from that of the stock component(s) being replaced.

The daily driver vehicle receives budget-oriented products and modifications for moderately improved driveability, reliability, durability, and performance. The high-performance street car is the next level up. Handling, acceleration, braking, and engine performance are significantly improved by choosing a compatible and complementary set of upgrades. The high-performance street car often evolves into the third vehicle

type, which is the streetable track-day car. This type of car maximizes performance for both the road and track. It is still street legal and practical for limited use on public roads.

I discuss various upgrade options within a given vehicle system and then recommend a typical approach using products that are consistent with it. Throughout this book I take a systems integration approach so the various parts installed are compatible with one another, regardless of their manufacturer. This is meant to achieve the highest performance in the most simple and cost-effective way.

SHORT-BLOCK AND ROTATING ASSEMBLY

When most people think about performance the first thing that usually comes to mind is more power. Improving the performance, control, and driveability of first-generation Mustangs is much more than increasing horsepower and torque.

In this book, I cover what you can do to not only make more power, but also to improve the driveability, reliability, and durability of your engine. I only discuss engines originally offered in first-generation Mustangs and focus this coverage on the Windsor small-blocks and some of the Lima and FE big-blocks. I do not cover common passenger car 6-cylinder engines or rare engines such as the Boss 302, 351, or 429.

In other chapters I also get into engine swaps, crate engines, and the logic for them. For now I assume you're going to modify your existing engine or use a similar short-block. I discuss parts that go on the engine (such as a water pump) as well as the related vehicle components (radiator, fan, etc.). I can't get specific about each possible engine/component so I keep the discussion generic.

I explain various modifications, the types of options available for each, and when they should be used. My general guidelines should help you narrow down your choices to a certain type of part or modification. You still have to do your own research to choose the specific part and manufacturer that's best for you.

Short-Block

With regard to the short-block and its associated components (crankshaft, rods, pistons, etc.) I assume that nothing will be changed for your daily driver unless repairs are needed. Your existing short-block is either in good shape, rebuilt/blueprinted, or replaced with a crate short-block.

Installing a crate engine is often the best option. High-quality machine shop services don't come at a cut-rate price. In many cases a ready-made crate short-block is less expensive than performing all the machine shop procedures, buying parts, and assembling an engine. In addition, the crate engine will suit

The classic Ford Windsor engine is the foundation for many high-performance small-block build-ups. The aftermarket offers a high-performance replacement for every component of the engine. With the right rotating assembly, heads, cam and intake, this Windsor small-block can easily produce 600 hp without power adders. (Photo Courtesy George Reid)

your specific performance goals and your budget. You don't have to wait as long for a crate, plus you benefit from a proven and properly matched combination of components. Manufacturing processes have been validated over hundreds or thousands of prior products.

If you still decide to do a rebuild because you have a numbers-matching engine or want to control the process more closely, make sure you find a reputable machine shop that has positive references from people you trust. (Mike Mavrigian's *Modern Engine Blueprinting Techniques* explains the proper steps for blueprinting and balancing. It will help you understand your options at the machine shop so you can make better decisions.)

For high-performance street applications, a crate engine that produces about 500 hp with 6,500 or less RPM is commonly available. Most stock Windsor/small-blocks and FE 390-ci or larger big-blocks can generate this amount of power and are affordable. When you buy a crate short-block from a reputable source, such as Dart Machinery, Coast High-performance, or Ford Racing, etc., you can be assured of this, whereas a given machine shop may not have the proper knowledge and/or equipment.

Of course, some stock blocks are better rebuild candidates than others. In fact, many builders use the later 5-liter small-blocks rather than the older 289/302 blocks because parts are more plentiful and affordable. These engines also have better materials and machining, plus hydraulic roller cams. A reputable crate-engine or short-block supplier uses the best block because they don't want any returns or warranty claims. They

generally rate their products for a maximum output. They have produced hundreds, if not thousands, of each combination for virtually any use, so they have a huge database of information.

Connecting Rods

A typical short-block for a high-performance street car uses a stock-type iron block and forged I-beam connecting rods. These rods are sufficient for mildly to moderately modified engines up to 500 hp when upgraded with stronger (ARP or similar) rod bolts. With power levels of 550 or more a stronger, forged H-beam rod with precision-ground alignment sleeves and larger, stronger ARP cap screws suffice. This design is far superior to using the shoulders of the rod bolts for locating the connecting rod caps. Solid dowel pins are stronger but aren't usually needed in this situation. You should usually use a full-floating piston pin with a bronze bushing at the small end of the rod with a small and properly located oiling hole for the pin.

Many other variables, such as the materials used, as well as the specific manufacturing methods and processes chosen also must be addressed. Select a crate engine that matches your needs and budget to have these correctly decided for you. Carbureted and EFI engines are offered with a variety of camshaft, cylinder head, induction, and internal part options to match your requirements. If you decide to build a short-block you need to research such factors and discuss them with the machine shop to determine what's best for you.

The bottom line regarding connecting rods is that a simple I-beam

rod with upgraded/ARP bolts generally suffices for a 450-hp small-block (550 hp for big-blocks) with proper balancing, blueprinting, and assembly into a good block. If you're making 600 hp (800 hp for big-blocks) and/or going to higher RPM, you should upgrade to the H-beam rods/cap screws.

For a streetable track-day vehicle with even more power (up to 800 hp with aftermarket small-blocks, 950 hp for big-blocks) you'll likely go right to a solid-doweled H-beam rod. However, if you'll be experiencing much higher RPM a specially

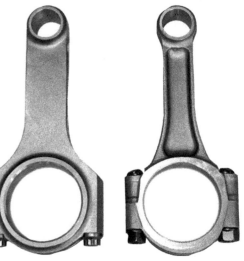

Stock-type cast-steel I-beam rods (right) are suitable for 500 hp or so, but you need to factor in vehicle weight, gearing, RPM, and other aspects. You can upgrade to forged steel for most street applications up to about 800 hp, but if you're building an extreme-performance engine you may upgrade to billet steel or aluminum rods. The H-beam (left) already has many design enhancements and is much stronger than most I-beam designs. It's not always lighter, however. For most of the vehicle applications in this book the H-beam rod provides the best value, strength, and durability.

machined and doweled lightweight I-beam rod may be best. It should be made from a superior alloy (4340 or 300M) steel and upgraded to use stronger cap screws. This setup can be stronger than an H-beam rod yet significantly lighter to perform better at the higher RPM. These rods can often withstand more than 1,000 hp.

If maximum RPM in a small-block with an output of 500 hp or less is expected they can be further machined and lightened. This would likely only be the case where a very light steel rod was needed instead of an aluminum rod. The latter aren't advisable for street or other long-term use due to their tendency to fatigue and stretch with time. Stick with the H-beam for most street and road race uses.

Pistons

Piston selection can be complicated. In addition to choosing pistons that fit and are strong enough, you also have to consider compression ratio and compression height. For a daily driver you'll likely use a cast, stock-replacement piston although there are advantages to upgrading to a hypereutectic piston. The latter are lighter and stronger so they hold up better. They're more dimensionally stable, thus providing a better seal, improved performance, reduced oil consumption, longer life, lower noise (particularly on cold starts), and lower emissions.

Hypereutectic pistons cost a bit more than regular castings but less than forgings. For a moderately modified engine of 400 hp or less they can be a good choice if you don't significantly increase engine output. With significantly more power, you'll likely want to use forged pistons.

The options for forged pistons are numerous, so here are a few of the things to consider when choosing one. Piston material, ring choices, and coatings need to be researched independently because there are so many options available for many engine packages. The correct diameter and compression ratio are most critical, and you need to correctly determine bore size, stroke, and combustion chamber volume. The compression height (where the top of the piston is relative to the top of the bore) and the top shape are piston-specific factors. In general, you want the piston to travel as far up in the bore as possible without creating clearance problems with the valves or the head. The thickness of the head gasket can influence this but it's usually best to have the top edge of the piston at or very slightly below the top edge of the bore.

Compression Ratio

Piston dome shape largely affects compression ratio (CR). Your options are dished, flat-top, or domed. Dished types keep the compression ratio lower and provide the least restriction to mixture flow. If you can get the CR you want with a dished piston it's often the lightest and best choice for in-cylinder motion/mixing. This helps increase the burn rate for better combustion efficiency. With aluminum heads and 93-octane pump gas, a CR of 10:1 to 10.5:1 is generally feasible for street use without the need for octane boosters. This can often be achieved with a mildly dished piston. This CR is about optimal for a street-performance car though generally not possible for a daily driver with stock replacement parts (about 9.5:1 max).

For a streetable track-day car, engines are built with a higher CR for increased output and to prevent preignition/detonation. The CR is really only limited by rules for a particular event or series. Unless you're willing to always use special fuels, octane boosters, etc., the highest CR you should consider for a street car with aluminum heads is about 11.5:1 because the quality of pump gasoline can vary.

To achieve a higher CR you likely need a flat-top or (more likely) a domed piston. Flat-top pistons often need to be "fly cut" to provide extra clearance for the valves, especially when high-lift cams and/or large-diameter valves are used.

Combustion chamber shape and valve location are also factors. Some cylinder heads, such as the Trick Flow Specialties Twisted Wedge

Most cast pistons are only suitable for a mildly modified daily driver; if you're building a high-performance engine they are inadequate. Hypereutectic pistons withstand moderate power levels of 450 hp or so, unless a power adder is involved. At higher power levels and/or with a power adder you need forged pistons, such as these from Probe Industries.

heads, rotate the combustion chambers and slightly change the angle of the valves to unshroud them for better flow. Special pistons are thus needed to properly match the new valve locations.

Pins and Rings

You need to consider piston pin height, especially for a stroker engine. The same bore and stroke can be achieved with a variety of rod length and pin height combinations. Piston speed, rod angles, thrust pressure, and many other parameters must be considered, especially with higher power levels. You also need to decide whether or not the pin will extend into the oil ring groove, which is usually to compensate for an increased stroke. This can result in an additional leak path for oil and combustion pressure.

Oil ring technology has improved greatly to make these leaks less of an issue but it's best to avoid them, particularly for a street-driven and/or road race vehicle. Doing so provides better ring sealing, combustion efficiency, and performance.

With regard to other piston-related items, it's usually good to have a small oil hole under each piston pin boss for extra oiling. In very high-output, high-RPM engines it may even be necessary to install oil jets, which squirt additional oil under each piston to help cool them. In general, a street-driven vehicle should use a production-style ring pack with standard-tension rings. Low-tension rings can be fine for a race car where maximum power is desired and the increase in oil consumption is not a concern. Likewise, neither very thin rings nor reducing the number of rings is a good idea for a street car. Gapless rings can provide a better seal as long as they are properly fitted and installed.

If you use a crate short-block/engine these choices will be made for you. Otherwise you should check with piston and ring manufacturers, the shop you're using, and others for recommendations. In any case, make sure the ring gaps are sized correctly to each individual cylinder and they are properly staggered away from each other on each piston.

Piston pin choices are to use a 1018 steel (or similar) stock replacement pin for a daily driver or a mild street performance car. Move up to a stronger and lighter 8620 steel tapered-wall pin for most street performance applications. For very high-output street performance cars and streetable track-day cars a 52100 bearing steel pin has the lowest weight and highest strength, for about twice the cost of 8620 pins.

Coatings

Using piston coatings is another aspect to consider because it offers anti-friction coating on the piston skirts. This OEM technology allows a reduced piston-to-bore clearance to improve combustion efficiency, especially when the engine is cold. It also reduces noise on initial startup and improves piston stability under virtually all conditions. This coating is generally not very expensive and is particularly appropriate for forged pistons where a larger bore clearance is required because forgings tend to change shape more than cast or hypereutectic pistons. An anti-friction coating can allow you to have the added strength and (sometimes) lighter weight of a forging while not sacrificing too much piston-to-wall clearance and sealing.

Other coatings, such as heat barriers on the piston crown and/or harder coatings for the piston pins, are generally not needed for the engines in this book. Similarly, hard anodized top ring grooves, exotic/ultra lightweight skirt designs,

In addition to the type of aluminum alloy and the overall design and shape of the piston, specialized coatings can also improve performance. An anti-friction coating can be applied to the piston skirt to minimize friction and wear, and also allow for a desirable tighter fit in the bore. (Photo Courtesy Probe Industries)

A raised-pin boss (often required with a stroker) can cut into the oil ring groove, depending on the specific components used (such as rod length) and the amount of increased stroke. This usually results in some additional oil consumption, blowby, and wear. This may be acceptable in some cases but it probably doesn't work for a car that sees any significant street usage. It's possible to avoid this with the proper rod length and a limited RPM range.

special pin locks, gas ports, etc., are also neither advisable nor needed for street cars. Leave them to racers.

Rotating Assembly

The rotating assembly is a crucial part of the engine package. For a daily driver you only need to use what you already have, or its equivalent, if it needs to be rebuilt or replaced. A cast crankshaft along with OEM main caps and balancer do just fine for a near-stock power level. If you're doing a rebuild, some minor cleanup in terms of chamfering the oil holes on the crank and making sure the fillet radii are revised can reduce the potential for stress concentration. If there's no other damage all you really need to do is a balancing job if you intend to keep the engine and further upgrade it.

The stock bearing caps and bolts are fine as long as they're not worn or damaged. You should, however, upgrade to a better bearing set for the mains, rods, and cam just to get the benefit of greater durability.

The cost difference between a "performance" bearing set and a direct-replacement set is minimal but the performance bearings generally have a stronger backing material with added clearance for the crank journal edges as well as thinner/ stronger, yet superior, facing materials. Some silicon-based facings can actually help to micro-polish the crank journals over time to improve performance and longevity.

Additionally, performance bearings generally have longer oil grooves (where applicable) to enhance lubrication while still providing enough bearing surface area to handle the higher loads of high-performance use. They also tend to be more resis- tant to corrosion and embedding of debris, which should improve durability in long-term use. Full competi- tion/race bearings should be avoided because of their much higher cost and their tendency to trade durabil- ity for load capacity.

Block Selection

If you want even more power for a high-performance street car or a streetable track-day car, you almost surely need an aftermarket block for the Windsor small-blocks (except for possibly a 351-based engine with not much more than 650 hp). Aftermar- ket blocks, such as the SHP blocks from Dart Machinery, are capable of handling far more power (more than 600 hp) due to many design changes they incorporate relative to even the best stock blocks.

The Dart SHP small-block (8.2- or 9.5-inch deck heights), for example, is an all-new precision-machined casting with much closer tolerances than the comparable OEM block yet it also retains the ability to bolt on the original (or comparable aftermarket/upgraded) components. Other design changes include thicker decks, cylinder walls, and other sur- faces for strength and improved sealing as well as revised/scalloped coolant passages. All of these increase total coolant flow and equalize the flow at each cylinder. This prevents hot spots and/or insufficient coolant flow, which can reduce power and increase detonation.

The oiling system has also been upgraded to a "priority" design, which directs oil to the main bear- ings first for greater dependability, especially under higher accelera- tions and turning. A really neat fea- ture is that the head bolt holes are all blind, tapped holes that don't open up into the coolant passages. This not only stops potential leaks but it also ensures more accurate torque readings because you don't need any sealant on the head bolts (or studs). Stronger, splayed, four- bolt steel (versus iron) main caps are used on the three center main bear- ing bulkheads to greatly increase strength and stability without the need for a main bearing girdle. The crankshaft is held much more sol- idly and securely, thus reducing flexure and the potential for bearing damage and/or failure.

The Dart SHP blocks also allow for the use of later-model OEM-style roller hydraulic camshafts because the bosses for the "spider" retaining plate as well as provisions for the "dog bones" and roller lifters are pres- ent. Roller hydraulic camshafts can generally provide significantly better performance without the driveability and other tradeoffs of a flat-tappet cam. They also last much longer and are not as noisy, nor should they require periodic adjustment.

Aftermarket blocks, such as Dart's SHP small-block, retain the stock motor mounts and you can still bolt on just about any OEM and aftermarket component, plus you have much, much higher strength, durability, and performance poten- tial compared to stock components. Such a block certainly sets you back a few more pennies than a stock block, but it's the only way to go once you get beyond a certain power and/ or RPM level. Dart also offers even stronger versions (Iron Eagle, etc.) of the small-block Windsor, which are intended for even more extreme and/ or competition use. A lightweight aluminum version is also available (see Chapter 6).

A main cap girdle, such as this one from CHP, is a good way to add strength to a stock-type two-bolt main cap block. These girdles strengthen the whole bottom end by tying the main caps together so they reinforce each other. This stabilizes the block and crankshaft. You can also use beefier ARP main studs instead of bolts to gain further strength and reduce distortion of the block and main caps.

Aftermarket engine blocks, such as this Dart SHP block, are much stronger than OEM Windsor small-blocks. They're made from a superior iron; an aluminum block saves 90 pounds. Both iron and aluminum blocks feature numerous design improvements including thicker decks, four-bolt (splayed) mains with steel caps, and reinforcements. (Photo Courtesy Dart Machinery)

You can stay with a stock block for a big-block engine up to 800 hp or so as long as you're not revving it too high and you upgrade the rotating assembly. However, it's usually best to go with a stroked 351-based crate engine instead of a big-block, even if the latter is what you already have. It's often much harder to find upgraded parts, including crankshafts, for big-block engines (except for the 460). You can make big power with a big-block and it is even easy to do. At higher power levels, costs rise and parts availability drops. A big-block rarely achieves the overall refinement possible with a stroked Windsor.

Crankshaft Selection

For a high-performance street vehicle, you can still use a cast crankshaft if you're using a stock block and the power level is 600 hp or less (800 hp for a big-block). You want to upgrade to a better crank, however, at the higher end of that range.

A crank cast from high-carbon steel is a relatively inexpensive upgrade from a stock cast crank yet it is all you need with a stock block. A stock block will likely fail before the crank, especially if lighter rotating parts (pistons, rods, etc.) are used. For the main caps you can still use the stock caps although you may want to go with stronger studs and nuts from ARP rather than reusing the stock bolts. ARP studs are made from a much stronger material and they distribute the load better within the block while also ensuring a more accurate torque reading. Using premium fasteners, such as those from ARP, protects against damage and failure. Buying a complete engine set from ARP provides these benefits and ensures you have the correct fastener types, sizes, and lengths.

For even more bottom-end strength with a stock small-block you can use a main bearing girdle. This steel brace ties the main caps together to spread the loads that each one encounters. The effect is to reinforce each individual cap. It can really stabilize a stock-block engine with two-bolt main caps; highly rec-

ommended if you're near 600 hp. Big-blocks are a deep-skirt design, which inherently performs a similar bracing function.

Once you've decided on an aftermarket small-block such as the Dart SHP or a big-block to make up to about 600 (small-block) or 800 hp (big-block), you need to think about the type of crankshaft you need. At these power levels a cast crank no longer gets the job done; it's time to step up to a forging. Forgings made from 5140 or 4130 steel are generally good up to about 700 hp, depending on the specific type of use (drag racing versus road racing, etc.).

For higher outputs up to 1,000 hp or so a heat-treated 4340 alloy forging is probably the best way to go. At these high power and/or RPM levels the material used is critical but so are the manufacturing processes and design elements. First make sure you have the right alloy for your situation and then narrow down your options by comparing the type of heat treatment used, the type of hardening (nitriding versus induction, for example), the surface finish and polishing specs of the finished crankshaft, and design features such as the rolling of the fillets and the shape of the counterweights, etc.

As your short-block is being assembled be sure to use an appropriate assembly lube, such as those from Joe Gibbs Driven, Royal Purple, or Red Line. All the bearings (main, rod, cam) should be coated with lubricant to ensure there's no damage on initial engine startup. Engine assemble lube stays put and offers superior protection against wear until the oil pressure rises enough to take over. This lube also blends into the oil and does not clog filters or oil passages.

Balancer Considerations

A final component to consider here is that of the harmonic balancer. Production engines are usually externally balanced, which means the balancer and the flywheel/flexplate must be matched to properly dampen the torsional vibration pulses of the crankshaft and prevent destructive resonances. Internally balanced engines are referred to as having zero or neutral balance; they don't require any imbalance on the balancer or flywheel/flexplate. Ford used mostly 28- and 50-ounce balancing specifications, which relate to the counterweights attached to (or integrated into the design of) the balancer and flywheel/flexplate. Later 5.0L engines, for example, are 50-ounce balance engines while most of the early small-blocks had a 28-ounce balance spec.

Many aftermarket crate engines and short-blocks are neutrally internally balanced so there's no external counterweighting. This requires more precise internal blueprinting and bal-

A stock cast crank (bottom) is fine for a daily driver or a moderately modified street car of 500 hp. Higher-performance street cars can still use a cast crank, but it needs to be an aftermarket cast-steel crank that's much stronger than a stock version. Metallurgy and manufacturing processes have greatly improved to produce a stronger crank. Most cast cranks have a tensile strength of 70,000 to 80,000 psi. They include many special features to further improve strength, durability, and reliability under higher loads. However, if you're building an engine of 600 hp or more you should use a forged-steel crankshaft. Forged cranks (top) handle the dynamic load and resist cracking and failure. The 4130 and 4340 forged-steel cranks have a tensile strength of 125,000 to 145,000 psi.

ancing but it is worth it because the engine is able to be balanced to a finer specification with less total weight, particularly in terms of rotational inertia. This helps improve engine responsiveness and also eliminates the potential for a counterweight to fall off and cause extreme imbalance and vibration, which could result in engine failure. Bottom line? Know the balance spec of your engine and use the appropriate components. They all must match.

For a daily driver an OEM direct-replacement balancer is usually more than sufficient for its mild level of modification. These can be purchased fairly inexpensively at most major parts stores and are a good thing to replace even if you don't need to rebuild or replace your engine. The reason for this is that virtually all stock/OEM balanc-

ers consist of two metal pieces with a rubber layer between them. Over time the rubber can deteriorate to the point where the metal parts shift relative to each other, thus creating an imbalance and the resultant vibration. Because the timing marks for the ignition are also on the outer metal ring such a shift also causes an error in setting the ignition timing. If there are any signs of the rubber layer having cracks or the metal parts having shifted (such as the outer ring being cockeyed so that it appears to wobble while the engine is running), the balancer should be replaced.

The high-performance engines require an upgraded balancer to match any changes made to the short-block and to better handle the higher forces and RPM. In most cases, an upgraded aftermarket balancer of the same basic design as the

OEM part suffices. The Professional Products balancer, for example, is an excellent choice because it has a removable balance weight. The materials and tolerances have been improved to handle higher stresses and speeds plus there are additional timing marks for more accuracy. This particular part complies with SFI specification 18.1, as is required by many sanctioning bodies before a vehicle can participate in their events.

For more serious competition vehicles there are other balancers that use silicon gel, rotating weights, and other proprietary design approaches, which do an even better job of canceling torsional vibrations, making more power, and reducing bearing wear. They are really only necessary with very high power levels and at very high RPM. Their cost is significantly higher and they are usually not designed for long-term/street use and/or harsh climates.

Professional Products makes this balancer, which has a removable 50-ounce imbalance weight. It can be used with an internally or externally balanced engine depending on whether the weight is used. An upgraded balancer, such as this one manufactured to closer tolerances, is better able to handle higher RPM without the outer ring shifting or the rubber layer failing.

unwanted movement. Those made by Energy Suspension also have an internal metal interlock feature to provide additional safety should the polyurethane material fail; these tabs still restrain the engine to a limited range of motion until repairs can be made. In some cases it may be necessary to add a supplementary torque strap or chain to further restrain engine movement

under very high torque conditions. This also helps prevent damage to the polyurethane and serves as a redundant safety feature.

Adjustable mounts can be used to change the location of the engine slightly by lowering it a bit and/or moving it slightly front to back. This can help with handling by locating the engine mass in a more favorable position plus it can also help resolve clearance and packaging issues.

For maximum flexibility, strength, and safety fabricated solid mounts or an engine plate can be used. These are very hard to live with on the street due to the extra noise and vibration they transfer to the rest of the car. The engine plate can also make servicing spark plugs, etc., much more difficult. Realistically, these should only be considered for the streetable track-day car or for true race vehicles.

Adjustable mounts that have some polyurethane cushioning in them are a much better choice for regular street use.

Motor Mounts

Stock rubber motor mounts tend to fail over time by developing cracks, which allow increasing amounts of unwanted engine movement. In extreme cases a mount can fail completely, thus allowing the engine to move to the point of preventing proper function of the clutch (especially with the stock clutch linkage) or even causing a stuck throttle.

On a daily driver with few modifications a new set of stock-type mounts normally do just fine.

For a high-performance street car you want to upgrade to polyurethane mounts, which further reduce

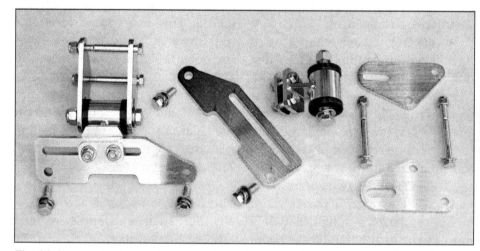

The highest-output street engines benefit from using a more specialized motor mount design, such as this from Ron Morris Performance. They use some polyurethane for cushioning for less noise and vibration in street use. These motor mounts are suitable for engines up to about 1,000 hp. They're adjustable so they provide flexibility as to where the engine sits, thus helping to minimize interference issues while allowing a lower center of gravity for better handling.

CAMSHAFTS, CYLINDER HEADS AND VALVETRAIN

Any internal combustion engine requires the properly timed and correct amounts of three basic things to function: air, fuel, and spark/ignition. Relative to air, the combination of the camshaft, valvetrain, and cylinder heads have the greatest influence over its potential for flow through the engine. Of course, the intake and exhaust systems play a role as well, but their contribution is secondary (see Chapter 3). All early-production Mustangs came equipped with overhead-valve pushrod engines so this chapter covers upgrades applicable to these engines only.

I cannot make specific camshaft/valvetrain recommendations because of the many variables. I can, however, state that a roller hydraulic camshaft almost certainly is the best option for most of the vehicles covered in this book. In the case of a daily driver, it's unlikely a new camshaft or most other valvetrain modifications are cost effective.

The streetable track-day car almost always gets a new camshaft along with other valvetrain modifications. The cylinder heads, camshaft,

and valvetrain are interdependent so they need to be upgraded as a system; they provide a new level of performance. Most vehicles are first modified by upgrading the more readily accessible, bolt-on components such as the intake, exhaust, carburetor, etc.

When all of this has been done the choice is then between leaving the stock engine alone (other than maybe just installing some higher-ratio roller rocker arms), installing a

power adder (nitrous, supercharger, etc.), or taking the engine apart to replace the cam, valvetrain, and/or heads. Installing a new combination requires a much higher level of commitment to performance and requires more skill and more knowledge, though not necessarily more cost. You need to determine your budget and performance goals.

You can get similar performance going either route for a similar setup, though some power adders, such

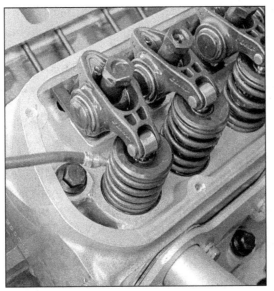

Modifications to the stock valvetrain are necessary when going to higher RPM and they can provide additional performance. The Comp Cams Pro Magnum steel roller rockers shown here are not only stronger to handle the higher valvespring loads associated with a performance camshaft but they also reduce friction and wear compared to stock parts. They free up horsepower and provide much longer life. It's always a good idea to squirt on some oil before installing the valve covers.

as nitrous, are more intermittent in their usability. An "all-engine" solution provides increased performance under all conditions, whenever you want it, but often reaches a point where the engine is too peaky in nature. A mild to moderate performance engine typically relies on bolt-on parts and/or a power adder, with perhaps the only "internal" engine change being the use of higher-ratio roller rocker arms. Once you decide to go beyond moderate performance, power adder or not, you inevitably need to make changes to the internals to safely, reliably, and fully achieve the higher power/performance levels you're after.

Camshafts

Flat-tappet camshafts have no place in a modern street/strip/track engine and solid roller camshafts are suitable only for pure race cars. Today's advanced roller hydraulic cams are the ideal choice for most high-performance street engines. They offer the advantages of roller design and internal hydraulics allow them to self-adjust. You get the best of all worlds. You can run very aggressive camshaft profiles with minimal friction and periodic adjustments are not required.

Modern hydraulic roller camshafts essentially provide racing technology for the street but do so without the need for the continuous maintenance of solid rollers. The latter still have their place with the highest-revving and/or highest-output engines used mostly in drag racing. Hydraulic roller cams are now generating very high flow rates, power, and performance while remaining totally streetable.

Many hydraulic roller camshafts are available for Ford small- and big-block engines. A wide range of manufacturers offer so many combinations for various applications and setups that it's impossible to cover all the relevant combinations. I assume you will use a hydraulic roller camshaft because very few vehicles need a solid roller. Simply put, more lift is better as long as the valves don't contact the pistons. More valve lift is essentially free performance because the engine breathes better with no real consequence in terms of driveability, idle quality, etc.

Older camshafts needed more overlap and duration to provide higher lifts and flow. Advances in roller hydraulic camshaft ramp design make it possible to achieve pretty high lift without the need to also have excessive overlap and duration. In general, you should go for as much lift as you can while still ensuring an adequate margin of clearance so the valves never hit the pistons. This must be verified. Any reputable engine/machine shop knows to check this and a crate engine manufacturer will surely protect against it to prevent returns due to engine damage.

For most street-driven vehicles valve lift in the area of about .550 inch is plenty for some pretty high-power/high-performance levels. The optimum figure, of course, depends on the power level desired, the intended use, the other components being used, and the camshaft timing events (including how it was installed, i.e., advanced, retarded, or straight up). Keep in mind that valve lift (versus cam lobe lift) is affected by the rocker arm ratio used. On an otherwise stock engine going to a higher rocker ratio increases valve lift to improve flow but usually not

enough to cause a problem with clearance.

However, it's best to start with a standard (usually 1.6:1) rocker arm ratio for a new cam. Then, if still more power is desired and it is safely possible to do so, you can easily change to higher-ratio (1.7:1 or so) rockers on the intake and/or exhaust valves to see if that helps. The rocker swap alone doesn't normally require that you remove the manifold and heads, etc.; just taking off the valve covers should do it. The reduced friction of the roller-style rockers frees up some otherwise wasted energy while also providing longer life due to less wear.

Changing from a 1:1 ratio to a 1.7:1 ratio, for example, increases lift at the valve from .550 to .585 inch, though in some rare cases it may also be necessary to change the pushrod length if the higher lift at the valve causes interference

Ford Racing, Edelbrock, Crane Cams, and others offer roller timing sets for the small-block Windsors and 385-series big-blocks. This Crane Cams roller-style timing set needs to be used in any high-performance Ford engine build. The double-roller chain is stronger and more durable than OEM-style chains. The sprockets of this timing set are also made from 4140 billet steel that's been nitrided for extra strength and hardness.

problems between the rocker arm and the valve.

The type of hydraulic roller lifters you use depends on whether you're using a newer or older OEM block or an aftermarket block. The newer (5.0L, for example) OEM blocks and most aftermarket blocks have provisions to use OEM-style hydraulic roller lifters. If that's the case, regular OEM lifters (or compatible high-performance/race versions) are used for moderate- to high-power engines. The limitation is usually either RPM or the type of block being used. Stock-type blocks can usually be modified to accept the OEM system. Two holes are drilled and tapped in the valley area to accept the bolts for the lifter retaining plate (the "spider"). This setup works reasonably well up to about 6,500 rpm with a cam of .550 inch or less lift.

If you have a block that doesn't make provisions for these lifters all is not lost. Crane Cams and others offer retrofit hydraulic roller lifters that look just like the solid roller lifters of old, except they have hydraulic internals. These drop into an older-style block and are even simpler to install than the newer, OEM-style roller hydraulic setup because these don't require a spider or "dog bone" lifter guides. They also have precision-fit plunger assemblies and other features that provide increased RPM potential.

Crane's Retrofit Series, for example, can also be used to replace OEM-type hydraulic rollers for potentially higher RPM because they are more stable at high revs. Sufficiently strong, hardened (to prevent wear from contact with the guideplates), compatible pushrods need to be specified by length after the rest of

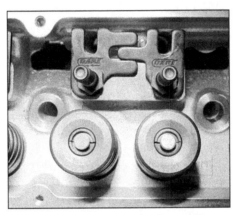

Comp Cams, Dart, and others offer stud-mounted rocker arm hardened guideplates to help improve valvetrain stability. These from Dart Machine are used to keep the pushrods properly located relative to the rocker arms. The plates restrict the lateral movement of the similarly hardened rocker arms. These Dart plates are unique in that they're adjustable to allow precise and independent centering of each pushrod under its respective rocker arm.

the valvetrain has been assembled. When only production components are used a standard-length pushrod can be used. However, even when combining components from the same aftermarket manufacturer it is still necessary to determine the cor-

All major valvetrain manufacturers offer roller rocker arms. Roller rockers reduce friction over conventional rocker arms and you often see an increase in horsepower. Ideally, the rocker tip/roller should be slightly off-center at rest, pass over the center of the valve tip as the valve opens, and reach a point about the same distance from the center (on the other side) at full lift. You also want to ensure there's no interference between the rocker arm and any of the other components throughout the full range of its motion.

When using non-OEM/direct replacement components, verify that the pushrod length is correct to avoid problems. This is especially true with an aftermarket block and/or a block or heads that were machined (such as for a change in deck height). Use an adjustable checking pushrod (shown) to determine the correct length/geometry. Vary the length of the pushrod to achieve the correct placement of the rocker arm tips over the valve tips while closed with the proper lifter preload adjustment.

rect pushrod length for your particular engine before installing them. This is due to the unpredictable combination of components and tolerances involved plus the need to ensure the rocker arm geometry is correct to avoid interference.

Springs

The camshaft and its maximum lift has the greatest affect on choice of springs. To some extent, the mass of all the components between the camshaft and the valve tip also comes

Beehive springs provide better valve control at a reduced weight when compared to standard springs. In addition, these springs are less susceptible to harmful harmonics. The oval-shaped wire allows a shorter spring height for a given pressure rating while the tapered profile and smaller retainer reduce mass to allow higher RPM use. This type of spring is commonly used on production engines and race engines. (Photo Courtesy Crane Cams)

into play but this is more of a concern to racers running at extremely high RPM than it is for those with street cars.

The correct springs provide just enough seat pressure and open pressure at maximum lift (using the correct installed height), without any spring bind. Excessive spring pressures not only cause unnecessary stress on the valvetrain components but also hurt performance and increase the likelihood of component failure. You can use a single, dual, or beehive spring but it needs to be suited to the head and the particular engine setup. It's best to follow the recommendation of the camshaft supplier or, if the springs come with the heads, verify their compatibility.

Assembled cylinder heads typically come with springs and hardware optimized for a particular use in terms of rev range, spring pressures, and so forth. They work well with the majority of camshafts aimed at the same purpose but it's always best to verify that with the camshaft manufacturer beforehand. There's no need

to use exotic spring hardware unless you're going to really high revs.

For the vast majority of engines covered here a good-quality steel retainer is fine for a rev range of about 6,500 rpm or less plus they last indefinitely. Lightweight titanium retainers with special valve locks may be required at the super-high RPM of race engines. The same goes for lash caps, spring locators, and stud girdles. Hardened-steel spring cups should, however, always be used on aluminum heads to prevent the springs from wearing away the surfaces they rest on.

Valvestem Seals

The basic choice for valvestem seals is between so-called umbrella seals (usually what's used in production) and more-sophisticated Teflon/PC seals (commonly used in racing). Umbrella seals work well for most of these engines as long as they are made from Viton or a similar high-temperature-rated material, which works better than rubber and lasts longer, especially in a higher-output engine. Teflon seals are even more effective at keeping oil away from the valvestem, possibly too much so in street use.

Depending on the type of valveguides, not enough oil may get between the valve and the guide with PC seals, thus potentially causing premature wear. Installing PC seals requires the cylinder heads to be machined around the valveguides so they fit. This is an extra expense that may not be justified on a street performance car, yet it may be more feasible for a streetable track-day car, which sees less street use and where the valveguides can more likely be modified to ensure the appropriate

Street-driven vehicles rarely need correctly rated conventional dual springs along with steel retainers and locks unless you plan on going to very high RPM and/or use a very aggressive camshaft. Dual springs provide some extra safety and redundancy. If one of the coils fails, it can prevent the valve from dropping into the chamber. Aluminum or titanium retainers are only suitable (justifiable) for race use, as are special keeper/lock designs. (Photo Courtesy Crane Cams)

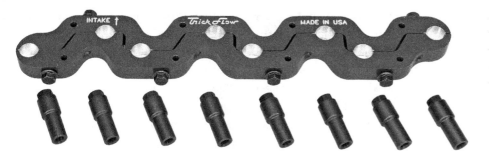

Should very high valvespring pressures be needed an additional means of increasing valvetrain stability and reducing unwanted deflection is to use a rocker arm stud girdle. It ties the rocker arm studs together so they reinforce each other. This requires longer adjustment nuts and taller valve covers. (Photo Courtesy Trick Flow Specialties)

amount of oil reaches them under all conditions. It really comes down to a tradeoff between maximum sealing and maximum valveguide life. Other factors such as spring pressure and maximum RPM also influence the choice.

Umbrella seals control oil well in many cases, especially when they are made of a superior and more heat-resistant material such as Viton. They just slip on with no machining required and are very inexpensive. They are suitable for a daily driver and probably most high-performance street cars. Teflon/PC seals (not shown) generally provide better oil control, but may allow too little oil to reach the guides. The guides are often machined with spiral grooves to help retain enough oil on the valve-stem to prevent excess wear. (Photo Courtesy Comp Cams)

Cylinder Heads

It's common practice when upgrading the camshaft and valve-train to also upgrade the cylinder heads, at least to some degree. By changing the cam, you inevitably need to increase the flow through the heads to get the most benefit from the cam and other upgrades. To achieve optimum performance the engine and its various components need to be treated as a system. All the various parts are matched to achieve the best balance of performance, driveability, and durability. This

aspect is neglected far too often by those who just throw parts together without evaluating their compatibility. It's almost always a question of balance between the desired outcome and the characteristics of the components. On the high end of the power and RPM scale things can surely get a lot more extreme than I address here.

Head Gaskets

You must ensure the head gasket bore size is correct (especially on a stroker engine) and that the gasket thickness is what you want in terms of durability and compression ratio. Standard "blue" composite, Teflon-coated gaskets are fine for most naturally aspirated engines. When power and RPM become very high and/or a power adder is entered into the mix, it's best to step up to a multi-layer steel (MLS) gasket set (such as those from Cometic). MLS gaskets don't require grooves to be machined into the head's deck surface but they do have certain requirements for the surface finish of the block and the heads.

To better utilize the superior sealing qualities created by MLS gaskets and the thicker deck surfaces of AFR,

MLS gaskets, such as these from Cometic, are a huge improvement over older gaskets. Steel's natural strength and resistance to heat is far more durable than other materials. When multiple thin layers of the proper type of spring steel are stacked they have a greater ability to maintain a seal under extremely high combustion pressures. They naturally flex to maintain a seal, yet return to the nominal position when the load is removed.

Dart, and other aftermarket heads it's also best to use ARP head studs instead of bolts. They're made from a vastly superior steel alloy that's much stronger and stretches much less even when the highest cylinder pressures are encountered. Studs are also inherently superior to bolts because they help distribute the clamping load more evenly over the deck surface and within the block, and this greatly reduces head gasket failures.

A bolt twists and stretches as it's installed, which can lead to less-accurate torque readings. A stud only stretches as the nut is tightened so the torque reading is more accurate. This improves durability and sealing plus it also helps reduce the distortion of the cylinder walls. That improves sealing and performance while also reducing oil consumption. The proper lubrication and torque figures must still be used but studs are just better at clamping things together. They also can speed up engine rebuilds at the track.

Cylinder Head Comparison

Because the daily driver doesn't justify a cylinder head upgrade for the expected power level and budget the following is a discussion of a street performance car and a streetable track-day car only. And because there can be some overlap between these vehicle types based on power level they each have a different head. The Dart head has a 347 stroker and the AFR head has a 427 stroker. Both are aluminum so each saves about 30 to 40 pounds per head compared to iron. Generally, they also allow up to about .5 more compression ratio to be used because aluminum heads get rid of combustion heat more efficiently. (Nowdays the only reasons to stay with iron heads are for originality or to lower cost.)

Example One: Dart Machine

Dart offers the Pro1 series of cylinder heads in several configurations. The 170- and 195-cc heads (62-cc combustion chambers) are best suited to moderately to highly modified street cars. The 195-cc version provides enough flow to reach the limitations of the stock engine block and other components. The 195 head is better suited to a more heavily modified (bolt-ons with a more aggressive cam plus more displacement/CR and/or a power adder) street car. The 170-cc version is best suited to a mildly to moderately modified (some bolt-ons and a fairly mild cam) smaller engine and/or when low- and mid-range torque are more of a priority than top-end power.

These heads were developed using Dart's "wet flow" technology, which provides higher flow numbers and better atomization of the air/fuel mixture. It considers the differences between designing a head with a more representative air/liquid mixture and just using dry air. This better simulates how an actual air/fuel mixture behaves as it flows through the head and can significantly affect port shape in pursuit of the best

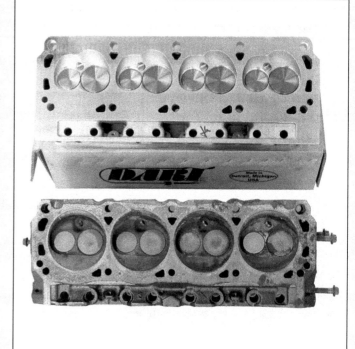

This comparison of an OEM 5.0L head (bottom) and an aluminum Dart Pro1 head (top) reveals many differences. Besides being about 30 to 40 pounds lighter the Dart head also has a revised, more-efficient, and faster-burning combustion chamber design (while still retaining the stock volume, 62 cc in this example). Valve sizes are bigger for better flow and both valveseats have been precisely machined for better flow and durability. The port shapes and volumes (195-cc intake, 65-cc exhaust) have been optimized for their intended power level. The exhaust ports have been raised slightly (.125 inch) to aid flow, yet these heads still can accept virtually all stock components or their aftermarket equivalents. They also have other design enhancements such as a thicker deck and superior materials.

Valve Covers

To top off your new heads you want to use a stronger cast-aluminum valve cover set and silicon-metal gaskets instead of the stamped-steel and cork OEM-style components. The cast covers not only look much better but they are more rigid to reduce the chance of leaks.

The perfect complement to cast covers is composite gaskets, which have a metal core covered with silicon gasket material. The metal cores usually have built-in stops to prevent overtightening of the fasteners while the silicon is usually molded with robust knife-edged sealing surfaces, which can be used over and over because no gasket sealant is needed. The covers also come off very easily.

For engines with a 5.0L EFI-style intake manifold that extends over the head a lower-profile valve cover is generally needed for manifold clearance. Check internal clearance to the cover too.

The change in combustion chamber design of many aftermarket cylinder heads can require the use of some different components. This Dart Pro1 head requires the use of a spark plug with a longer reach (left) than the plug type used with the stock head (right). If the stock-reach plugs were used the result would likely be misfire because the plug gap is sunk so far into the head. (Photo Courtesy Dart Machinery)

real-world flow and performance. Airflow and fuel flow are measured to help optimize each head not only in terms of maximum flow but also in terms of how well a fixed air/fuel ratio is maintained across the full flow range.

Besides the difference in intake port volume (that's what the numbers 170 and 195 refer to), the higher-flowing 195 head also has a bigger intake valve (2.02 versus 1.94 inches). These heads retain the standard valve angles and port spacing so all OEM-compatible bolt-ons

should fit. They're made from a virgin 355-T61 alloy for greater strength and less risk of casting problems. They benefit from heart-shaped combustion chambers that increase combustion efficiency and burn rate. They also reduce the potential for dangerous preignition or detonation.

The exhaust runners have been raised .135 inch to improve flow through the 1.60-inch valve. The exhaust valveseats have been hardened and radiused to improve flow. Similarly, the intake valves rest in multi-angle valve-seats to improve flow into the cylinders. All of the valves are located by long-lasting manganese-bronze valveguides.

Dart Pro1 CNC heads further improve on the standard Pro1 heads by using precise CNC machining to ensure each port and chamber is just like the others (dimensionally) and

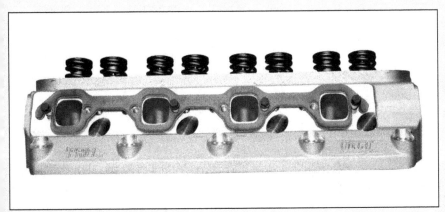

The slightly raised exhaust ports of the Dart Pro1 heads shouldn't cause any problems with the fit of headers. These heads (as well as the CNC versions) come with dual-exhaust bolt patterns to allow the use of headers with wider bolt spacing. This reduces the restriction coming out of the port because the header tubes are not pinched to provide bolt clearance.

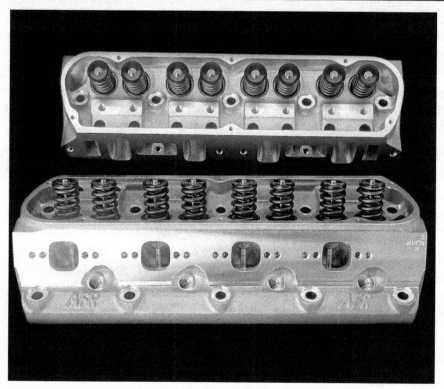

When building a high-performance Windsor small-block, the AFR Renegade is an option. These heads have large 2.08-inch intake valves and standard CNC machining. These 205-cc heads flow more than the previous version of 225-cc heads yet are still suitable for street use because they don't sacrifice mid-range flow or velocity to get the higher maximum flow numbers. This greater "area under the curve" allows AFR to claim their heads generally outflow similar heads of most competitors while their full-CNC heads cost only a small amount more than the as-cast heads of competitors.

AFR also offers a 220-cc Renegade head meant for large displacements and even higher RPM ranges. While the 220-cc versions may be a bit marginal for street use the 205s are ideal because of their high flow even at low lifts and revs.

thus should flow nearly the same, which is very desirable. The Pro1 CNC heads are available in 210- and 225-cc port volumes and are obviously meant for high power levels and RPM in heavily modified engines with aftermarket engine blocks and more aggressive cams.

Example Two: Airflow Research

The AFR 205-cc Renegade heads are a different animal with a different purpose. They are still a street-worthy OEM-style bolt-on head that accepts all of the components meant for a stock head but they're meant for significantly higher power levels. The interesting thing about these 205-cc AFR heads is that this generation outflows the previous-generation 225-cc heads. The technology employed by AFR somewhat separates flow from port size in that a smaller port volume can be used to maintain better low-speed/part-throttle performance without losing too much flow at the top end. AFR strives for more "area under the curve" by maintaining relatively higher flow at lower valve lifts as well as just at peak lift.

Larger port-volume heads are still the preferred choice for maximum output, mostly competition-oriented vehicles where general street use and lower RPM performance are not priorities. The two things that make the greatest contribution to this capability are the larger, 2.08-inch 21-4N lightweight intake valves (exhaust is 1.60 inches and is made from superior 2132 stainless steel) and the full use of CNC porting on every head.

The larger intakes allow for more flow through the increased "curtain area" as the valve is opened. The use of CNC machining for the ports and combustion chambers improves flow by producing more-complex shapes and a smoother surface finish than an as-cast head. It also does so the same way every time, thus ensuring greater consistency from cylinder to cylinder and head to head. This allows for optimum tuning because the fuel and spark requirements for each cylinder are much more similar, eliminating the need to tune for the worst-case cylinder. Even the best hand porting cannot duplicate this level of consistency or accuracy on a port-to-port, head-to-head basis.

As expected, the AFR head shares much of the technology seen in the Dart head: It was developed using wet flow technology, the deck is extra thick (.750 inch), the exhaust ports have been raised slightly (.125 inch), the intake valves get a multi-angle valve job, and the exhaust valves are

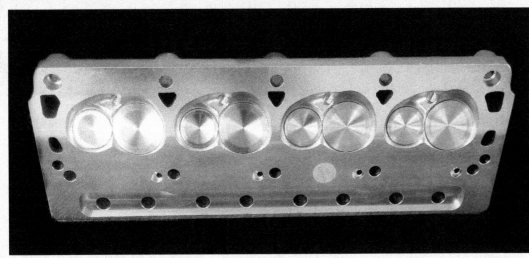

The completely CNC'd combustion chambers on the AFR Renegade heads make a very significant contribution to performance. The consistency between chambers is a critical asset; 58- and 72-cc versions are available. The heart-shaped chambers improve combustion speed and efficiency. Also, the AFR chambers have a smoother finish to aid in-cylinder motion and minimize the potential for sharp edges, which can cause hot spots that lead to detonation. The valves have been significantly unshrouded to aid flow in and out of the cylinders. Note the funnel effect around the exhaust valves.

radiused. In keeping with its higher flow and RPM goals the AFR head also has lightweight valves with 8-mm stems to allow better flow (by creating more flow area) and potentially

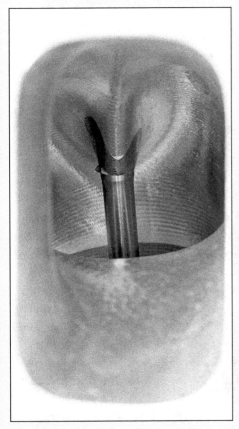

Precision CNC machining can create very complex and efficient port shapes. They also can be almost identically reproduced over and over again, on the same head or any number of heads. This greatly improves the performance potential when both heads are so close in specification.

higher RPM use with less risk of damaging valve float. The lighter valves allow for the use of lighter springs, retainers, and so forth, which can help reduce the reciprocating mass of the valvetrain. This improves valve control so the camshaft profile reduces float and allows more RPM.

The springs are a small-diameter dual design made from chrome silicon vanadium with nickel that's given a special heat-treating process. AFR claims these springs perform as well or better than even "beehive" springs up to about 7,000 rpm, plus they provide the additional benefit of redundancy in the event of failure.

For the most extreme applications, AFR offers even stronger, higher-rate, larger-diameter springs that can be used up to .710-inch lift. These are of a similar material and construction plus they undergo a two-stage shot-peening process to further increase their strength and durability.

AFR's heads all come with more-durable and more-reliable bead-lock keepers (which spread the spring load more evenly and are less likely to fail). They also have special hardened-steel spring seats with integral locators (to protect the head surface and keep the springs properly centered around the valveguides and their high-quality Viton valvestem seals). AFR's clean-sheet-design heads are free from the restrictions of the OEM head design and are fine for all but the most radical engines/vehicles intended to be driven on the street, however rare that may be. ■

INTAKE, EXHAUST AND FUEL SYSTEMS

Properly matched camshafts, valvetrains, and cylinder heads with great flow characteristics don't perform at their maximum potential unless you're able to efficiently get sufficient air and the fuel to them in the correct amounts. Not coincidentally, the air intake and fuel systems are responsible for these duties.

In this chapter, I discuss the path of the incoming air from where it enters the vehicle, through the throttle(s), and then into the cylinder heads and out the exhaust while also providing guidelines for each vehicle type. I address the fuel system in a similar manner; from the fuel tank to where the fuel enters the intake air. I concentrate mostly on carburetion because that's what all of these cars originally came equipped with.

I also discuss some cost-effective options for electronic fuel injection (EFI) retrofits. (Completely custom EFI systems are not within the scope of this book and only provide a meaningful incremental benefit in competition/racing use.) The EFI systems I discuss are focused on providing better driveability, starting, and efficiency relative to carburetors while also having similar, if not better, performance for a reasonable cost, and with fairly easy installation.

Intake System

The stock air intake systems of early Mustangs were, for the most part, not much to write home about. They were made for the masses with little attention to performance potential, except for the relatively rare performance engines not covered here. Most were a closed-element design with heated inlet air to help the engine run better when it was warming up in colder conditions. In warmer climates a common trick was to flip the lid upside down to improve airflow.

An open-element air cleaner was available in some cases, which allowed the engine to breathe better than the closed-element design. It was, however, still forced to ingest underhood air, which is hotter and less dense, therefore offsetting some of the benefit. The noise level also increased but that was usually considered a good thing.

Cold-Air Intakes

One option in terms of stock setups was a cold-air/ram-air type such as those with dual snorkels, which

A cold-air intake helps produce maximum performance and it's better if there is some degree of ram effect. This setup used on the Agent 47 Harbinger 1969 retro racer is a perfect example. The duct is located in a very high-pressure area on the front of the car for ram effect. A filter with large surface area and low restriction is used to keep dirt and debris out of the intake air.

were routed to the fenders to get colder outside air. Another option was the well-known shaker-style hood scoops, which pulled cold air into an enclosure around the carb(s) and sealed to the bottom of the hood. Retrofitting one of these to a car that didn't have them, even a mildly modified daily driver, should improve performance noticeably, particularly under certain weather conditions.

Duplicating the OEM setup exactly can be costly but it ensures you're a lot less likely to have issues with water ingestion, dirt, or other debris getting into the engine. There are many aftermarket variations of these options.

For a high-performance street car or a streetable track-day car, some form of intake upgrade is required

The dual large-diameter ducts of the Agent 47 system allow a lot of cool pressurized air to reach the engine. The rubber material of the ducts also helps to slightly insulate this air from the underhood heat so less makes its way to the engine.

When a MAFS-based EFI system is used, all the intake air must go through the sensor so only a single duct can be used. The duct size can be fairly large as long as the sensor is matched to it. This is a ram air setup on a 1965 fastback 347 stroker equipped with an EEC-IV. Placing the filter inside a box behind the grille ensures a good supply of cool, pressurized outside air. The larger (97 mm) Abaco/DBX digitally programmable sensor sits right behind the filter on the other side of the box. The sensor has a very large and smooth bell-shaped opening to aid flow into it, plus the straight ducting behind helps ensure accuracy.

This EEC-IV installation system in a 1965 draws cool outside air into the filter box behind the grille (under the ZEX decal), passes it through the Abaco/DBX MAFS, and then straightens it out by a length of large-diameter ducting before it reaches the throttle body. There's also a nitrous nozzle along the way. The thick rubber and plastic ducting (filled and smoothed inside) provides some insulation from heat to help keep the air cooler and denser for better performance.

to eliminate the restriction of the stock system and to have the higher flow you need for the higher power level. A minimally restrictive cold-air intake system that benefits from at least some ram effect/pressurization as vehicle speed increases allows all the other flow enhancements to realize their greatest potential.

Always use a less-restrictive but still effective permanent air filter (dry or oiled gauze, metal mesh, foam, or some combination of these) to avoid the performance loss that occurs as paper elements become dirty. Be sure to clean the filter when needed and carefully re-oil it if applicable. But remember that too much can cause issues with a mass airflow sensor (MAFS).

It's generally not very beneficial to insulate the ducting from the cold-air inlet(s) to the engine but an open-mesh screen should always be used to keep any larger debris out of the engine. Make sure all of the joints are sealed but still leave a means for rain/water to escape.

Carburetor

Holley and other carburetors delivered fuel to many Ford small- and big-block engines. These ranged from a simple 1-barrel carb on 6-cylinders to dual 4-barrels as a dealer-installed option on some high-performance models. In most cases, a well-chosen single 4-barrel delivers just as much performance, or more, and it is a lot easier to tune and maintain while also being more driveable.

There are far too many carburetor options to provide a specific recommendation but there are some general things you can look for to help you make a better choice. Of these,

the CFM rating (essentially the maximum amount of air it's capable of flowing) of the carb is the first thing to nail down. Many people tend to think more is better; that putting a big carb on an engine always makes it perform better. Not true. Quite the contrary, actually. An oversized carb doesn't improve performance but it significantly degrades driveability and fuel mileage while also making the engine harder to start and more prone to fouling.

It's usually better to err on the side of caution and go with a slightly smaller carb rather than one that may be too big. Power may suffer very slightly but throttle response, driveability, and so forth is markedly better.

Selecting a Carburetor

Some very general guidelines for the CFM rating for a given small-block situation are that less than 600 cfm is almost always more than enough for a mildly modified daily driver. For a street-performance car with mild to moderate mods a 600-cfm carb works in some cases but a 680- to 700-cfm carb is probably called for when there are a few more modifications. By the time you get into upgrading the cylinder heads, cam, and so forth you're probably ready for a 750-cfm carb. This is also good for most streetable track-day cars of about 600 hp or so. If you have a highly modified street-performance car with larger displacement or a streetable track-day car with more than 600 hp you may want to look at going to a carb with more than 800 cfm.

Other things you must consider are engine size, maximum RPM, level of modification, fuel, power adder

usage, vehicle weight, transmission type, and gear ratios. Considering at least these main factors help ensure a wiser choice.

The brand of carburetor is less important than its features. Some are generally only needed for street use (such as a choke) while others are meant solely for the track (extra tunability provisions such as screw-in air bleeds, plus easy assembly and disassembly features, etc.).

A daily-driver carb needs to have all of the provisions in terms of vacuum and PCV connections, a choke, a simple idle circuit, and vacuum secondaries. The choke can be electric (for simplicity) or manual (for greater

Quick Fuel Technology (QFT) offers several different series of carbs. The HR (hot rod) series is available in CFM ratings ranging from 580 to 780 for models with vacuum secondaries and 600 to 850 for those with mechanical secondaries. These carbs are aluminum and use separate float bowls and metering blocks. They use four-corner idle, screw-in idle feed restrictors, and air bleeds. They also have glass fuel-level windows and adjustable center-hung floats. The vacuum secondary models allow for adjustment using only hand tools with no need for an assortment of springs or the risk of torn diaphragms. (Photo Courtesy Quick Fuel Technology)

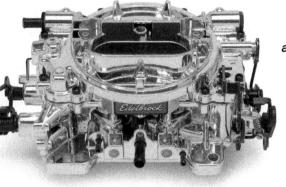

Edelbrock's Thunder AVS carbs provide simplicity with excellent street-ability. They don't provide as many tuning options as some other brands but they build on the features of Edelbrock's Performer series carbs by adding a Qwik-Tune Secondary Air Valve to the virtually identical features shared with the Performer carbs. This tunable air valve allows you to adjust the secondary opening rate with simple hand tools. Metering changes are made by simply swapping in new metering rods. (Photo Courtesy Edelbrock)

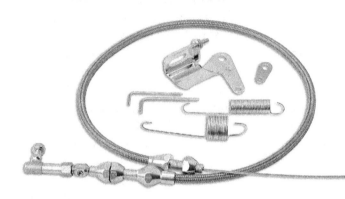

Stock throttle linkages can stick/bind and not operate smoothly. Replacing the stock throttle linkage with one of Lokar's throttle cable kits ensures smooth, reliable throttle actuation. These cable kits provide extra flexibility in the way they're routed and more precise adjustment. (Photo Courtesy Lokar Performance)

control). There's no reason to try to reuse the OEM choke setup because the electric choke works much better and is far easier to adjust.

A high-performance street car likely has an electric choke and adjustable vacuum secondaries at the lower end of the power range and probably migrates to mechanical secondaries and a manual choke at the higher end. In most cases, a more sophisticated "four-corner" idle setup probably provides the extra adjustability needed for a stable idle with the more aggressive camshaft likely being used. The materials used are also better (billet aluminum and higher-quality gaskets, floats, and so forth), as is the design of other components such as the metering blocks, power valves, and boosters.

A streetable track-day car is usually just a larger evolution of what is used for a high-end street performance carb. It has a higher CFM rating, a manual choke (if any) plus all of the adjustability, tuning, and design features needed for optimum performance and durability during track use. It also very likely uses mechanical (instead of vacuum) secondaries and special bowl and float designs.

Some of these features may also be common to some high-performance carbs.

Intake Manifold

After the air and fuel have been introduced to each other in the carburetor the mixture passes into the intake manifold and makes its way to each cylinder. Although this sounds relatively simple, it is not. First and foremost, you ideally want each cylinder to receive the same amount of air/fuel mixture for each combustion event. This is impossible for a number of reasons so you just try to come as close as you can.

On a relatively well-designed, single, 4-barrel manifold you can get down to about a .5 air/fuel ratio spread across all eight cylinders under peak power conditions. This varies greatly with engine speed and load for no other reason than the differing positions of the throttle plates in the carb(s) affects the path of the mixture. The end result is that you have to tune (jet) for the leanest (weakest) cylinder to prevent detonation, which makes the other cylinders richer than you want. That lowers peak performance and wastes fuel (lower MPG).

Aftermarket manufacturers do their best to design intake manifolds with even flow distribution but they are limited by the location of the carb(s) versus the intake ports on the head as well as the size and shape of the intake runners of the heads. A single-plane manifold may have a straighter shot at each port but that doesn't always ensure more even distribution. When a dual-plane manifold is used to improve low-end performance the increased

This Edelbrock RPM Air Gap dual-plane manifold is optimized for an RPM range of 1,500 to 6,500. The runners have been raised above the floor of the manifold (the "air gap") to remain cooler and transfer less heat to the mixture. The exhaust passage for the choke has been eliminated so a manual or electric choke must be used. The intake runner cross-sectional area and the height of the carb-mounting flange have been increased to produce more top-end power with minimal loss at lower RPM. This type of manifold is exceptionally good for a moderately to heavily modified street-driven high-performance car. (Photo Courtesy Edelbrock)

A single-plane manifold is often preferred for 600 hp or more. This Summit Racing Street and Strip Stage 4 manifold provides gains in the 3,500- to 7,500-rpm range. This is more of a strip/track-oriented manifold in that it has four ports for coolant temperature sensors (two in front, two on the rear coolant crossover), cast-in bosses for nitrous nozzles or fuel injectors, and a larger, more-open plenum. The runners are separated from the manifold floor to keep the intake mix cooler. (Photo Courtesy Summit Racing)

complexity inherent in the design can also make balanced distribution more difficult to achieve. The higher-flow velocity of the dual-plane manifold (due to normally lower volume runners, among other things) can help atomization in general but not necessarily distribution.

Daily drivers and mildly to moderately modified high-performance street cars normally use a dual-plane manifold because this design is best for the 1,500- to 6,500-rpm range in which they are mostly operated. A more heavily modified high-performance street car and a streetable track-day car usually benefits from a single-plane design to get the more even distribution and bet-

ter performance in a range of about 3,000 to 7,500 rpm.

Pure race manifolds, which may be hard to tolerate in street use, can go beyond this RPM level but are only appropriate for the highest power levels when there is little concern about significant street use.

EFI Conversion

The conversion from carburetion to fuel injection offers many potential benefits. Among them are better mixture distribution, idle, throttle response, driveability, and gas mileage, plus lower pollution. The knock on fuel injection has been that it was complicated, costly, and didn't make

as much power as carbs. It's safe to say these concerns have been almost completely eliminated with modern aftermarket EFI systems. (I don't discuss mechanical fuel injection because there's little, if any, benefit for street use and the cost is usually high.) EFI systems are now very simple to install and can even be "self learning" to a large degree so the task of tuning is greatly simplified.

Many systems just involve the removal of the carburetor and fuel pump so they can be replaced with a higher-pressure electric pump, a different fuel-pressure regulator, and components such as a throttle body (or multiples) and sensors. The simplest systems look very similar to a regular 4-barrel carb and even use a similar-style air cleaner. Most of the electronics are tucked out of sight so the original underhood appearance changes very little in many cases. At least one oxygen sensor needs to be installed in the exhaust and the fuel line usually needs to be upgraded with a higher pressure rating.

With many systems a laptop or other computer isn't needed because the systems are self-learning. If you like to tune, the possibility of using a laptop is still generally available. These throttle-body systems have an air/fuel mixture flowing through the intake manifold so they are still subject to less-than-perfect balance between them.

However, the fuel is better atomized by the fuel injectors integrated into the throttle body and the fuel metering is much more precise and adaptive to temperature, barometric pressure, and numerous other parameters that are ignored by a carburetor. This allows the EFI system to continually re-optimize the mixture to compensate for changes in these

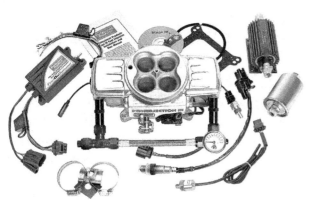

The Powerjection III kit from Professional Products provides throttle-body fuel injection. You have to install an electric fuel pump in the tank, install sensors, use high-pressure fuel lines, and adapt the system to your wiring harness. You hook up all the wiring and check everything for leaks and other problems before you turn the key to start it. You can use it in a "blow-through" configuration with a supercharger or turbocharger because it has a built-in 2.5-bar MAP sensor that can read up to 25 psi of boost. The Powerjection III is good for up to about 550 hp with the standard parts. A larger throttle body (1,200 versus 750 cfm), larger fuel injectors, and a more-powerful fuel pump can raise the power capability to about 700 hp. (Photo Courtesy Professional Products)

factors while also continually monitoring the effects of the changes made through the oxygen sensor.

Fuel Injector

To get the full benefit of EFI requires that you no longer inject fuel into the manifold like a carburetor. Instead, you point a fuel injector at each intake valve and spray the fuel directly into the intake port. This does several good things. First, by only flowing air through the intake manifold the distribution is instantly better because air, being a gas, is naturally inclined to distribute itself more equally. In addition, spraying the fuel right at the valve means there's no chance of the fuel puddling on the floor of the intake manifold or wetting the walls of the runners to any significant degree. This also helps distribution as well as overall metering. Finally, if you fire the injectors individually (sequentially, as opposed to groups) you can also realize better throttle response and further improvements in overall fuel control.

Modern fuel injectors running at higher pressures do an excellent job of atomizing the fuel into a fog that's more easily burned. Individual injectors at each port are better than fewer larger ones farther upstream because each one has to deliver less fuel and can thus be more precise and responsive. As the oxygen sensors read the composition of the exhaust gases they can make the necessary corrections to the fuel flow more quickly and more accurately by doing so one cylinder at a time. Combined with the same ability to compensate for other factors such as temperature and pressure, a sequential EFI system provides the potential for extremely accurate, precise, and adaptive fuel control with built-in learning capability and diagnostics for a very reasonable cost.

Engine Control Unit

The amount of fuel to be injected into the engine depends on the amount of air it ingests, just as with a carburetor. With EFI, however, the amount of air is just input data to the engine control unit (ECU), which is used to determine how long each injector stays open when it fires, thus determining how much fuel is injected.

There are two main ways to provide this data to the ECU: Measure it directly or calculate it based on other information. The first approach requires the use of a MAFS, which uses a very ingenious method of measuring air mass directly, based on how much electricity it takes to maintain a constant temperature on a wire that's been placed in the airflow path. This has the advantage of being a direct measurement instead of a calculation. It also is able to compensate for modifications that improve airflow as you make them.

If you put in that new cam or exhaust system and the engine flows more air as a result the MAFS sees it and the ECU can act accordingly. Similarly, if the engine wears a bit and flows less air it can take care of that too. This ability to continually measure and correct the airflow is one of the main reasons Ford, for one, uses a sequential MAFS-based control system in virtually all of its new US production vehicles (at the time of publication).

The knock against this approach is you must have a MAFS and place it somewhere close to the engine. It also needs to have a certain length of straight ducting immediately after it to ensure an accurate measurement. This need to have/position a MAFS and use a single inlet duct for the intake air can sometimes be problematic. Still, for the majority of high-performance street cars a sequential MAFS-type system provides the best overall performance and driveability for a reasonable cost. Fortunately, the EEC-IV system used

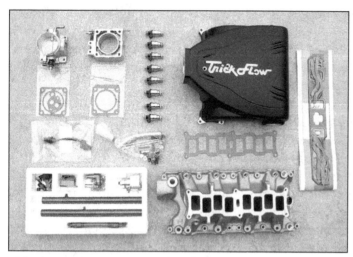

This assortment of aftermarket upgrades can replace their respective standard 5.0L components. The Trick Flow Specialties (TFS) Track Heat intake manifold is similar to the OEM manifold but has been revised to flow much better in the 1,500- to 6,500-rpm range while providing even more balanced distribution to each port. The higher-flow (36 lbs/hr) TFS TFX injectors provide significantly better response and atomization compared to stock injectors. Using the basic EEC-IV control system with various component upgrades gives the benefit of a proven OEM system with more and better features, which is also scalable for higher power and is ultimately very cost-effective because you change the system very little as you make more modifications.

You can upgrade a MAFS to make an EEC-IV perform better. The stock Hitachi sensor is relatively restrictive because of its basic design and small bore. It's also not the best in terms of accuracy under some conditions, particularly if the intake ducting isn't done right. The first aftermarket MAFSs from companies such as Pro-M solved these problems by redesigning the sensor body, so it was much less restrictive and had a larger bore. These parts still used the OEM sensor's electronics though they were modified and tested to yield much better accuracy and precision.

When different fuel injectors are installed, however, the electronics must again be modified (usually by sending it back to the manufacturer) to match the new injectors. Abaco's DBX line of digital MAFSs eliminates this limitation while also making comprehensive tuning and recalibration much simpler. Using an even larger and less-restrictive bore Abaco installs four sensors inside the housing so the product is virtually unaffected by the configuration of the ducting or other things such as reversion, which can throw regular sensors off. (Photo Courtesy Abaco Performance)

by Ford on production V-8 Mustangs from 1989 to 1995 lends itself very well to retrofitting older carbureted Mustangs with EFI.

These systems can very easily be adapted to older vehicles. When supplemented with aftermarket performance parts they produce very high power levels with better performance than most aftermarket systems. Better still, as modifications continue to be made and/or other changes occur the system can readily be retuned as needed by simply swapping in higher flowing fuel injectors and then recalibrating the ECU. Products such as the TwEECer make the latter process much simpler by either interfacing directly with the EEC-IV ECU to selectively modify its input and output signals or by using a special/digital MAFS made by Abaco Performance.

The Abaco MAFS has the ability to be programmed as needed to revise its internal "transfer function," which is used to provide air mass data to the ECU. This is a better approach than having to get a new MAFS or having the one you have recalibrated by the manufacturer. The Abaco MAFS can be reprogrammed as often as you need for best performance, whereas regular analog MAFSs must have a specific combination.

Here is a 75-mm Professional Products throttle body and EGR spacer installed on a TFS intake manifold in the same manner as OEM components. Provisions exist for all related OEM components, such as the EGR valve, idle air control (IAC), and throttle position sensor (TPS). This combination is completely compatible with the other OEM (or aftermarket replacement) parts yet it provides much better performance and efficiency.

If you extrude hone the intake manifold, this process removes the rough casting from the interior surfaces and balance flow for the best possible cylinder-to-cylinder air/fuel distribution. It removes and/or smoothes any surface imperfections leaving a very smooth and uniform surface finish. This greatly enhances flow, and each runner can then be treated individually to achieve virtually identical flow through all runners.

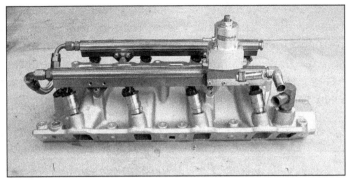

The Professional Products high-flow fuel rails and adjustable regulator have been installed on this Windsor. TFX injectors were mounted on the TFS lower intake. These components are an improvement over stock parts. Note how the fuel injectors are precisely aimed in line with the ports to ensure minimal wall wetting or potential for fuel to migrate back up the runners. The fuel rails can accept the stock-type fuel couplings or the fittings can be replaced with those that accept AN hoses. Fuel pressure adjustment is by turning the center screw and then tightening the lock nut.

TFS TFX fuel injectors are a far-superior design compared to OEM EEC-IV 5.0L injectors. The most obvious difference is three exit holes instead of a single pintle type of exit. The revised nozzle design improves atomization and reduces the potential for deposit buildup. TFX injectors use disc-type control valves and improved windings for better response with less noise. Stainless steel bodies with Viton O-rings ensure superior durability and sealing while internal 1/2-micron-thick filter screens protect the injectors from dirt and debris. Each TFX injector is fully tested for quality and comes with an OEM-compatible EV-1 type of connector.

EFI systems can also use individual runner-type intake manifolds and can do so very effectively. Because only air is being throttled, there are fewer potential variables compared to multiple carbs so the effect on balance is less. There is still the need to ensure each cylinder receives the same amount of air but this is easier. The short runner lengths are less restrictive than those of a conventional manifold and can thus improve responsiveness and maximum power. The downside of many such installations is they usually end up ingesting hot underhood air.

A design that allows the stacks to protrude through the hood or to be enclosed in a "box" (which seals to the underside of the hood and allows only cooler outside air to be taken in) is better for performance. The use of a hood scoop to create a ram effect is a further improvement if the flow is evenly distributed to each inlet.

Racers prefer the second approach because they don't usually want the restriction of a single-duct MAFS system, however slight it might be. Many aftermarket manufacturers, and even some OEMs, prefer to calculate the air mass using the "speed density" method. You calculate air mass based on measurements of engine RPM and manifold pressure along with a volumetric efficiency correction factor determined during the calibration process. This gets you pretty close (at least during steady running); then you still use the oxygen sensor data to refine your calculation.

Speed density systems don't have the requirement of using a MAFS or

Sequential MAFS-Based System

A very easy way to retrofit a sequential MAFS-based system to your older Mustang (or other vehicles) is to purchase a complete kit such as this one from Pro-M Racing. This system uses mostly 2005–2010 OEM Ford components and a few special items to make it work on older, previously carbureted cars. Some improvements over the older EEC-IV system include the ability to use wideband oxygen sensors as well as the original narrow-band type, full OBD II diagnostic capabilities, customizable datalogging, and the ability to easily reflash/recalibrate the ECU via a simple USB connection.

When you get the system it has been calibrated based on the information you provided about your engine. When combined with the inherent capabilities of a sequential mass-air system to adapt as needed you should have an optimized calibration soon after the start. If you change things later, you can just enter the changes (such as new injector size) via the proprietary software provided for installation on your laptop. If you want to do a full-blown calibration/mapping program, you can, but it's usually not necessary.

The Pro-M Racing system truly is "plug-and-play" from the start. The single-plane manifold has been modified to accept the fuel injectors and rails while maintaining a low underhood profile. Both the manifold and the 1,000-cfm throttle body can support very high-power outputs. The throttle body retains an IAC motor for idle control. A compatible distributor, coil, and full, high-quality wiring harness are also provided with all necessary sensors.

Perhaps the most ingenious aspect of this kit is the use of a modified GM MAFS, which mounts directly above the throttle body. This allows it to sense the mass of the incoming air without the usual limitation of the ducting having to conform to certain requirements. Other MAFS options are also available for different applications (such as a blow-through system with a power adder) but this standard sensor (shown here below the fuel injectors) allows a more classic underhood look without sacrificing performance or driveability. A signal conditioning box is included to convert the digital GM signal to be compatible with the Ford electronics. Because the kit takes care of fuel and spark, you just need to get enough fuel to the rails at the right pressure.

Pro-M also sells pre-bundled packages, which have everything you need: an OEM-level sequential, multiport, MAFS system, which provides dramatic improvements in starting, driveability, fuel economy, and more. It can automatically adapt to changing conditions and modifications plus it can be easily upgraded with new fuel injectors, etc., as needed. You can easily recalibrate at any time via laptop, if necessary, to optimize for any new modifications you make. ■

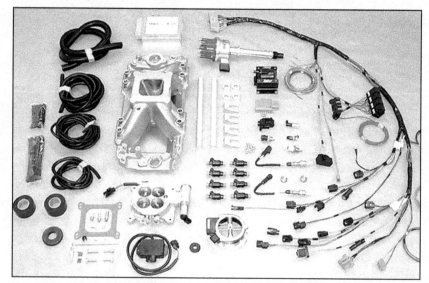

All components of the Pro-M Racing MAFS-based system are shown here. The wiring harness, distributor, intake, throttle body, ignition box, and all the necessary parts to complete the installation are included in this kit.

A new high-quality EEC-IV wiring harness from companies, such as Ron Francis Wiring or Painless Performance is necessary. They use superior more-modern materials, which provide better durability and connectivity. These aftermarket harnesses can often be bought in special configurations made for use in older vehicles. In this photo you can clearly see the labels/tags used to identify individual circuits. The color coding and looming of the wiring is also more simplified. (Photo Courtesy Painless Performance)

needing straight ducting, etc. This makes them better suited to crowded underhood areas and the use of more complicated intake manifolds (such as multiple carbs) and/or a power adder with positive manifold pressures. A speed density system can make virtually any amount of power, whereas a MAFS system eventually becomes impractical beyond a certain (though still very high) level.

At the highest levels, say 800 hp or more, the speed density system may make a bit more power. This can matter to a racer, but it's usually not worth the tradeoff in terms of driveability and long-term adaptability, if the car is still driven on the street. Racers are constantly tuning their cars anyway so they are recalibrated on a frequent basis to compensate for changes. For a high-performance street car or a streetable track-day car this level of interaction may not be desirable or practical.

Fuel System

Whether you use a carbureted or fuel-injected approach you still need to pay attention to the details to get maximum performance, especially with a lot of modifications. An incorrect manifold gasket or cheap fasteners, for example, can negate all of the improvements you're attempting to make, or even result in expensive damage to your newly improved engine. One precaution that can be taken (especially if there are no special features such as sealing beads, etc., on the gasket) is to apply a thin film of RTV or another suitable sealant around the ports and water passages. Be careful not to apply too much; you don't want any of the excess getting into the wrong places. This better holds the gasket in place during assembly and further reduces the chance for leaks with negligible risk of other problems.

Stainless steel ARP fasteners for the intake manifold and other external engine components can be part of a complete engine kit or can be purchased separately. In addition to not corroding they are stronger, have

a more compact head design for easier access, and were manufactured to tighter tolerances than cheaper bolts.

Reliably getting the fuel to the carb or EFI system in sufficient quantity under all conditions is also necessary for maximum performance. As power levels increase so does the amount of fuel that must be transferred. Likewise, higher acceleration and cornering forces cause more movement of the fuel within the tank, thus potentially moving the fuel away from the pickup. Under some conditions it can suck vapor instead of liquid, with the expected negative results.

Although you always want to be able to use all of the fuel in your tank, with EFI it's also critical to preventing damage to the fuel pump and other components. That's why virtually all modern production vehicles equipped with EFI have fuel tanks with internal sumps and/or baffling to keep fuel around the pickup as much as possible. In a high-performance street car or streetable track-day car it will inevitably be necessary to upgrade the fuel supply system to better cope with the need for

Always use a premium gasket, such as this Edelbrock intake example. It isn't the least-expensive option, but it's made from high-quality materials and has desirable features such as the imprinted bead around the port opening. You need to make sure they don't block the ports. Sometimes it's just a matter of repositioning them. Sometimes you may have to trim them to match the ports.

higher fuel flow under more-extreme dynamic conditions.

The stock fuel tank and lines are usually sufficient for a daily driver unless it's been more extensively modified to produce significantly more engine power or generate much higher cornering forces. When an upgrade is required it normally involves installing a new tank with an internal sump and/or baffles such a those made by Tanks, Inc. When much-higher performance levels and/or event rules require, a fuel cell may be needed for safety and better fuel control. In any case, care must be taken to ensure the fuel pickup is also upgraded to reduce restriction to the fuel pump inlet. Not doing so can reduce the fuel flow rate significantly and also cause pump damage or failure.

A higher-output fuel pump (such as those produced in the United States from Aeromotive) is needed along with upgraded fuel lines, filters, and fittings, etc., to reliably provide the needed fuel. An in-tank pump is normally adequate for most street-driven vehicles while a larger-capacity external pump is needed at the higher power levels and/or when a power adder is used.

Aeromotive's Phantom Fuel System effectively converts a stock fuel tank to EFI, or to a higher-volume in-tank pump (with better fuel pickup) for a carbureted engine. Cut a hole in the top of the tank with a 6- to 12-inch depth, trim a few pieces to fit, install the baffling/foam into the tank along with the lower retaining ring, and then install the pump and mounting bracket assembly into the tank and on top of the foam sealing ring. The result is a quiet, high-volume pump that runs cool, keeps the fuel cooler, and doesn't run dry even in very extreme maneuvers. (Photo Courtesy Aeromotive)

If your Mustang is going to be used for competition, you need to install a fuel cell that has a safety bladder. Fuel Safe offers premium-quality fuel cells for first-generation Mustangs. The aluminum outer containers are TIG welded, and the fuel bladders are FIA FT3 approved. The bladders contain full safety foam baffling for excellent fuel pickup and inhibit the possibility of an explosion.

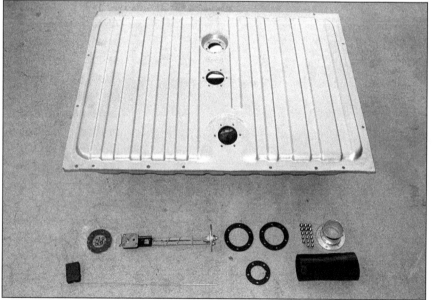

For a conversion to EFI, it's best to get a fuel tank that's been modified to accept the necessary hardware, such as this one from Tanks, Inc. This 16-gallon fuel tank is a direct bolt-in for 1964½–1968 Mustangs. It's been designed with an internal 4.3L sump and baffling that keeps the fuel pump pickup fully immersed even under the most extreme dynamic conditions. The electric fuel pump module/bracket is installed through a hole in the top of the tank that's been located over the sump. You can use one of the pump modules available from Tanks, Inc., or the pump of your choice so long as the mounting bracket is compatible. A standard five-hole aftermarket fuel sending unit can be installed in the top hole for a fuel gauge.

If an external pump(s) must be used, it is critical that the size of the outlets from the fuel tank/cell be large enough to not cause a restriction. The higher the engine output and fuel flow requirements, the bigger the outlets need to be. Any reasonably powerful street performance car should have at least one -8/.5-inch outlet. As fuel demand increases the outlet size (and fuel line diameter) should also increase to avoid restriction, which may reduce the amount of flow and may cause the pump(s) to overheat or fail.

Aeromotive's Eliminator pump is their highest-flow pump meant for continuous/street duty. (Only their Pro Series pumps, which are meant for short-time use, flow more.) The Eliminator pump can support up to 2,300 hp carbureted and 1,900 hp with EFI. Those figures drop about 26 percent with boost. The pump has a dual-chamber pumping mechanism and, like its smaller in-tank brother, is especially good at having higher flow at higher pressures. (Photo Courtesy Aeromotive)

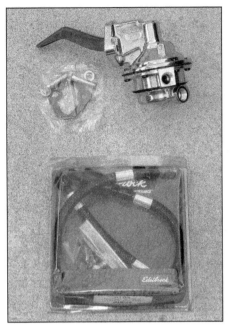

In some cases you have to use an electric pump because the timing covers on later engines (such as the 5.0L) have no means to drive a mechanical fuel pump. An excellent example of a mechanical fuel pump upgrade is this 110-gph Edelbrock Performer RPM Street. It's good up to about 600 hp on a carbureted engine (EFI systems can't use it). This pump greatly increases flow and also provides larger ports for larger fuel line fittings. This pump runs at 6 psi (no regulator needed) and also features a "clockable" lower housing, which allows you to rotate it as needed to get the best alignment for the inlet and outlet ports. Also shown is an Edelbrock high-flow fuel pump to carb hose kit.

Aeromotive Stealth 340 is a small, yet very powerful, in-tank fuel pump. It can be installed in virtually all fuel tanks/cells likely to be used in these engines. It flows enough fuel to make about 1,000 hp carbureted or 700 hp with EFI, even under boost. It's a turbine-style pump so it's very quiet and durable. It comes with a filter sock to pre-screen the fuel and prevent pump damage. It can be used with carbs or EFI. (Photo Courtesy Aeromotive)

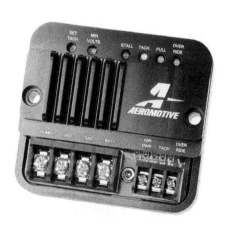

Aeromotive's Billet Fuel Pump Speed Controller (FPSC) is a good addition to any vehicle with an electric fuel pump but is especially beneficial with EFI. The FPSC monitors engine speed and modulates fuel pump speed to better match demand. Unlike other systems that do this by reducing the voltage to the pump (and can lead to damage and possible failure), the FPSC duty cycles the pump power circuit to harmlessly reduce output. (Photo Courtesy Aeromotive)

Nitrous Oxide Injection

Once you've upgraded the fuel supply system to get more fuel to the engine you may also want to consider adding a simple and relatively inexpensive way to allow the engine to use the extra fuel supply to provide even more power, at least for brief intervals. This can be done very effectively with the installation of a nitrous oxide injection system.

Supercharging and turbocharging are other examples of "power adders" that provide extra air mass, thus allowing more fuel to be burned to create more power. These are not discussed here due to their high cost and frequent need for custom installation procedures. Besides, the injection of pressurized nitrous oxide along with additional fuel can provide tremendous increases in power for short periods of time. This is because nitrous contains much more oxygen per unit mass than does air so injecting it instantly adds additional oxygen into the combustion chamber, which in turn allows more fuel to be consumed. This creates higher cylinder pressures that translate to more power.

Nitrous can be injected into each intake runner or from a plate underneath the throttle body/carburetor. It can be introduced with the additional fuel (a "wet" system) or it can be injected alone with the additional fuel coming from elsewhere, such as the fuel injectors on an EFI engine (a "dry" system). It can also be injected in multiple locations and in multiple stages to achieve different performance levels and benefits based on intended use.

In drag racing, for example, a two-stage system may inject a smaller amount during the beginning of a run to help prevent excessive wheelspin and then add the remaining amount

Nitrous Express (NX) specializes in later-model EFI-equipped vehicles and have also applied their technology to products for older carbureted vehicles. Systems with power-boosting capabilities from as little as 50 to several thousand horsepower are available. The Gemini wet plate system (shown) is capable of adding up to 500 hp at the wheels. This "next-generation" system has some very unique features. NX claims this system and its advanced plate design are especially beneficial to carbureted Fords.

later in the run once more-stable traction has been achieved. The Nitrous Express Gemini Plate System uses a specially designed, billet Spraybarless plate mounted underneath the carb. It provides 50 to 500 additional horsepower for a limited

The Gen-X Accessory Pack offered by NX has everything you need to complete your nitrous installation, including an automatic bottle heater. The heater has a pressure transducer to provide feedback used to keep the bottle pressure in an optimal range, regardless of the ambient temperature. Also included are a liquid-filled pressure gauge for installation on the bottle valve, an NHRA-approved pressure-release fitting (with a replaceable pressure disc), blowdown tube (for venting nitrous to outside the car if the bottle pressure should exceed 3,000 psi), fuel pressure safety switch (stops nitrous flow if fuel pressure drops too low), and all the associated hardware and connectors. (Photo Courtesy Nitrous Express)

time. This superior design provides exceptionally balanced distribution along with excellent atomization to deliver maximum performance and efficiency. The high-quality components provide the required flow and have exceptional durability.

These NX Lightnings are advanced solenoids. NX redesigned the flow path inside the solenoids to eliminate unnecessary turns and changes in direction while maintaining a more-constant cross section for the still-liquid nitrous. By raising the inlet port and using a bottom exit, NX eliminated several 90-degree turns and one expansion area. These solenoids have a bypass port that allows you to hook up a purge valve directly to the nitrous solenoid for a neater appearance and more effective venting.

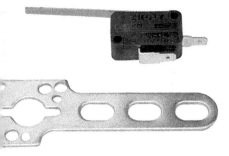

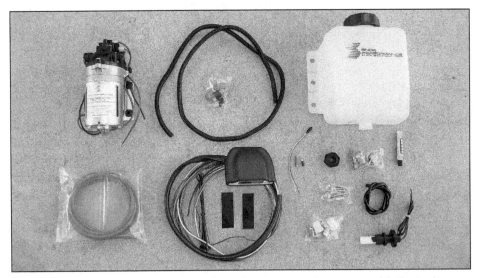

Water/methanol injection systems have become much more sophisticated over the years. This Stage-3 Boost Cooler from Snow Performance is a perfect example. Snow uses a special, very high-pressure Ultra High Output (UHO) pump that provides greater flow potential and allows for better atomization with smaller droplet sizes. It receives the mixture from standard (shown) or optional, larger reservoirs, which have a bottom outlet for all the fluid.

Plate-type systems provide enough nitrous for most high-performance street and street/strip applications plus they're easier to install and tune. This Gemini Twin Plate uses a perimeter spray system, which acts like a direct-port system in the sense that it directs the plumes toward each runner (in a single-plane manifold) to get a superior mixture balance at each port/cylinder and between them. This approach combines the benefits of direct-port systems (mixture balance and response) with the benefit of injecting farther upstream (more mixing and cooling).

Regardless of the type of system chosen, the mounting position of the bottle is critical to getting all the nitrous out of it. The valve end must be raised and the bottle lined up along the centerline of the car so liquid nitrous covers the internal pickup tube (at the bottom of the bottle) even under hard acceleration. Never mount the bottle sideways (90 degrees to the centerline) or level.

Water/Methanol Injection

Water/methanol injection systems allow increased ignition timing and/or compression ratios, thus improving performance. In essence this can compensate to a degree for inadequate fuel quality and/or octane. This is particularly true in certain areas of the country, such as in California, because these systems can be used to compensate for the availability of only 91-octane pre-

mium pump gas. The injection of a water and methanol mixture (along with the potential addition of other additives such as nitromethane) primarily has the effect of cooling the intake charge through the process of converting the injected water into steam during combustion. This lowers the peak combustion temperature while also increasing the burn rate due to the increased surface area of the fuel droplets coating the water droplets.

When a combustible liquid such as methanol is included in the mix

the additional energy from its combustion is added to that from the combustion of the primary fuel mixture. This results in a greater total release of energy over a longer period of time and the extra performance comes without the higher pressure spikes that lead to detonation.

One of the more sophisticated injection systems is manufactured in the United States by Snow Performance. This Stage-3 system uses true 2D mapping to ensure the precise delivery of the correct amount of liquid under very high pressure so it is

The LCD display mounts with Velcro strips, usually on top of the dash, in the driver's line of sight. The display shows boost pressure, fuel injector pulse-width, and the percent of maximum flow at any given time. The parameters for the mapping are all quickly and easily programmed from the driver's seat using two buttons (shown). A mixture flow gauge is also available for standard gauge pods.

more evenly distributed throughout the intake charge and is more quickly and completely ignited.

A unique control unit allows for mapping based on manifold pressure and fuel injector pulse width (in the case of EFI) in any proportion desired by the user. The control unit can also be programmed to operate only under specific conditions and to also provide a warning should the included reservoir run out of liquid. These features allow for extremely accurate metering of the injected liquid, which can reduce the amount of liquid used and/or needed to achieve the desired result. This generally yields better performance in the low- and mid-range load points because they are not receiving more liquid than is really needed, as is common with less-capable systems.

Failsafe Gauge

Even after you've made all the upgrades to the air intake and fuel systems you can never be totally safe from mishaps that are beyond your control and unexpected. Being able to watch what's going on with your air/fuel ratio on the road while datalogging it with some other parameters (such as RPM, boost, etc.) for subsequent evaluation can help. The ability to immediately act on it to protect your engine is even better.

AEM Performance Electronics has developed just such a device for any vehicle: the universal Digital Wideband Failsafe Gauge. It provides a highly accurate Bosch wideband oxygen sensor (which never requires

A wideband oxygen sensor helps you tune your engine combination for the best performance. AEM's Digital Wideband Failsafe (DWF) gauge displays air/fuel data and datalogs it along with other information. It provides a warning to protect the engine should the data fall outside the ranges you've set. The DWF uses a proven Bosch UEGO-type sensor for gathering the air/fuel data and an onboard vacuum/pressure sensor, which can read up to 29 psig. Both parameters can be simultaneously displayed on the gauge in real time by using the 24 tricolor LEDs around the edge and the full-color LED display screen in the center. A low-level signal output triggers a failsafe strategy through an external device (such as the ECU). An RPM signal input is used while tuning. (Photo Courtesy AEM Performance Electronics)

any open-air calibration to be performed) and an internal datalogger capable of storing up to three hours of data for subsequent playback using the included software.

The gauge can simultaneously display boost pressure for pressurized cars. Best of all, the gauge can be programmed to provide a warning and an output signal that can be used to retard spark if the air/fuel ratio or manifold pressure/vacuum falls outside of the ranges that you've programmed into it. There's also a trigger function to begin datalogging automatically.

Exhaust System

After upgrading your engine to get more air and fuel into it you also need to upgrade your exhaust to get the extra spent gases out of it. For a daily driver this may just mean converting to dual exhausts and/or putting on a less-restrictive set of mufflers and at most, maybe a set of headers to go with them.

For high-performance street cars and streetable track-day cars, however, a complete makeover is needed. Functionality, performance, and durability under more extreme use are the

main priorities. For most street cars a 2.5-inch exhaust should be used.

The streetable track car usually has larger (more than 3 inches) tubing and less concern over the noise level or appearance because the car also probably sits a bit lower and has a lot of undercar reinforcements such as subframe connectors. It may also be necessary to use oval instead of round tubing to maintain sufficient ground clearance. It's also more likely that the exhaust terminates before the rear axle to not only reduce weight and restriction but also to avoid interference with the axle and suspension.

For example, Doug's headers are manufactured with a machined sealing bead and a thick flange, and are stitch welded at the port. To minimize exhaust leaks the company includes a set of its own proprietary header flange gaskets so all of that good work doesn't go to waste if inferior gaskets are used. Doug's gaskets are super thick and made from a specially formulated material that can withstand temperatures up to 1,100 degrees F as well as up to 3,700 psig/255 bar of exhaust pressure. Each gasket is also precisely matched to the port shape of its respective header.

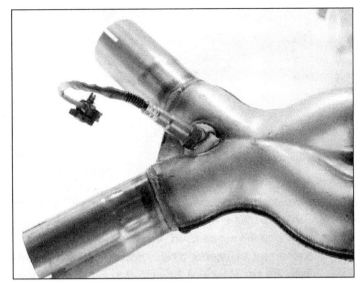

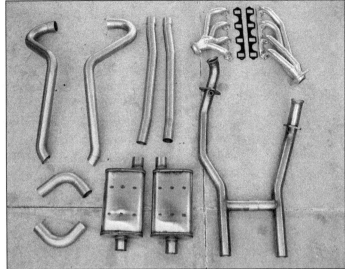

Whenever you use a wideband sensor to monitor the air/fuel ratio take care to be sure it is located where it can "see" the exhaust from all cylinders. On an X-pipe (shown) a good location is just before the merge. On an H-pipe the middle of the crossover is good. With open headers you should really use one per collector, but in any case, the sensor should be as close to the collector flange as possible. In addition, always tilt the sensor so water doesn't ruin it.

Installing an aftermarket exhaust system yields considerable performance. Even on a minimally modified car the reduced backpressure can provide more power and better throttle response along with a much better sound. In many cases fuel economy can even improve a bit. The key is to match the exhaust to the engine, particularly the cam and intake. A full package such as this one from JBA is easy to install because all the parts are compatible and complementary, rather than from different sources.

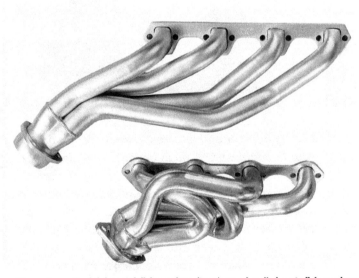

Here is a "mid-length" header (top) and a "shorty" header (bottom). In general, the longer the header, the better it fits. For a mildly modified engine you don't really see much of a difference, but as power levels rise it's best to go longer if you can. Fortunately there are plenty of options for full-length headers for older Mustangs. In most cases a shorty header meant for a 5.0L also works in an older car. With small-blocks there's a lot of crossover.

This 1965 fastback with a 347 stroker small-block and a T5 manual transmission has a typical high-performance street car exhaust. As you can see, the long-tube headers fit with no problem even though a hydraulic clutch is used and there are oxygen sensors in the collectors. This Magnaflow system uses 2.5-inch stainless steel tubing and an X-pipe design, which, thankfully, tucks up rather neatly under the driveshaft. One of the issues with X-pipes is they can sometimes hang down relatively low depending on where the "X" is. H-pipes are less prone to this problem but they generally don't perform as well as X-pipes.

This small-block Windsor kit has multiple options for configuring the rear part of the system. The quickest option is to simply install turndowns on the muffler outlets (shown). This reduces restriction but causes a lot more noise inside the car. You also have to worry about the fumes getting into the car at low speeds or when sitting still. The main reason to use this type of setup is a lack of clearance around the axle due to intrusion by the suspension and/or other components such as a fuel cell. In that case you probably use a "turbo"-style muffler (shown) for clearance.

A variation on the middle location of the exhaust is to angle it outward to exit just after the tire between the body and the suspension. This eliminates fuel heating concerns and it better directs noise and fumes away from the car. It takes a little effort to aim the exhaust so it's not flowing right at the suspension or tires but it possibly avoids damaging them from the heat.

Once you've found a good position, you can use a minimally compliant hanger as close to the exhaust tip as possible to prevent any excess movement. This takes the exhaust all the way to the back of the car so that the noise and fumes are not "captured" underneath the car.

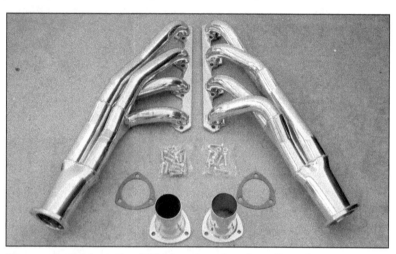

These small-block Ford Windsor headers from Doug's are rare because they do double duty by being designed for a full race car and for the street with a much lower power level. A good compromise for such dual-use situations is to use a Tri-Y design instead of a race header with larger tubing.

The Tri-Y design of this Doug's small-block header has relatively large 1¾-inch primaries, which then merge into two oval-shaped sections (made from 2-inch tubing) before they finally merge into the 3-inch collector. This approach provides markedly better performance in the low- and mid-RPM ranges with only a small loss in peak power compared to a standard 4-into-1 long-tube header.

This greater "area under the curve" provides noticeably better performance and driveability on the street with a relatively negligible effect on the track (for a street car). In fact, in road race situations where there are many slow, low-RPM corners. Tri-Ys can actually result in better lap times because you can often come out of the corners harder.

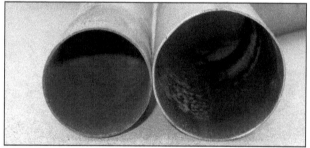

Having a larger and less-restrictive collector on your headers isn't of much benefit if you slap on a set of reducers to decrease the tubing diameter significantly. The 3-inch tube (right) has 44 percent more flow area yet the pipe diameter is only .5 inch (20 percent) larger than the 2.5-inch tube (left). A 1/4-inch drop in diameter isn't a big deal but it still should be avoided if possible. Larger drops can really cause a significant loss in power so you're probably better off going with a smaller header that has a matching collector to get back in torque what you lose on the top end.

Unless you can tuck the larger pipes up farther or can "go NASCAR" and flatten the round tubing into an oval shape you have to be careful to avoid scraping or otherwise damaging the pipes.

IGNITION AND STARTING

As you pack more air and fuel into the cylinders, you significantly increase the cylinder pressure and the charge motion within the cylinder prior to ignition. This can make it less likely for the spark to occur with enough energy for combustion, or to occur at all. Even for a mild-performance car, minor upgrading of the ignition system can result in better starting, throttle response, performance, and fuel mileage. This is mainly due to normal wear over time, which results in higher resistance in the spark plug wires, a larger gap at the plugs themselves, wear at the distributor cap and rotor, and, if you're still using them, the breaker points. All of these components are easy enough and relatively inexpensive to replace, but breaker points do not belong on high-performance cars.

Ignition System

If your vehicle has breaker points and you want to get away from them you can install an ignitor conversion kit, such as one from PerTronix. They use a magnetic pickup with associated electronics to replace the points. You no longer have to be concerned with their periodic wear and need for

adjustment or replacement. The kit installs discreetly inside your stock distributor; the only evidence of it is the two external wires instead of the usual one. The ignitor provides maintenance-free performance superior to that of points due to the increased spark energy levels resulting from longer dwell times allowed by the electronics.

When combined with a compatible coil, better plug wires, and better spark plugs the strength, consistency, and reliability of the ignition system is greatly improved.

Spark Plugs

Spark plug choice is critical because it can yield the greatest benefit. A plug that's too cold can get

Newer technologies such as this PerTronix Ignitor kit replace the points and are maintenance free for life plus they provide a hotter and more-reliable/stable spark. When you add the fact they also fit entirely inside the distributor and are thus completely out of sight except for one extra wire, it's a no-brainer.

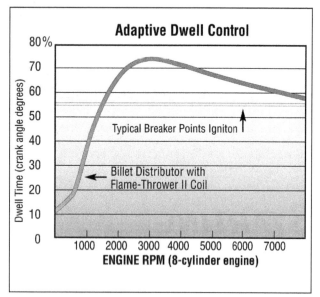

Adaptive Dwell Control

Dwell Time (crank angle degrees)

Typical Breaker Points Igniton

Billet Distributor with Flame-Thrower II Coil

ENGINE RPM (8-cylinder engine)

This graph clearly shows how the combination of a PerTronix ignitor breakerless conversion kit and matching coil greatly outperform their stock counterparts. Even with the OEM coil there's a huge benefit from the ignitor alone. This is mainly due to better stability and longer dwell time, plus the elimination of bounce and wear. (Illustration Courtesy PerTronix)

voltage requirement for the spark. Iridium plugs last significantly longer than regular or even platinum-tip plugs for not much more cost than the latter.

Enthusiasts often avoid platinum-tip plugs because they tend to not remove the heat as quickly as even a copper-core regular plug. Their purpose is long life, not performance. A properly gapped iridium plug can last up to 100,000 miles on the street, especially with ignition upgrades.

Amplifier Box

Improvements made for daily drivers also apply to high-performance street cars. However, the higher cylinder pressures associated with the higher power levels of the latter likely require the use of an ignition amplifier box along with a compatible, even higher-output, coil.

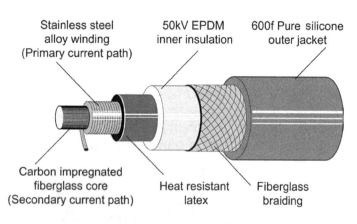

Stainless steel alloy winding (Primary current path)

50kV EPDM inner insulation

600f Pure silicone outer jacket

Carbon impregnated fiberglass core (Secondary current path)

Heat resistant latex

Fiberglass braiding

Stock spark plug wires become burned or cracked from exposure to the elements, which can lead to arcing. At some point the resistance rises enough to cause weak sparks or even misfire. The best way to correct this is to use a spiral-wound wire set, which has a much lower resistance metallic conductor that supplements the carbon core. This allows more energy to reach the plugs so they fire more reliably under all conditions.

Other design features incorporated into better aftermarket wire sets include an 8-mm-diameter radio suppression wire with a spiral-wound metal core, which is the most common choice for high-performance street use. Larger diameters and extra outer insulation may be needed in more extreme cases. (Illustration Courtesy PerTronix)

With very high cylinder pressures it likely becomes necessary to use an ignition amplifier box such as this PerTronix Second Strike unit. Unlike most ignition amplifier boxes this unit provides two sparks across the full RPM range. It doesn't revert to a single spark above 3,000 rpm or so. This box also provides the capability of varying when the second spark event occurs, thus allowing you to better optimize it to the characteristics of your engine for maximum benefit. (Photo Courtesy PerTronix)

fouled with deposits and cause misfires. A plug that's too hot can cause detonation and engine damage. For most high-performance street and streetable track cars a standard-style plug of the correct heat range is fine. Plugs with iridium-center electrodes outlast and outperform conventional plugs. Manufacturers such as Autolite

market less-expensive iridium plugs but they lack some of the features found on those by NGK and Denso.

The thin iridium-center electrode coupled with a tapered ground strap creates optimal conditions for ignition. These provide an open area that allows the flame front to propagate rapidly; smaller electrodes reduce the

Amplifiers greatly increase the total spark energy and the duration of the spark for more complete combustion. The longer spark duration is the result of firing multiple sparks instead of just one. This provides additional opportunities for combustion to occur (or reoccur) because the chances of an ignitable mixture being near the spark plug at the time the spark occurs are increased. These devices usually require hard-wiring larger-gauge wires directly to the battery to supply extra current for their faster-acting electronics to build more and hotter sparks in the time available. Amplifiers generally intercept the ignition trigger signal, amplify and/or multiply it, and then send a higher-voltage signal to the ignition coil to increase the voltage and the total spark energy. The coil must be compatible with the box to work best.

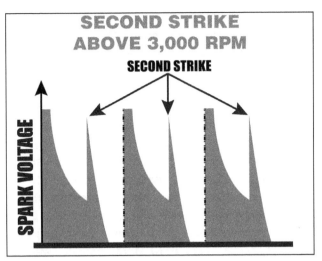

The PerTronix Second Strike retains its multi-spark capability throughout the entire RPM range. This unit provides the benefit of an extra spark at much higher revs plus it allows you to adjust when the second spark occurs. The amount of the delay (or offset) is represented in degrees of crankshaft rotation.

The CAO rotary switch on the outside of the box adjusts the delay. You can precisely vary the timing of the second spark from 2 to 18 degrees after the first to obtain optimum performance. (Illustration Courtesy PerTronix)

Distributor

It's also probably beneficial to replace your distributor with a superior aftermarket unit. They have more-robust construction and materials with tighter manufacturing tolerances compared to a stock unit. The absence of the accumulated wear of the older unit virtually eliminates excessive spark scatter and timing errors, which plague the stock distributor, especially over longer periods of time.

If you're using an EEC-IV control system for ignition and fuel control you can gain some performance by also upgrading the TFI ignition module attached to the distributor. The stock modules have a tendency to overheat and cause the car to run roughly or even shut off until they cool down. In some cases they fail altogether and the engine doesn't run. Aftermarket TFI modules are designed to not have this issue plus they also have upgraded electronics, which produce more spark energy.

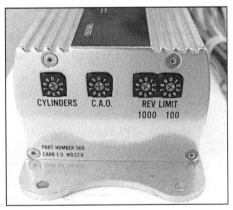

The PerTronix Second Strike unit has adjustments for the number of cylinders of the engine, the crank angle offset (CAO), and an adjustable "soft" digital rev limiter, which is far more accurate (within .01 percent) than analog products. Second Strike first randomly drops a single spark event. The RPM limit is adjustable in 100-rpm steps via the digital rotary switches (no need for external resistors). There are only five wires to hook up.

When using an amplifier box it's imperative to use a properly matched coil. PerTronix recommends their Flame-Thrower HV coil for the Second Strike. It's an efficient E-core design capable of producing upward of 60,000 volts without internal shorting or other problems such high voltages can cause. The vacuum potted coil body is mounted in a 6063 T5 aircraft aluminum bracket that acts as a heat sink. It not only helps keep coil temperatures down but also makes it rugged enough for hot and vibration environments. These coils have brass terminals for better conductivity and are available in three primary resistance values, including .45 ohm for the Second Strike and most CD-type boxes.

For non-computer applications PerTronix and others offer greatly upgraded distributors, which look better, work better, and last longer than stock versions. This PerTronix Plug-n-Play Billet Distributor is far more durable and accurate than the OEM distributors it directly replaces. It comes with an Ignitor II/III module already installed to eliminate breaker points while also providing the advantages of adaptive dwell and a hotter, more-reliable spark. The polished, CNC-machined housings contain tempered-steel shafts, which twist less to provide better accuracy and longer life. The shafts are held by an upper ball bearing and a longer, oil-impregnated lower bushing, which reduce friction and vibration, especially at higher RPM. The advance weights are precision stamped to provide more consistent timing. High-dielectric distributor caps and rotors with brass terminals (for better conductivity and corrosion resistance) are standard. (Photo Courtesy PerTronix)

you to use different curves for street and track use, thus providing better performance for each instance than would a single, compromised curve.

Eliminate the Distributor

One upgrade that can be beneficial in many cases is to eliminate the distributor altogether. Compu-Tronix has developed a retrofit distributorless ignition system based on the technology used on many later-model OEM vehicles.

The distributor is replaced by an electronics module, which provides signals to two coil packs that use the "waste spark" method to fire the spark plugs twice as often as usual. This eliminates the need for a distributor, cap, and rotor, thus also eliminating the rotor/cap air gap. This greatly improves the accuracy of the spark timing, especially at much higher RPM where its very fast electronics allow it to maintain virtually full output across the entire RPM range. Not having air gaps in the distributor, etc., which slow down and weaken the spark current, is a big factor.

If you're using a TFI-type system it's a really good idea to replace the OEM Ford TFI module because they're prone to overheating. Once they overheat the engine runs rough and misfires (if it keeps running). When the module cools down it works again, usually. To avoid this and gain extra performance, replace it with a high-performance module, such as this PerTronix Flame-Thrower. It uses superior components that aren't affected by normal underhood conditions. They provide faster internal response, which provides maximum dwell, higher spark energy, and more-accurate timing. (Photo Courtesy PerTronix)

Ignition Improvements

For the streetable track-day car there are further upgrades to consider. These include an even hotter ignition box and coil along with an even more sophisticated distributor

MSD claims to have virtually eliminated play in their billet distributors, thus improving spark accuracy and suitability for high-RPM use. The billet aluminum body is CNC machined to a tolerance of .001 inch. The internal polished and coated steel shaft is made of a superior material with improved manufacturing methods to keep it from flexing at higher speeds/loads. The magnetic sensor and the external TFI module (on 5.0L/TFI versions) are also upgraded to ensure better performance and reliability. (Photo Courtesy MSD Ignition)

that allows for the use of different timing curves (on carbureted applications). The matched High Energy components from Crane Cams are an excellent example of race-quality products that are also completely at home on the street. The adjustable timing curve feature, in fact, allows

Having a total of four 60,000-volt coils at your disposal is another plus. Because there are more coils each has more time to fire, even after the wasted spark is considered. There's enough time, in fact, to maintain full output up to 12,000 rpm should you need to go so high. Compu-Tronix claims this allows the DIS8 to provide more total spark energy than any single-coil system with a distributor.

The synch module and coil packs are sealed from the elements and use OEM-type Weathertite electrical connectors for a good seal without corrosion. This is an excellent option for a high-performance street car where a lot of spark energy and limited tunability is needed in a reasonably priced, maintenance-free system.

Of course you can take this distributorless concept even further by using a coil-per-plug setup and eliminating the waste spark to get the best of all worlds. This is now being used on most production vehicles, not only for performance reasons but also for better fuel economy and lower emissions. It's designed into the powertrain control module and provides incredible timing accuracy, spark energy, and durability in new vehicles.

High-Resolution Crank Trigger

The ultimate system uses a high-resolution crank trigger for the best timing accuracy and consistency. Retrofitting such a system to an older car, although not impossible, is complicated. In very simple terms you need sensor inputs you

Beyond the Distributor

The Crane Cams system goes beyond a high-performance street-only system. The distributor shares many similar features but things are taken even further. Instead of a magnetic Hall Effect sensor the Pro-Curve billet distributor uses a photochemically etched stainless steel optical-triggering disc. It provides better accuracy (within .5 degree) yet still provides a magnetic-trigger compatible-output signal through its connector. There are also 27 pre-programmed advance curves in the all-digital internal electronics to provide plenty of tuning options. These are chosen by quickly and simply adjusting the two rotary switches on the exterior; no weight or spring changes are required.

Other features include a strong, stainless steel shaft and the choice of a larger cap for minimal crossfire potential or a smaller cap for tighter packaging. Both are high-dielectric with all-brass fittings.

The Crane HI-6R/Digital Multi-Spark CD Ignition box has a very high primary spark energy (1,200 mj) and voltage output (450) for each multi-spark sequence. It also has built-in timing retard for use with an optional external-adjustment module. In addition, the RPM limit adjustment comes standard on the box via two rotary switches that allow adjustments in 100-rpm steps. It uses a non-damaging sequential rev-limiting strategy and is made to take extreme abuse by virtue of it being fully potted to better protect the more-reliable surface-mounted electronics. Rubber shock mounts are also included to reduce internal vibration.

The matching coils are Crane's LX92, which is an E-core design Crane claims can provide up to 12 times more spark output than an OEM/stock coil. Its closed magnetic path greatly reduces inductive losses to generate more secondary energy and voltage at the spark plugs. The coil is epoxy encapsulated and mounted in an aluminum bracket that acts as a heat sink. It also uses heavy-gauge low-resistance wiring for better heat dissipation and durability. With all this spark energy available and just looking for something (or someone) to jump to, the coil also has an insulated primary connection to reduce the possibility of arcing on both circuits.

Finally, superior plug wires are needed to further prevent arcing while also suppressing RFI/EMI and delivering maximum energy to the plugs. Cranes's 8.5-mm Fire Wires do this with an extremely low resistance rating and reactive core technology, which is a further evolution of the spiral-wound metallic concept. Dual-layer pure silicone-on-silicone construction and 550-degree F plug boots can take the heat. ■

You can eliminate the distributor altogether and retrofit an aftermarket retrofit version of proven OEM technology. The Compu-Tronix DIS8 distributorless system, which includes a couple of coil packs, an electronics/synch module and a couple of small wiring harnesses, replaces the distributor. This is a "waste spark" system because it actually fires two sparks per cycle: one at the end of the compression stroke for ignition plus another at the end of the exhaust stroke.

You can eliminate the distributor altogether and retrofit an aftermarket version of proven OEM technology. The DIS8 distributorless system by Compu-Tronix replaces the distributor with a couple of coil packs, an electronics/synch module, and a couple of small wiring harnesses. The module goes where the distributor came from; the coil packs can go virtually anywhere as long as the wiring harnesses from the module can safely reach them and the plug wires can likewise safely reach where they need to be (shorter is better). This type of ignition is known as a "waste spark" system because it actually fires two sparks per cycle: one at the end of the compression stroke for ignition and another at the end of the exhaust stroke.

don't have, very fast electronics for each cylinder, and a control module to use all of this properly. Making it compatible and functional isn't easy; making it work well is even harder. The cost, effort, and expertise involved are much greater than the potential benefit for most street cars.

The much-higher power levels and the likely use of a power adder on a streetable track-day car may make it necessary to use a colder-range spark plug. It may also be beneficial to use a spark plug designed to better cope with such extreme use.

For example, multiple ground straps help ensure reliable ignition. ZEX racing plugs have a larger primary ground strap (with a copper core) surrounded by three smaller ground straps. This design helps ensure a spark remains possible even when very high cylinder pressures and charge motion velocities are encountered. This also adds a degree of redundancy and safety so that engine damage and/or injury may be prevented should there be a problem with the primary ground strap.

Other spark plugs with multiple electrodes are usually not meant for high-performance or racing use because their designs tend to shroud the spark too much and they use platinum electrodes. Platinum is fine

for long life in a stock engine but it tends to melt more easily, especially with power adders.

Starting System

A strong starting system is necessary when the compression ratio has been significantly raised and when a lot of spark advance is being used, particularly at warmer ambient temperatures. In addition to the function of starting the car the battery also serves as somewhat of a dampener for the electrical system, which can help to minimize large voltage excursions that can affect the ignition or other electrical/electronic systems. EFI systems must have a stable voltage level to function optimally even though they can still work at fairly low levels due to their voltage compensation capability.

Conventional batteries are fine for normal use but a better solution is absorbent glass mat (AGM) batteries. They are more resistant to vibration, heat, and similar issues, which can kill a regular battery. They're more "power dense" so they can be lighter and/or more powerful for a given application. Best of all, they're essentially maintenance-free and virtually spill-proof so they can be mounted in almost any position.

Optima Batteries

A daily driver benefits from a battery upgrade not only in terms of more reliable starting but also in the ability to run accessories, such as the audio system, with less fear of running the battery down too far. Optima's family of batteries are a great solution because they are readily available and reasonably priced while also providing very high cold-cranking and reserve power levels.

The RedTop battery is optimized for higher cranking power in a smaller, lighter package.

Optima also offers the Yellow-Top line, which still has very high cranking power but trades some of it off to achieve significantly higher reserve power levels. This is basically how long you can run on the battery with the engine off. If you have very high-drain accessories, such as audio and video equipment, this may be more of a priority to you.

Enersys Odyssey Batteries

The above also applies to the high-performance street car plus it likely has the additional burden of a higher compression ratio. Enersys Odyssey batteries are extremely compact for their capacity. They share the ability to provide very high cranking and reserve power levels,

The Odyssey AGM battery uses 99.99-percent virgin lead to achieve greater power density. It features cast, welded, and bonded cell plate connectors; tin-coated brass-alloy terminals; and optional metal cases to endure very severe operating environments. Shown here is Odyssey's etched billet-aluminum mounting kit. It mounts the battery much more securely than generic mounting kits and includes inner cushioning pads to help protect the battery from vibration and extend its life.

thus making them very well suited to remote mounting. Because they are a sealed gel cell/AGM construction they can also be mounted in virtually any position with no risk of leakage.

Odyssey claims their batteries have a design life between 8 and 12 years with a normal service life between 3 and 10 years depending on the application. This compares to 5 years and 1 to 5 years for a conventional battery. Even though these batteries may cost a bit more up-front they can be less expensive over time because they don't need to be replaced as often.

Furthermore, Odyssey batteries hold their charge much better, allowing up to two years in storage before needing to be recharged (versus only 6 to 12 weeks for conventional batteries).

A final benefit is that when an Odyssey battery finally begins to fail it does so gradually so it is less likely to leave you stranded.

Lithionics Batteries

A streetable track-day car has little, if any, need for reserve capacity to run accessories with the engine off. It needs maximum cranking power with minimal size and weight. For such applications and where cost is less of a consideration a lithium ion formulation likely fits the bill, at least at the track. It probably isn't the ideal choice even for minimal street use, especially in colder climates. For the ultimate lightweight battery a carbon-fiber-encased lithium ion battery such as one from Lithionics Battery may be what you're looking for.

Lithium ion batteries have several advantages over conventional lead acid and AGM batteries. For a given cranking power rating they usually weigh about half. They also last much longer; sometimes they're able to endure up to 10 times as many recharging cycles. They're also a completely sealed, no-maintenance design and hold their charge very well in storage. They usually can retain about 75 percent of their initial charge after one year.

Lithionics products have other unique features such as NeverDie and dual-voltage capability. Because all lithium ion batteries require internal electronics to ensure proper charging and safety, Lithionics has also programmed in a special feature that monitors the draw of the battery and puts it into a special sleep mode if you leave the headlights on, etc. It ensures at least 20 percent of the battery capacity is retained to allow starting the vehicle under all conditions. You simply push the NeverDie button on the battery and you're ready to go. You don't need to worry about being stranded by a dead battery.

The dual-voltage feature is very useful for extremely hard-to-start engines because it provides an additional connecting lug just for the starter circuit with a 16v output to provide more effective starting power. A normal 12v (12.8v, actually, with lithium ion) is also provided for everything else. The higher voltage per cell (3.2 versus 2v) allows for faster recharge times (two to four times) and much less voltage "sag" (the amount the voltage drops under load) on start-up. This prevents damage to vehicle electronics during start-up and also ensures more stable/consistent performance, especially with more-sensitive EFI systems.

Powermaster Starters

A high-torque starter motor can offset weight by potentially allowing a smaller and lighter battery to be used while still retaining sufficient starting capability. Reserve capacity, however, is lower but recharging time is much quicker.

If you consider a starter upgrade you should also consider an indexing high-torque starter, such as those from Powermaster, to gain clearance with headers and nearby parts while also reducing weight.

LUBRICATION AND COOLING

Taking the time to evaluate your oiling system and make improvements where necessary not only protects your engine by preventing problems but it can also be a source of even more performance gains. The cooling system of a vehicle is critical in removing the additional heat created as you increase engine output to improve vehicle performance. In this chapter I briefly take a look at where some opportunities may lie within these systems to protect against problems and also make some gains.

Oil Pan

The oil pan holds the oil and makes sure oil is available to the oil pump pickup under all conditions. Forces are placed on the oil and the oil pan's design and baffling must ensure that the oil pickup remains submerged.

The pan design can be relatively simple because a common street car isn't subjected to high-g loads. The pump pickup generally is not uncovered for very long (or at all) because these vehicles can't accelerate very hard. As performance increases, however, as it does with a higher-horse-power Mustang, the oil pan needs enhanced baffling to compensate.

High-Performance Oil Pan

A high-performance oil pan has greater capacity and the incorporation of baffling to help keep the oil near the pickup under all conditions. The increased capacity surrounds the pickup with more oil so there is enough left around the pickup to feed the engine until the dynamics change and the rest of the oil returns.

For a drag racing application, the pan is deeper to further submerge the pickup and add baffling to the rear of the sump to help keep it filled under hard acceleration. Additional baffling is also usually put at the front edge of the sump to help retain the oil under hard braking.

Little attention needs to be paid to what happens to the oil while turning because, hopefully, that only occurs at slower speeds at either end of the strip. A drag race pan doesn't usually make a very good street oil pan because the extra depth can be problematic in terms of ground clearance.

Road Racing Oil Pan

A better alternative for a street performance car/track-day car is an

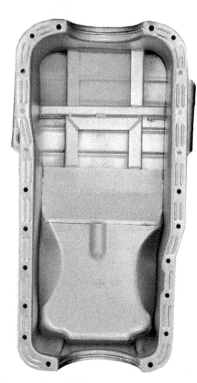

Aggressive driving requires aggressive oil control. This road race oil pan from Milodon includes special baffles, trap doors, and extra capacity to help keep the oil away from the spinning component (thus reducing "windage" losses and increasing net power). They also keep the oil near the oil pump so it gets picked up. This ensures stable oil pressure and less risk of engine damage. Deep pans may be fine at the track but reduce ground clearance on the street.

oil pan designed for road racing. Such pans are normally not much deeper than a stock pan yet they achieve their added capacity by having a sump that's wider and in some cases a bit longer than stock. This gets you the added oil capacity without much, if any, loss in ground clearance.

A special oil pickup tube is required for use with this pan design, and it can be further optimized to be less restrictive than the stock pickup. You can use a metal standoff over the pickup screen to ensure a minimum amount of clearance between the pickup screen and the oil pan floor. Once you correctly relocate the oil pickup for the new pan design you can determine the placement of the baffling.

For a small-block road race pan, Milodon, for example, effectively uses a series of chambers and trap doors to allow the oil to flow only in certain directions under specific conditions. This tends to keep more oil around the pickup while also allowing quicker replacement of the oil when the vehicle direction changes. Baffles are strategically placed to control the oil in all directions. The combination of this baffling with the extra oil capacity is extremely effective in preventing the oil pickup from being uncovered and sucking in air.

Oil Accumulator

The Accusump by Canton Racing Products provides a reliable supply of oil in high-performance applications, especially those with very rapid and extreme direction changes. This device stores a specific amount of oil under pressure while the engine is running. It is connected directly to the engine oiling system, preferably as close to the oil

pump output as possible. Should there be a drop in oil pressure it causes the oil in the Accusump to immediately begin flowing back into the engine to provide pressurized oil until normal pressure returns. Once that occurs oil is pumped back into the Accusump so it is ready for the next drop in oil pressure.

By installing a driver-controlled valve between the Accusump and the engine the driver can close the valve before the engine is shut off, thus capturing the volume of pressurized oil in the Accusump. Before the engine is again started the valve can be opened to provide oil to the engine during startup. This can greatly increase engine life and reduce the potential for scuffing, etc., until the oil pressure rises to its normal level.

The Accusump is available with various capacities to be used in different ways. A smaller one, for example, can be used as a pre-oiler for turbochargers to greatly prolong the life of their bearings at start-up and in the event of a temporary drop in oil pressure.

The Accusump can be mounted virtually anywhere there is space for it. Other than a couple of mounting brackets and the need to run some relatively large braided line or hose to the engine there's not much involved in installing and using one.

A pressure gauge and air valve mounted on the unit are used to adjust and monitor the internal pressure (directly proportional to the engine oil pressure).

For its price an Accusump is very cheap insurance against a big repair

This Accusump oil accumulator unit from Canton/Mecca stores a quantity of oil under pressure so that if engine oil pressure drops, the oil from the Accusump is immediately forced into the engine to compensate and prevent engine damage. When normal oil pressure is restored the oil is forced back into the Accusump to be ready for the next such event. With the installation of a valve in the line to the engine the Accusump can also be used to pre-oil the engine before it is started, thus greatly reducing one of the major sources of engine wear. (Photo Courtesy Canton/Mecca)

bill and/or bodily harm should an engine fail.

Dry Sump Oiling System

For the most extreme streetable track-day car the ultimate oiling system is a dry sump type. This system gets its name from the fact that external pumps are used to scavenge the oil from a very shallow oil pan so it can be directed to a large reservoir for de-aeration. A separate pressure pump stage supplies the minimally aerated and (optionally) cooled oil through a filtration system and then back to the engine under pressure.

The main advantage of a dry sump system is that the shallow oil pan allows the engine to be mounted

An upgraded oil pump, such as this Melling unit, can provide an extra margin of safety compared to even a new stock pump. A higher-volume pump is often the best choice because it circulates oil more quickly and helps cool it better. A high-volume pump can help compensate for larger bearing clearances. A high-pressure pump is called for when high RPM and relatively tight bearing clearances are the norm.

much lower, thus lowering the center of gravity. This works well in a race vehicle with a tubular frame but it may not be feasible in a production vehicle unless significant changes are made to the front structure.

In cases where there are few limitations with regard to cost a dry sump system can be especially appealing not only for the better engine location but for the increased performance, which comes from the vastly better evacuation of oil from around the spinning crankshaft. This greatly reduces "windage" losses inside the engine and can free up a significant amount of power otherwise lost as parasitic drag. Dry sump systems aren't cheap, but they are extremely effective.

Wet Sump Oiling System

A wet sump system is suitable for most mild- to high-performance street engines. You can gain significant performance by keeping the oil away from the rotating assembly that creates drag. To some extent a deeper oil pan accomplishes this but the real gains come from the installation of a windage tray and/or oil scraper.

These devices attach to the main cap fasteners and/or along the oil pan rail. Their purpose is twofold: They provide a barrier between the spinning crankshaft and rods, etc., and the oil (mist and/or liquid). They also try to remove as much oil as possible from those spinning components so it can be directed back to the oil pump pickup as soon as possible. Pretty significant gains in power (sometimes 20 hp or more) can be realized if this is done well. The use of a bearing-cap girdle can sometimes preclude the use of a windage tray and/or oil scrapers but if there's any way to accommodate it, you should.

A high-volume oil pump is generally a good idea simply because it helps ensure the engine has enough oil at any given time. A high-volume pump is especially needed when

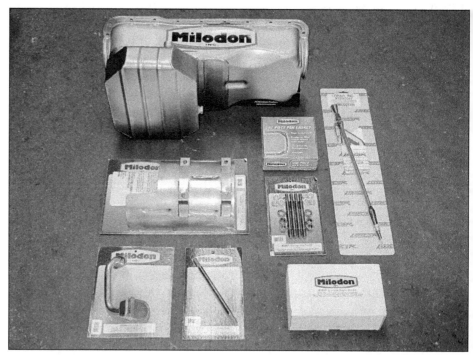

Upgrades for a wet sump system include a windage tray (and correct installation/stud kit) to further keep oil away from the rotating assembly, a stronger/hardened oil pump shaft to further protect against breakage under hard use, a single-piece silicone pan gasket (with built-in spacers to prevent crush), and a really trick Lokar locking (and flexible) dipstick, which screws right into the oil pan for a leak-proof seal at both ends. It even has a mounting bracket.

A properly designed windage tray does its job of keeping the oil and mist away from rotating parts. The main bolts (or studs) must be replaced with special ones made for the tray. Fortunately, Milodon uses high-quality fasteners similar to ARP's, which provide a similar level of strength and safety. The retaining nuts must be located high enough to keep the tray from contacting any moving parts (usually the rods) while remaining level. You might have to modify the tray due to the stud tips being closer together with the splayed four-bolt mains.

larger bearing clearances are being used, though this is likely only in a competition engine. Street-driven vehicles need engines with relatively tight bearing clearances. Still, the extra volume can help with cooling the bearings as well as offering better protection overall.

A high-pressure oil pump is generally only needed when very high RPM are experienced and/or when you have things such as oil cooling jets for the pistons, which require higher pressure to work properly. Having more pressure than you need is just a waste of energy.

A high-volume standard-pressure pump is usually the best option for street-driven performance/track-day cars. If you use such a pump it is also a good idea to upgrade to a hardened pump driveshaft because the extra force needed to drive the high-output pump can cause premature wear or even failure of a standard shaft, especially under higher-RPM conditions.

A one-piece pan gasket is simply much more convenient and seals are much better than older, multi-piece cork gaskets. Make sure you get the type that have the hard inserts to prevent overtightening, which can damage the soft gasket and/or create leaks.

A flexible dipstick provides more mounting options, it looks better than a metal tube, and the positive seal keeps proper crankcase pressure with everything looking neat.

Oil Type

The importance of using an appropriate engine oil cannot be understated, nor can the need to change it as necessary. For high-performance applications a synthetic blend of the proper weight generally suffices. However, when you have a power adder and/or very high power levels it's best to use a full synthetic. Companies such as Red Line and Royal Purple specialize in high-performance lubricants and generally offer a superior product.

Such oils are formulated for higher film strength to compensate for higher loads and RPM. They are more resistant to foaming or degradation from high heat (especially important when turbochargers are used). They also provide superior corrosion and sludge resistance (thus providing the potential for longer change intervals).

Other specialty oils include those with unique formulations. Some include extra amounts of ingredients such as the zinc and phosphorus required for older vehicles with stock, non-hardened valveseats.

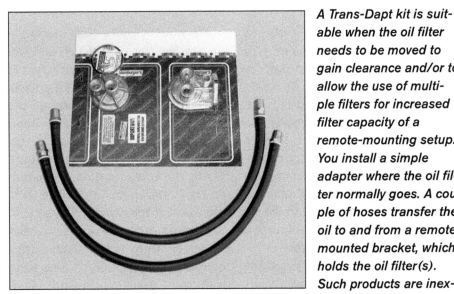

A Trans-Dapt kit is suitable when the oil filter needs to be moved to gain clearance and/or to allow the use of multiple filters for increased filter capacity of a remote-mounting setup. You install a simple adapter where the oil filter normally goes. A couple of hoses transfer the oil to and from a remotely mounted bracket, which holds the oil filter(s). Such products are inexpensive and easy to install. They can also speed up filter changes significantly.

A remote oil cooler keeps the engine oil temperature in an acceptable range (usually below 250 degrees F). This is suitable for extended high-RPM and competition use. The best products, such as this SuperCooler from B&M Racing, use a "stacked plate" design that's more efficient and robust with less pressure drop than cheaper tube-and-fin designs. These products install very similarly to a remote oil filter setup. (Photo Courtesy B&M Racing)

Thermostat

As you increase engine output to improve vehicle performance you also create, usually in direct proportion, additional heat that the cooling system must remove from the engine. In most cases, especially the early 1964½–1966 cars with smaller radiators, you soon exceed the capacity of the stock cooling system and experience overheating problems. Fortunately, there's no shortage of steps that can be taken to improve your car's cooling performance.

A lower-temperature thermostat is the easiest and least costly move to make. This reduces the temperature of the engine coolant, which can provide a little extra performance by reducing the temperature of the intake charge so it is denser. Dropping one step in temperature (from 205 to 185 degrees or from 185 to 160 degrees) is usually enough to make a noticeable difference. Dropping more than one step is usually not advisable because it may require adjustment of the fuel mixture (carburetor jetting, choke, etc.). It also significantly degrades the performance of the heater and/or defroster, which can be an issue in cold and humid climates.

For a carbureted engine you can often use a thermostat rated as low as 160 degrees F. For EFI-equipped engines, however, there can be problems with the function of the ECU when using thermostats rated below 180 degrees F or so.

Replacing the thermostat is a standard repair/maintenance operation, requiring only the new thermostat, a new gasket, and perhaps some RTV or other sealant to provide extra insurance against leaks.

Radiator Cap

Be sure to verify that the radiator cap has the correct pressure rating for your application and that it seals properly with the radiator neck. You might also want to increase the pressure rating slightly for high-performance situations because this can help reduce the formation of bubbles in the coolant when it encounters the hotter spots inside the engine (such as near the exhaust valves).

Making more power likely raises the temperature at these areas, thus increasing the potential formation of bubbles. A higher-pressure radiator cap somewhat offsets this to help maintain maximum cooling by promoting the presence of more liquid coolant in these areas, which has a greater ability to remove the extra heat generated than does the presence of bubbles. This can be further ensured by using a coolant additive such as Red Line's Water Wetter or Royal Purple's Purple Ice to alter the characteristics of the coolant so that it is better able to remove and transfer heat from the engine.

These additives can lower coolant temperatures by 20 degrees F or more. They can allow the use of water only versus a water-coolant mix because they also include corrosion inhibitors and other additives needed in a street-driven vehicle. Using 100-percent water with one of these additives has a higher heat transfer capability than a water-coolant mix and thus can provide the greatest cooling capacity as long as potential freezing is not a concern.

Whatever coolant you decide to use it's a good idea to install a filter to clean and monitor it.

Mechanical Fan

Factory fans were almost always fixed-blade steel fans, which worked reasonably well, especially when they had many blades. These fans had two issues, however: They were dependent on engine speed and they created a lot of drag on the engine.

The first issue becomes a problem when you're stuck in traffic on a hot day, possibly with the A/C on. The low engine RPM means low fan RPM, which means there is not much airflow right when you need it most. This is because of the high ambient temperature plus the added heat load the A/C system puts on the engine and the cooling system.

The drag of the A/C compressor means more fuel is burned and thus more heat is created by the engine to be removed. The A/C condenser is almost always located in front of the radiator so the heat it throws off goes right into the radiator. This reduces its effectiveness due to it getting some already heated air along with the cooler ambient air.

The only way to resolve these issues (other than relocating the condenser away from the radiator, which is rarely feasible) is to flow more air through the condenser and the radiator. Because the stock fan is tied to engine speed this is not possible unless you want to be constantly revving the engine, which is only marginally helpful.

A good solution is to have a better fan and/or more fans that are not as dependent on engine speed for airflow. The simplest approach is to change the stock mechanical fan for one that moves more air at a given engine speed. Unfortunately, a flex fan does not do this; it actually flows less as the blades flatten out at higher RPM and should therefore never be considered for a street-driven vehicle.

You can use an OEM fan with more blades, say from a larger engine and/or one that came equipped with factory A/C. This flows more air at any given speed but is still directly dependent on engine speed to create flow. This option should only be considered if you have a very minimal cooling issue and you want to spend as little as possible.

A better option is to use a clutch-type fan from a later-model vehicle such as a 5.0L engine from a Fox-Body (1979–1993) Mustang. The fan is oversized in terms of airflow potential so there's plenty of reserve capacity to keep the engine cool. The

installation of a later-model thermostatic clutch fan can often prove to be beneficial in terms of freeing up some power and also providing better cooling, even if a fan shroud doesn't fit.

The thermostatic nature of such fans allows them to basically freewheel or slip somewhat when maximum cooling isn't needed, thus taking less energy from the engine to drive them. However, when more cooling is needed the amount of slippage is reduced to where the fan is essentially connected almost solidly to the engine, thus providing much greater airflow.

A greater number of fan blades along with their greater surface area and steeper pitch provide much greater maximum flow yet deliver it only when it is needed.

A fixed-fan's flow rises with RPM even if it's not needed. They are a bit heavy, they may require some adaptation to fit on older cars, and they usually require a custom fan shroud because they are much larger than stock-type fans. However, once they've been installed the only

maintenance is to clean any dirt or dust off of the thermostatic coil so it can function properly. These fans can be relatively inexpensive if bought used.

Electric Fan

A slightly more costly and complicated solution to cooling challenges is to replace your mechanical fan with an electric fan. This has several advantages. First of all, its operation is completely independent of engine speed. It comes on via a manual switch or, more commonly, a sensor mounted on the radiator turns it on when a certain preset temperature is reached. Many fans also provide a means to switch the fan(s) on whenever a certain event occurs, such as the A/C compressor turns on or a nitrous system is activated. It can be completely automatic.

Electric fans come in many shapes, sizes, and airflow ratings. Most have built-in shrouds. The more powerful fans usually require that they be connected directly to

Flex-a-lite and other companies offer high-flow aftermarket fans that can be actuated in a number of ways. A thermal sensor, which contacts the radiator core, can be manually adjusted (via the knob on top) to turn on the fan at a wide range of temperatures, as the need dictates. The fan can also be turned on manually from a switch near the driver or it can be triggered by any number of events such as turning on the A/C, actuating a nitrous system, or reaching a certain manifold pressure. It only works when it's needed, thus eliminating any drain on the engine when it's not running.

The majority of engine-cooling fans are mounted between the radiator and the engine and thus "pull" air through the radiator core.

"Pusher" fans mounted on the external side of the radiator can also be beneficial. When heat exchangers are mounted before the radiator they raise the temperature of the air reaching the radiator, reducing its cooling capability. Increasing the airflow rate can help offset this. The increased airflow from a pusher fan can improve the efficiency of the A/C condenser and/or auxiliary coolers because more air flows through them instead of some going around them.

the battery (often via a relay) because they draw a lot of current. Most can be attached directly to the radiator core after the mechanical fan has been removed.

Fans mounted between the radiator and the engine that draw air through the radiator are known as "puller" fans. Fans mounted in front of the radiator (and also the condenser on A/C-equipped cars) force the air through the radiator and are thus known as "pushers."

Pushers are generally less efficient than pullers but they can be effective at increasing the performance of a puller when the radiator core is especially thick. They can also improve the performance of the A/C system by forcing more air through the condenser.

Radiator

The cooling system upgrades discussed thus far are applicable to any of the vehicle types being discussed in this book though they are aimed mainly at daily-driver and street-performance vehicles. When power levels rise significantly beyond stock levels, A/C is retrofitted, indoor extra coolers are added, etc., virtually all of these upgrades and even more

are needed to remove the additional heat. The OEM radiator is probably no longer up to the challenge.

Fortunately, there is no shortage of high-capacity radiator upgrades for early Mustangs. Most are direct fit and can easily replace the OEM radiator while providing more cooling power. Special configurations are available for popular engine swaps such as the installation of a later 5.0L engine, which requires a change in the location of the hose fitting on the radiator. Its use of a serpentine-belt drive causes the water pump to rotate in reverse, thus requiring that the hose outlet be located on the opposite side of the car. Having a radiator that already accommodates this difference is convenient and less expensive than adapting it yourself.

In most cases an aluminum-core radiator is preferable to a copper/brass type due to its reduced weight and reduced cost. The aluminum radiator doesn't look stock so if that's a consideration you may want to stick with a thicker (three- or four-row versus the usual stock two-row) copper/brass radiator. An aluminum radiator is a bit thicker and requires a higher-flowing fan (and/or multiple fans) but the reduced weight and lower cost are worth it. They may

also increase the radiator thickness and its frontal area.

Aluminum radiators have more-efficient tube and fin designs so that those with 2-inch-wider tubes, more frontal area, and/or better fin design (internal and external) are usually able to dissipate more heat than a heavier three- or four-row copper/brass radiator using older technology. They also can still have internal transmission oil coolers and other features that allow them to be direct bolt-ins.

When buying an aluminum radiator avoid any that use epoxied joints because they can crack and leak. They also reduce the heat transfer potential of the core. Brazed joints are superior in heat transfer, strength, and durability. You must also ensure the filler neck clears the hood.

Cooling Module

For the highest power levels such as are seen in a highly modified street performance car and a streetable track-day car even more extreme measures must be taken to ensure proper cooling. This is especially true for the latter vehicle type because it will likely be operated at very high speeds and outputs for an extended period of time.

At the Silver State Classic open road race near Ely, Nevada, for example, it is quite common for many vehicles in this event to run at full throttle for almost the entire 90-mile course. This can be as little as 1/2 hour for the fastest unlimited class cars to about an hour for the slowest cars. Even at the slower speeds many stock vehicles have trouble with overheating. The faster you run, the more important it is to upgrade the cooling system if you want to have any hope of finishing without overheating. This requires not only upgraded individual components but also considerable effort to match the components to achieve optimum performance.

One way to ensure this is to use a cooling "module" instead of acquiring your parts independently. An excellent example is the Be Cool direct-fit Classic radiator/fan module. It's rated for 700 hp (they also have 1,000-hp modules with bigger fans as well as 400- and 300-hp versions). It includes everything you

The use of a coolant recovery tank such as this one from Mustangs Plus fits every first-generation Mustang. It prevents coolant loss and protects the environment because it doesn't immediately allow coolant to spill onto the ground when the radiator cap pressure is exceeded. The polished billet aluminum also adds more underhood appeal.

need: from radiator, fan module, mounting brackets, etc., to a matching hardware kit, billet radiator cap, and overflow tank. You also get all of the necessary wiring and other items you need for a "hassle-free installation" (their claim).

Be Cool guarantees this module drops your coolant temperature by at least 20 degrees F. They even double the warranty period to two years if you use only their Be Coolant Super Duty Antifreeze. It is a special biodegradable propylene glycol formu-

lation that lasts for 7 years/300,000 miles and protects aluminum and other cooling system components down to -26 degrees F. It has a boiling point of 267 degrees F at 15 psi and it's made in America.

Water Pump

The final thing to consider relative to engine cooling is the water pump.

Daily Driver Applications

For a daily driver there's usually no need to use anything more than a good-quality direct-replacement OEM-type pump if yours needs to be replaced. Just make sure it is made by a reputable company and has improvements in the impeller, bearing, and seal designs. Stay away from plastic and stamped steel impellers if possible. A cast impeller is almost always more efficient and more durable.

High-Performance Applications

As to high-performance street and streetable track-day vehicles, pump performance needs to increase. First of all, there must be sufficient coolant flow. This requires the impeller and pump housing to be designed for optimal flow. They're

Be Cool offers cooling modules and complete kits for substantially improving cooling capacity. If your rebuilt or crate engine now produces twice the horsepower, you need twice the cooling capacity. Be Cool offers 300-hp-rated radiators and 1,000-, 700-, and 400-hp modules. The modules include high-capacity aluminum radiators, dual or single fans, and all wiring and other hardware.

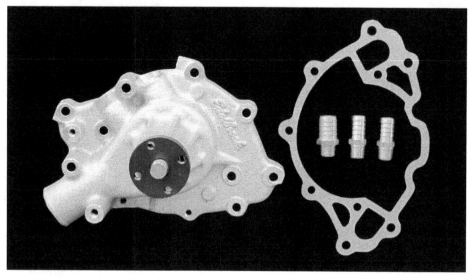

High-performance, computer-designed pumps such as this one from Edelbrock not only flow more with better balance but do so at a higher velocity. Powdered-metal impellers with larger vanes are precision cast to provide extra flow at low RPM. In addition, heavy-duty bearings and seals as well as a superior alloy and CNC machining help ensure better durability with improved cooling performance.

also manufactured to closer tolerances to achieve it and keep it over time.

Next, the higher-RPM use of these applications places more stress on the components so the highest-quality bearings and seals are required for durability.

Finally, achieving the best cooling and engine performance requires the coolant flow to be sufficient in terms of volume and pressure as well as balanced from bank to bank. OEM replacement water pumps place little, if any, emphasis on this but companies such as Edelbrock make it a priority.

Victor Series high-performance water pumps incorporate all of those design properties plus a precision-cast powdered-metal impeller with over-sized vanes for maximum flow and pressure. The design also ensures no more than a 1-percent flow difference from bank to bank.

For competition-oriented applications such as the streetable track-day car an even further upgrade is possible in the form of Edelbrock's Victor Pro Series competition water pumps. These add features such as a revised impeller entry for even greater flow, still more-robust components (thicker shaft and backing plate, billet hub, heavy-duty ball/roller bearing, etc.), and multiple hose connection options (standard hose, AN or NPT fittings, etc.). These pumps can also be used in high-performance street applications although the extra flow, strength, and expense are rarely justified in all but the most powerful and extreme instances.

Drag Race Applications

Electric water pumps make perfect sense in a drag race scenario where they can eliminate parasitic drag during the brief run down the strip yet they can run with the engine off to cool the car during the trip down the return road and in the pits. They also eliminate the need for a drive belt/pulley, which simplifies the front of the engine, saves some weight, and frees up space for extra belts, etc., to drive superchargers and so forth.

Although some electric water pumps have been used on production vehicles they are built for long-term durability. They are usually also computer controlled to vary flow based on engine coolant temperature and other factors. The electric water pumps offered by the aftermarket and for racing purposes are generally not as sophisticated and, if they were, they would be quite pricey compared to a mechanical pump. They also are not really designed for long-term durability nor are they well suited to frequent street use, especially in areas with extreme weather.

A rear crossover passage on the intake manifold, as shown on this Summit Racing Stage IV part, can improve cooling. It helps ensure more balanced cooling between the cylinder heads. Even with the most-precise water pump and engine block designs, a flow imbalance as the coolant rises from the block through the heads is not uncommon. The crossover helps ensure both heads consistently receive a similar amount of flow and cooling.

ENGINE SWAPS

In this chapter I cover the common engine swaps for first-generation Mustangs that increase performance potential. My philosophy is "There's no replacement for displacement" when it comes to increasing performance, but the key is how you get it. I discuss the tradeoffs of various options along with how good a given scenario is in terms of "Bang for the Buck" for the installation/conversion phase and once the car is being driven.

I cover the following engine choices: small-block Windsor (short-deck and tall-deck), big-blocks, modular engines (two-, three-, and four-valve V-8s; no V-10s), the 2011 and newer 5.0L Coyote engine, and the 2013 and newer 5.8L S/C GT500 engine. (No installations in original 351 Cleveland, 427 SOHC, or Boss, etc., vehicles are discussed, nor are these engines discussed as swaps.)

Given enough time, skill, and budget you can swap just about any engine into any car but that's not what I address here. My goal is to discuss reasonable, practical, and cost-effective options most owners want to and can afford to install. These options are feasible and deliver meaningful performance increases with few, if any, significant tradeoffs.

For a daily driver the pushrod Windsor engines are really the only reasonable option unless your car already has or had a big-block. Upgrading to a big-block or to one of the modular or Coyote engines is really only practical for street-performance vehicles where the desired performance level, novelty, and budget are the guiding factors.

For a streetable track-day car the intended type of on-track/strip use likely dictates the tradeoffs between weight, power, suspension, and driveline design, usually with less regard for total cost.

In any case, you should retain the ability to use the car however, whenever, and wherever you want. This is about hot rodding for the masses, not just the monied few.

Swapping a small-block Windsor engine into a classic Mustang is relatively easy because these cars were made to accept these engines. In this case, a Ford Modular engine has been installed. It has an enormous footprint and it's much wider than a common Windsor small-block. In order to make the Modular engine fit, you need to remove the shock towers, and that involves intricate metal fabrication.

Small-Block Windsor

The small-block Windsor engines are by far the easiest to swap into first-generation Mustangs. Because these engines were originally available in these cars it's a natural fit, except for the tall-deck engines in the 1964½–1966 cars. Even that combination can be made to work without too much trouble, though it's debatable if it is really beneficial.

The short-deck engine has plenty of room in the 1967 and later cars because they could be bought with big-block engines. The short-deck (8.2 inches) Windsor small-block engines ranged from 289 to 302 ci as original equipment in first-generation Mustangs. With the exception of a few special high-performance models most were simply designed to be light yet compact and reliable. Because the same basic engine layout was used well into the 1990s for the Mustang and other Ford products it's clear the basic design was a very good one. However, when higher performance is your goal it's often likely you expose shortcomings (thin walls, lack of reinforcements, etc.) that would rarely show up in normal use.

There are no hard-and-fast rules and no guarantees; every upgrade situation is different. A common belief is that a stock/OEM Windsor 5.0L block is good to about 500 hp in naturally aspirated form. Older 289/302 blocks (with the exception of the 1969/1970 Boss 302) are generally not as good to start with as the later 5.0L blocks for a number of reasons, not the least of which is they are not compatible with later OEM-style hydraulic roller lifters.

If you're going to use a power adder, you should at least upgrade to the superior Mexican, A302, or Ford Racing Boss 302 block. They have better metallurgy and reinforcements, which makes them stronger. Above 600 hp and/or heavy increases with a power adder, the A302 block should be the minimum considered. Realistically, it's then time to upgrade to a stronger aftermarket block such as the Ford Racing Boss 302, or an even stronger version from another supplier.

Short-Decks

The short-deck Windsor block has received a lot of support in the aftermarket because it fits easily in any of the first-generation Mustangs as well as later versions to the 1995 model year. Dart Machinery is one of the most respected producers of aftermarket Ford engine blocks (as well as crate engines, cylinder heads, and related items). Their products benefit from many advances beyond the original OEM designs.

For the Windsor family Dart offers four levels of engine blocks and any short-block, long-block, and complete crate engine based on them. These products range from the relatively affordable entry-level SHP blocks to the Iron Eagle variants to the all-out Race Series aluminum blocks. All are available in short-deck (8.2 inches) and tall-deck (9.5 inches) versions.

The SHP version is an iron block, which accepts most stock components and accessories, including the roller hydraulic cam setup (lifters, dog bones, and spiders) from 5.0L and similar EFI engines. It features thicker deck surfaces, scalloped outer water jackets (for better, more-even cooling), a priority main oiling system, steel main caps (four-bolt/splayed on numbers-2, -3, and -4), and blind-tapped head boltholes (to reduce water leaks).

These blocks are available in short-deck and long-deck versions with siamese-bore diameters of 4.000 or 4.125 inches (unfinished). The cylinder walls are cast extra thick to allow for bore diameters of up to 4.185 inches while still minimizing bore distortion.

Even with a more-complex, late-model, fuel injected, small-block engine such as this 5.0L there is still plenty of room. This 1966 is easily able to accommodate the 5.0L (or a 347 or larger stroker engine), even with the late-model's serpentine-belt drive and related accessories. This is an extremely popular swap because it's fairly easy, not very costly, and it provides significant benefits in power and MPG.

The Iron Eagle Sportsman shares most of its specifications with the SHP and adds a few features. The most significant of these is the option for multiple deck heights, which (in the tallest deck version) can allow for displacements of up to 468 ci due to its even thicker cylinder walls (.250-inch minimum versus .230-inch minimum for the SHP) and superior alloy (versus the SHP). These blocks are also available with 2.249- or 2.749-inch main bearings.

Dart's Iron Eagle blocks are intended for hardcore racers yet they still retain compatibility with most stock components. These blocks build on the specifications of the Iron Eagle Sportsman blocks by adding a low-restriction priority main oiling system along with front and rear external oil feeds to complement the complete stock-type system. Dual crossovers have provisions for restrictors to allow more precise allocation of oil flow when solid roller cams and/or roller rocker arms are used. Reducing oil flow to the rockers, for example, can reduce crankcase windage.

Other reinforcements include use of a premium alloy along with extra-thick deck surfaces, even thicker cylinder walls, extra webbing in the main bearing area, and the use of billet steel four-bolt main caps for all five main bearings.

The short-deck version easily fits in all years from 1964½ to 1966 because it's virtually identical in its outside dimensions to what these cars originally came with. It can make more than 500 hp and still have great driveability. Short-deck blocks are a platform that provides ample power for most early Mustangs. This engine family is suitable for the 1967–1970 models but in many cases they don't provide sufficient torque and horse-power for the larger, heavier 1971–1973 models.

Aftermarket blocks can be stroked to 347 or even 363 ci to make enough power even for these cars. The 1964½–1966 cars readily accept the shorter deck. You may have header fitment issues and this may require notching the header tubes. In addition the steering box and rod may have to be relocated when squeezing the tall-deck version into the smaller, narrower engine bay of these years. You're also relatively limited by tire size (as to how much power you can effectively get to the ground), unless you make some relatively extreme modifications to at least the suspension and body.

Tall-Decks

The short-deck block provides a light engine package in a relatively lightweight car for improved handling. The tall-deck block weighs about 80 pounds more than the short-deck version (cast in iron) and in most cases the extra output it provides really isn't usable in these smaller, lighter cars. You can stuff a tall-deck engine into the earlier cars but unless you modify/ remove the shock towers you have to settle for a less-than-optimal exhaust system.

Hood clearance is likely also an issue. For the 1964½–1966 cars a short-deck small-block is usually the best overall choice. If you want more power it is easy to modify one to 500 hp or more if you stroke it and/or use a power adder. Unless you're building a competition or show car that'll likely do.

For 1967 and later models, the tall-deck (351-based) Windsor may make more sense if you want to reach higher performance levels than are possible and/or practical with the shorter deck. The extra weight of the taller deck is less of a factor because these cars are heavier anyway, are suited for these engines, and you need more power for similar performance. Up to 500 hp you can still go with a stroked (347-ci) short-deck block and save some weight while also having a bit better selection of parts. For more than 500 hp with the short-deck use a power adder or step up to the taller deck and live with the weight penalty. You can, of course, also invest in an aluminum tall-deck block and get the power without much weight penalty, for a price.

A power adder on a stroked tall-deck can yield 1,000 hp or more. You still have a car that's completely driveable on the street, except perhaps

The Dart Race Series aluminum blocks have pretty much the same features as the Iron Eagle blocks but they're about 100 pounds lighter. Because they're cast from 355-T61 virgin alloy with pressed-in, dry ductile-iron sleeves there are some differences. For example, the use of these sleeves limits the maximum displacement to 463 ci even though they are relatively thick. Unlike many aluminum blocks these retain compatibility with most stock parts.

Even with long-tube headers there was no need to modify the shock towers on this 5.0L-based 347 stroker in a 1965 fastback; it was an easy fit. This engine has many other modifications and puts out more than 400 hp at the wheels (well over 500 rwhp when the ZEX nitrous system is on) yet still has exceptional performance, driveability, and fuel economy. This engine uses the OEM EEC-IV fuel injection system plus a programmable Abaco MAFS to simplify tuning. It also sports aftermarket A/C and many other modifications yet is reliable and easy to work on. (Photo Courtesy Coast High Performance)*

under harsh weather conditions. It all depends on what your goals and preferences are and what resources (time, skill, budget, etc.) you have. A modified 351-ci tall-deck engine can get to 600 hp without too much trouble and it can spare you the expense of the new crankshaft and other parts (rods, pistons, etc.) needed for a stroker. This really only applies if you already have a tall-deck block because there's little difference in price between comparable crate engines, either short- or tall-deck.

Big-Block

Installing a big-block in a 1964½–1966 Mustang is very difficult because the vehicle was essentially a pony car and not a muscle car. Physically the 390 FE and 385-series big-block engines are difficult to fit and you also need to upgrade the transmission, rear axle, differential, and other parts. It makes very little sense because the cars weren't available with them from the factory and you need to remove

the shock towers to make one fit. This requires substantial modifications and comes with quite a price tag.

You can make just as much power with a tall-deck Windsor with a power adder (not that you could likely use it effectively unless you also beefed up the body and suspen-

sion). A stroked Windsor can provide comparable performance with lighter weight. You also pay an ongoing penalty in lower stability, lower gas mileage, and even a reduced ability to make further modifications because you don't have room for them and/or there aren't many parts that fit this setup.

Installing an FE or 385-series big-block in a 1967 or later car, on the other hand, is a practical and feasible option. Because these later cars were available with big-blocks from the factory they have enough room for them (most, anyway) and there are plenty of modifications and parts for this combination. You'd still be better off with a tall-deck Windsor (whether stroked or not) in terms of cost, lower weight, and greater parts availability but if you want a big-block (for whatever reason) it at least makes some sense in these later cars.

If your 1967 or later car wasn't originally equipped with a big-block you can get the parts for one from a salvage yard or as new parts from

The larger 1967 and later cars were available with big-blocks so Windsors go right in, just like this 427W stroker tall-deck. This engine makes just a bit over 600 hp at the flywheel yet is totally streetable. When the NX plate system is activated, power exceeds 700 hp at the wheels. Reaching these numbers with a big-block is certainly possible but it likely costs more and adds more than 100 pounds to the front end. Making these numbers with a modular engine is much more difficult and costly because the shock towers must be cut. The 427W drops right in and can be further modified for more power and/or efficiency with EFI and other mods.

Ford's specialized engines, such as this Boss 429, are great for their legendary heritage, their appeal when you open the hood, and their performance if they're tuned right. Unfortunately, they are very tough to fit in many cars due to their size. From the factory, the shock towers had to be revised to accommodate the extra width of this engine. These engines are super expensive if they are original but "replica" engines, such as those from Jon Kaase Racing, are not inexpensive. The latter are a much better choice for performance not only due to their lower cost but to the enhancements in design and metallurgy, which have been incorporated.

aftermarket sources. Depending on your goal special aftermarket parts such as motor mounts can provide added strength, lowering and/or moving the engine back, and so forth to help improve performance and resolve issues such as hood clearance with certain manifold/carburetor setups.

If you're going for a particular look when you pop the hood, a particular sound when you get on it, or if you're trying to build a clone of a special big-block model, for example, a big-block in a 1967 and later vehicle may make sense. It goes in easily and can be a cost-effective upgrade relative to a small-block or even the original big-block if it is an engine with lower displacement or lower performance.

Modular Engine

On paper, the modular 4.6 looks attractive: aluminum block (mostly); aluminum heads in two-, three-, or four-valve configuration; plus lots of other features such as cross-bolted mains, overhead cams, and roller followers formerly seen mostly on more-exotic and/or racing engines. The two-valve versions are generally regarded as being the least desirable of the modular engine family in terms of their performance potential.

Size Challenges

The biggest impediment to installing a modular engine into a first-generation Mustang is not the performance potential of these engines but rather their size and bulk, particularly in terms of width. The numbers (according to Ford Racing) tell the tale: A short-deck Windsor is 18¾ inches wide, the tall-deck is 21 inches, regular big-blocks (no SOHC, Boss 429, etc.) are about 26 inches, and the SOHC (two- and three-valve) versions of the 4.6L modular engine are 25⅝ inches. They're almost as wide as the big-blocks! The four-valve modulars are a whopping 30 inches wide.

All modular engines are about 28 inches long; a big-block is about 32 inches long.

Differences in height are really hard to quantify because there are so many differences in oil pans, intake manifolds, carbs versus EFI, etc. In general, Windsors are shorter than the 4.6L SOHC and the 4.6L DOHC is the tallest of this bunch.

Modular engines are significantly wider than all of the Windsors and can sometimes even exceed the width of a big-block. This virtually disqualifies a modular engine from being a practical choice for 1965–1966 cars (unless time and cost are not issues).

Then there is the questionable rationale of trying to install a DOHC modular engine in a 1967 or later car when even a big-block would be an easier (and likely less expensive) fit.

In any case, the modular engine's reduced displacement relative to an older pushrod engine is something of a disadvantage, as is the initial cost of the engine and the reduced availability of performance parts. Furthermore, unless you convert to carburetion and some form of aftermarket ignition system to replace the OEM fuel injection, you also have the added difficulty of installing and tuning the full factory computer system or an aftermarket substitute for whatever you might choose to not retain.

Weight Challenges

A stroked tall-deck provides more displacement, greater performance potential, easier installation and tuning, generally lower overall cost, and even lower weight if you go with an aluminum block, heads, and intake.

Again, the numbers tell all: an iron-block 4.6L 2V weighs about 500 pounds; the 4.6L DOHC engines (all are aluminum blocks) weigh about 425 pounds. This compares to roughly 400 to 450 pounds for a short-deck Windsor with a

This Gateway Performance Suspension shock tower notching kit is one way to add more under-hood room for a larger engine. The panels replace the factory shock towers, so there is still some cutting and welding involved. These pre-formed panels save a considerable amount of time and effort, all for a very reasonable price. A modern strut-type suspension must be used with them, however, so it may not be practical unless you had already planned on making that costly modification.

The installation of a modular engine in these Mustangs requires extensive modification to the engine compartment for it to fit. This is due primarily to its significantly greater width than the older pushrod engines. The two-valve version (shown) is not as tight a fit but even it usually requires removal of the shock towers (shown) along with the installation of a completely different suspension system. The two-valve/SOHC modular engine can fit in the 1967 and later cars more easily because they originally had big-blocks available as an option. It's much more difficult to put one in an earlier Mustang and really is not practical except for a special show car.

production iron block and aluminum heads (more with an upgraded/aftermarket iron block, and about 60 pounds less with aluminum block) and about 600 pounds for an all-iron tall-deck (550 with aluminum heads, and 470 for block and heads). Big-blocks weigh well over 600 pounds, even with aluminum heads.

The lightest option by far, an all-aluminum short-deck, is the easiest to install and is capable of making more than 500 hp naturally aspirated (much more with a power adder). Even if you forgo the aluminum block to reduce costs (by $4,000 or so) you're still at the low end in terms of weight (more than the aluminum DOHC, but less than the iron DOHC).

Although an all-aluminum tall-deck may not be the most economical choice, it arguably offers the greatest performance potential with relatively easy installation while still likely being lighter than the iron SOHC.

A modified DOHC with a power adder can probably match a stroked-aluminum tall-deck in output but it is significantly harder to install, less reliable, and likely costs more.

Performance Challenges

The 4.6L 3V engine produced a respectable 300 to 315 hp while weighing 420 pounds. The 3V engine is a better candidate than the 2V in

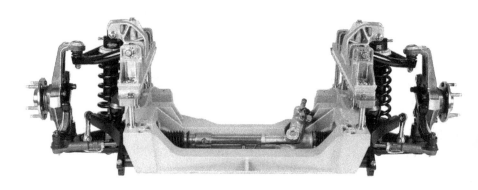

To maximize handling, you need to remove the OEM subframe. This Detroit Speed Aluma-Frame setup includes a complete coil-over suspension, rack-and-pinion steering, and even an ingenious (and much improved) method for making adjustments to the suspension geometry (caster and camber). Installation is surprisingly simple in that little cutting is required to mount the cross-member under the frame rails. Thick support plates with through-bolts are placed on top of the frame rails to secure it and provide mounting points for other components. (Photo Courtesy Detroit Speed)

The DOHC modular engines are much more difficult to fit in any first-generation Mustang, even the largest 1971–1973 models, because they're wider than a normal big-block. Given enough time and money, it can be done (shown). Doing it in a 1966 and earlier car, however, makes very little sense in terms of cost or even performance because of the extensive modifications needed. This installation was done with a very "OEM" look and uses mostly stock Ford parts (presumably from the donor car of the engine). This results in some compromises such as the front Monte Carlo bar. With DOHC engines in particular it's often better to use aftermarket and/or custom-made parts to minimize the need to make such tradeoffs.

The Ultimate Modular Engine

The 5.8L supercharged DOHC four-valve was introduced in the 2013 Shelby GT500. At 662 hp (J1349 certified) and 631 ft-lbs of torque it was the most powerful mass-production V-8 engine at the time.

It was basically an upgraded version of the 5.4L engine from 2012. The bore was increased to get to 5.8L, the compression ratio was increased by .5 to 9.0:1, and oil jets were added to help cool the pistons. It's very light due to its aluminum alloy, yet it's also very strong with its deep-skirt design, steel main caps, and six-bolt mains, etc.

The block has additional ribs and other reinforcements for strength but a unique feature is the plasma-sprayed cylinder bores. Instead of using heavy, less-stable, and less-conductive iron liners the bores are rough-finished, and then a special, long-wearing coating is applied via a plasma-spray process resulting in a metallurgical bond with the block. There's virtually no risk of the coating coming off. The cylinders are then finish-honed to their final dimensions. The very thin coating offers minimal resistance to the flow of heat so it transfers to the aluminum block more quickly and more evenly.

The integral bore design is similar to what is normally used in iron blocks, thus allowing for similar design techniques (bolt hole and boss location, cooling passages, etc.) to significantly reduce bore distortion and oil consumption.

Other upgrades include the use of a more-efficient and higher-flow TVS2300 supercharger, improved cylinder heads with MLS head gaskets, GT40 camshafts, and a redline increase from 6,250 to 7,000 rpm. ■

For the 5.4L/5.8L GT500 engines the 1969 and later models are really the best years to consider. They fit in the 1967 and 1968 models as well but with great difficulty. This 1969 has a 5.4L, and it is one of the modified and strong Ford Racing versions, which can make (and survive) much higher power levels than the production equipment. With an upgraded supercharger (shown) instead of the OEM unit these engines are capable of making well over 700 hp. If you use one of these 5.4L engines the best options are the later 2011 or 2012 versions because they have the highest stock output of the 5.4L engines as well as the 100-pound-lighter aluminum block.

The larger 5.4L engines are a difficult fit due to their added height and their considerable width. The addition of a supercharger does, however, minimize the need to make many additional modifications beyond the stock 500 hp. A simple pulley change along with a few minor intake and exhaust modifications can yield enough power to satisfy most needs. This swap should really only be considered for the 1967 and later cars (the later, the better) because of available space underhood. These engines are also complicated in terms of their electronic controls if the factory computer and wiring harness are reused.

If the older and larger members of the modular engine family don't seem to be a feasible option there is one more to consider: The 2011 and newer 5.0L Coyote engine. Or in this case, the Edelbrock 5.0 Coyote crate engine is a definite consideration. It is significantly more powerful (412 hp or more) than all but the 5.4L and 5.8L engines yet it is significantly less bulky than both of those and the older 4.6L DOHC engines. It is only marginally larger than either (two- or three-valve) 4.6L SOHC engine plus it only weighs about 20 pounds more. The complexity of the electronics, particularly those that control the Ti-VCT camshaft timing, make it very difficult to realize the full potential of this engine with a production-based control system. (Photo Courtesy Paul Johnson)

terms of maximum performance potential while offering comparable performance to a stock, older 4.6L DOHC with significantly easier installation. A modified 4.6L DOHC can provide greater maximum performance than the newer 3V but the durability and reliability of the former is somewhat suspect (there have been problems with the earlier thinner castings, bore distortion, etc.). It is surely a more difficult fit in a first-generation vehicle, even with notched shock towers. In many cases the shock towers need to be removed

altogether and a completely new front subframe and suspension is needed to make either of them fit.

5.0L Coyote

Although the 5.0L 4V Coyote engine is technically also a member of the modular engine family it needs a separate discussion. The Coyote was introduced as the standard engine in the Mustang GT; beginning with the 2011 model year there are many more of them in circulation. Their cost is less because of the lack of a supercharger. They are also significantly lighter (only about 450 pounds) due to their aluminum block and dimensions similar to the previ-

ous 4.6L SOHC engines (a little wider at 28 inches, a little shorter at 26 inches, and about the same height). The good news is that they were rated at more than 412 hp (444 hp for the Boss 302).

Because this engine is so much more sophisticated in terms of its degree of electronic control it's even more difficult to make everything work together because every car is different. The older vehicles just don't have most things the newer ones have.

For example, if you use the original unmodified factory wiring and computer you have the most trouble. Ford Racing does sell a stand-alone Control Pack for vehicles with manual transmissions (for more than $1,000).

Ford Racing Performance Parts (FRPP) offers Control Packs to facilitate the installation of a Coyote engine in non-emissions vehicles such as a street rod (and some first-generation Mustangs, depending on what laws apply in your area). This kit includes the major components, such as the specially calibrated and slimmed-down ECU, the necessary drive-by-wire throttle pedal assembly, a MAFS, oxygen sensors, and a wiring harness.

By necessity, the ECU has been calibrated to compensate for the lack of many sensors and signals found in the production car, which are rarely, if ever, feasible to incorporate into a non-emissions vehicle. The ECU and calibration allow the engine to function in such vehicles but, generally speaking, at a somewhat reduced level because full functionality cannot be retained.

This product includes a specially calibrated computer, the necessary drive-by-wire throttle assembly, a mass air sensor and inlet tube, a modified body harness (with a power distribution box and certain features omitted for use in non-emissions vehicles including the correct oxygen sensors), and other items. You need to ensure the vehicle has the proper fuel supply system (with a return line) and hook up everything else that's needed.

Even when you're done with the install and you get the car running, you have to do a full tuning and calibration exercise to get anywhere near the level of performance and efficiency the engine had in full production form. Unfortunately, you'll likely never get it that good because all of those things that were deleted to make the engine compatible in an older car were also things that helped it run better. When you change the components, change the vehicle (weight, gear ratios, aero, etc.), and remove some of the functionality of the computer (to not have it go into fault mode or throw trouble codes because many signals aren't there) you just aren't able to get it to run as well.

In time, the aftermarket will likely develop stand-alone computers and other components to resolve this problem, to some extent. But for now, there's no doubt a push-rod Windsor is easier to install and less expensive with more performance potential.

Crate Engine

Assuming that you've decided what type of engine you want, the next logical decision is how much work you want to do. Do you already have an engine that you want to overhaul and/or modify or do you want a new one? If the latter is the case you should very seriously consider the option of buying a ready-to-install crate engine rather than buying parts and/or a used engine, which would need to be worked on to be ready for use.

Crate engines are available from many companies, including Ford Racing, CJ Pony Parts, and Coast High-Performance. A crate engine builder that has been around for any significant length of time (such as Coast High-Performance) has a wealth of dyno data and has established what runs well on the street and what lasts—and what doesn't.

Companies such as Dart, Ford Racing, and CHP can afford to invest in the best equipment, people, and processes. This helps ensure high quality throughout the manufacturing and assembly process. This also combines the precision and consistency of CNC machining (which is far beyond what most engine shops can afford) with the expertise of a dedicated engineering staff and trained assemblers.

Special services such as multi-angle valve jobs, precision balancing and blueprinting, and deck-plate honing are generally done at extra cost when having an engine built at a shop. The crate engine builder can incorporate many, if not most, of such operations into their normal processes so every engine gets some degree of "special" treatment at a significantly reduced cost and with greater precision and consistency.

As you know, engines and other assemblies are available in various combinations for different uses and budgets. Most builders have what you need in stock so there's little delay before shipping your order, even custom orders.

Short-Block Assembly

There are many processes included in the way a 347 (short-deck) short-block is assembled. Following are photos of some of the unique features and techniques Coast High Performance (CHP) uses,

After all clearances have been checked the bearing shells are coated with a lubricant to ensure there's enough until the oil pressure builds up. (CHP likes to use a mix of assembly lube and ProBlend. Red Line also makes an excellent product.) The lubricant should have enough film strength to stand up to the pressures that are generated on start-up and is sufficiently tacky so it stays where you put it without being squeezed out or otherwise running off.

The finished CHP 347 stroker short-block doesn't look too different than most others except for possibly the inclusion of the main bearing girdle. Every CHP crate engine, short-block, or long-block comes with a build sheet detailing the final specifications. This "blueprinting" is included in their price (but is an extra-cost service when an engine is built by a shop). Careful matching and precision balancing of the components ensures each one closely meets your spec.

many of which they've learned over the years from their thousands of engines already in use.

Before CHP chooses parts they have been thoroughly researched, developed, and proven over the years to provide better performance and durability for the customer. They also try to minimize the potential for any in-use failures or warranty issues that would damage their reputation, not to mention their bottom line. CHP keeps learning and improving so both they and the customer benefit.

V-Belt versus Serpentine-Belt Systems

Stacking multiple belts next to one another for various accessory combinations adds weight, complexity, and overall length to the engine. The extra accessories require the mounting brackets be adjustable as well, thus making them inherently less stable.

The solution to these issues is a single "serpentine" belt. This multi-ribbed belt is much thinner than a V-belt so it's less affected by higher belt speeds. The multiple ribs increase the contact area of the belt relative to the pulleys, thus reducing the possibility of slippage. The single belt is made from better materials and is much stronger in terms of tensile strength, thus greatly reducing belt stretch during operation and over time. Serpentine systems are dynamically self-adjusting, thus providing stable belt engagement with less chance of coming off or breaking. The single belt also makes a shorter engine.

Vehicle manufacturers have almost universally abandoned V-belts in favor of serpentine belts for the primary drive of engine accessories. Unfortunately, most production systems are not easily retrofitted to older engines. Ford's small-block Windsor

engines are a notable exception to this in that the serpentine belt-drive system used on later-model 5.0L V-8 engines usually can be adapted to older engines with V-belts.

S.Drive Kits, for example, from Eddie Motorsports are available for conversions with or without power steering in several finishes ranging from a natural/polished look to gloss or matte black. These kits include everything needed for a conversion including a new alternator, water pump, power steering pump, and all associated pulleys, brackets, and other hardware. The cost is very reasonable and installation is fairly simple.

The result is a better-looking single-serpentine-belt system that reliably handles higher belt loads and RPM without needing periodic adjustment. The mounting of the components is much more stable and the packaging envelope of the drive system is reduced.

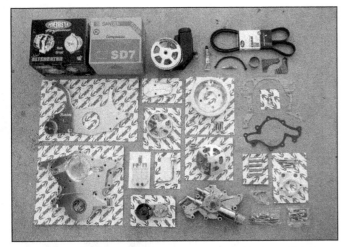

This S.Drive serpentine-belt conversion kit from Eddie Motorsports comes with everything you need to eliminate your old V-belt system and upgrade to the newer, better serpentine design. It includes a new Powermaster alternator, a compact and efficient Sanden A/C compressor, a Unisteer/Mavel Saginaw-type power steering pump, and a short-profile Ford Motorsports water pump. Besides allowing the engine to be shorter, the use of a tensioner and idlers provide much greater belt stability. It also needs less total tension so there's less strain and wear on bearings.

The first item to install is the custom CNC-machined billet aluminum timing cover. It goes on with the four lower bolts and four studs that go around the water pump passages (not shown). The ends of these studs, which go into the block, must be coated with an appropriate sealant if they protrude into the water jacket. The harmonic balancer and ignition timing pointer can also be installed once the timing cover is on. Grease the seal on the cover first and use threadlocker on the balancer bolt (use Grade 8 and a hardened washer).

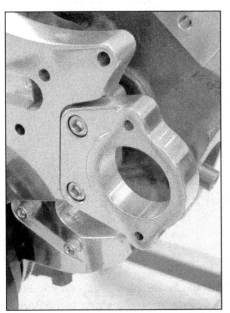

The water pump and gasket can then be installed over the four protruding studs. Use a gasket sealer on both sides of the gasket and tighten the bolts from the middle out (don't overdo it and crush the gasket). The power steering pump goes on with only two long bolts inserted through the spaces in the pulley. A series of four threaded standoffs must be screwed onto the studs protruding from the water pump. The shorter one goes on the lower right stud while the longer three go on the remaining studs. All must be installed with the grooved end near the engine.

In some cases you need a spacer (such as this one from Professional Products) between the balancer and its pulley. To determine whether you need one, hold the pulley against the balancer to see how well its belt grooves line up with those of the water pump and power steering pump. If they line up, you're good; if not, use a spacer. Once you determine the proper pulley alignment you can install the pulley with the four bolts and the supplied, special, dished washers. S.Drive kits are made only for four-bolt balancers though many (such as the Professional Products version) have dual-bolt patterns to accommodate either situation.

The supplied Powermaster high-output alternator goes on next with one short bolt, one long button-head bolt, and a spacer used with the long bolt. Test fit everything first because it may be necessary to trim the spacer to get it to fit between the alternator and the timing cover mounting boss. Install the short top bolt first.

If you use a dipstick that goes elsewhere, install the supplied plug into the dipstick hole on the timing cover to seal it off.

The belt tensioner is almost the last component to go on. It has two small pegs on its rear face, which go into two corresponding holes on the front support plate for proper alignment. Use the single bolt to keep everything tied together.

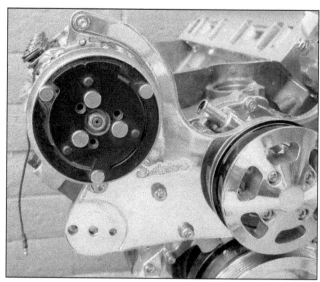

Install the A/C compressor on the other side of the support plate. It uses two short bolts and a large shoulder bolt for proper location. First loosely install the lower support-plate bolt and then get the shoulder bolt started most of the way in. Next install the upper support-plate bolt and fully tighten the rest. The A/C pulley goes on next with the three supplied bolts. Make sure it's lined up properly and that it turns freely. Tuck the electrical wire out of the way and, if you are using A/C, install the coupling plate on the compressor. Seal off the ports with caps until you are ready for hookup and charging.

After you install the tensioner cover and belt you are finished. This looks better than the stock setup plus it shortens the engine so there's less chance of interference with an upgraded fan and/or radiator. This setup remains stable at much higher RPM and the belt lasts much longer. Whatever belt stretching may occur over time is automatically compensated for by the tensioner.

TRANSMISSION

After determining your engine package the next logical step is to choose what type of transmission you're going to use. The transmission is the next component in the flow of power from the engine and, combined with the rear axle ratio, it determines your overall drive ratio (ODR). It's also appropriate to note the ODR changes based on transmission gear.

This brings up the issues of how many gears ("speeds") the transmission has and what the maximum ratio spread is between them. In general, more gears means a wider ratio spread. This is usually a good thing for a street-driven vehicle because it allows better acceleration in the lower gears while reducing the RPM at a given speed in the higher gears. This reduces wear, noise, and (normally) fuel consumption.

A high-performance Mustang benefits from a close-ratio transmission where the ratio differences between gears is reduced. This can be helpful in keeping the engine in a more beneficial RPM range and in reducing the effect of gear changes on the handling of the vehicle.

A wide-ratio transmission does the opposite and provides a wider ratio spread, which can provide some of the benefit of going to more gears without the transmission becoming bigger and/or heavier.

Conversions

Converting from an automatic transmission to a manual takes many steps and component installs. It's almost always easier to convert from a manual transmission to an automatic

because you don't have to install a clutch pedal or entire pedal box. It's a lot easier to ignore or remove than it is to add. It's also more difficult to route and anchor linkages and cables.

From Automatic to Manual

At a minimum, when you convert from an automatic transmission to a manual you need to install a pilot bearing in the end of the crankshaft, get a new block plate, choose a transmission and bellhousing, check to see if you need to change the transmission crossmember and/or driveshaft,

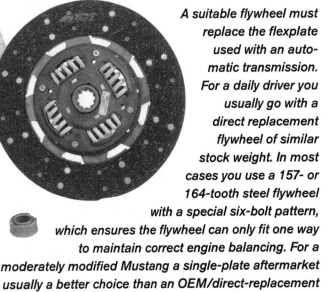

A suitable flywheel must replace the flexplate used with an automatic transmission. For a daily driver you usually go with a direct replacement flywheel of similar stock weight. In most cases you use a 157- or 164-tooth steel flywheel with a special six-bolt pattern, which ensures the flywheel can only fit one way to maintain correct engine balancing. For a mildly to moderately modified Mustang a single-plate aftermarket clutch is usually a better choice than an OEM/direct-replacement setup. (Photo Courtesy Advanced Clutch Technology)

choose a pressure plate and clutch disc, install a third pedal and make it functional (with either a linkage, a cable, or via hydraulics), choose and install an appropriate shifter, and figure out how to get the speedometer and any other connections (backup lights, clutch safety switch, etc.) to work. Whew! It sounds somewhat intimidating but it really isn't because these conversions are common and the necessary components are readily available.

Modern Driveline (MDL), for example, offers many conversion kits. In fact, the company specializes in 5- and 6-speed conversions for Ford vehicles, Mustangs in particular. Unlike some companies that just assemble parts made by others into a kit, MDL (in most cases) designs and manufactures their own components or has it done to their unique specifications. Examples of the former include cable clutch conversion kits, hydraulic clutch conversion kits, and conversion crossmembers. The parts are engineered to complement one another, and you need proven parts to complete the conversion to a modern overdrive (OD) transmission.

In the case of MDL you also benefit from their extensive experience with Ford. If you buy a complete conversion kit, the instructions include all of the detailed steps to complete the conversion for your specific car.

The following photos are highlights of installing an OD manual transmission into a car that originally had an automatic. This is not a step-by-step guide because there are too many differences among cars. It is an overview of some of the more critical things you need to address.

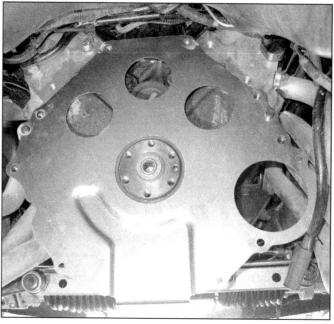

When converting to a manual transmission from an automatic it is necessary to install the appropriate engine block plate. An OEM aluminum component, such as this, is fine for about 500 hp; a thicker steel piece should be used with more than 500 hp. You must also install a roller pilot bearing in the hole in the end of the crankshaft. This locates the transmission input shaft and simply presses in. Always use a new part because it's relatively inexpensive and a worn part can cause clutch chatter.

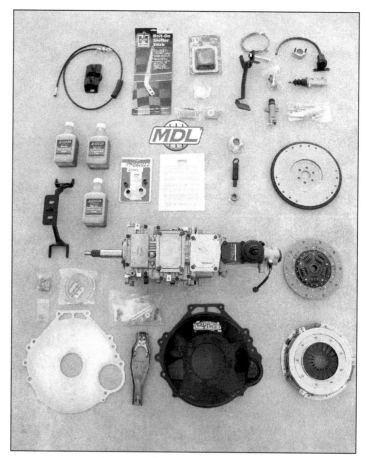

This Modern Driveline kit is for installing a Tremec TKO 5-speed manual transmission into a 1967 or 1968 Mustang. It includes the transmission, bellhousing clutch setup, hydraulic clutch actuator conversion kit, new transmission crossmember and mount, shift handle and related accessories, speedometer cable and gear, synthetic transmission fluid and, in this case, a complete pedal setup with roller bearing upgrade to convert a car that originally had an automatic transmission.

When installing a new clutch setup you must ensure the clutch disc is properly centered/aligned relative to the flywheel and pressure plate. Use the alignment tool that's included with the clutch kit (or it can be purchased separately). You can also use an input shaft from your type of transmission.

Another tip is to ensure that one of the splines on the input shaft (or clutch alignment tool) is directly at the top (12 o'clock) position while the pressure plate is being tightened. This eases installation of the transmission if you ensure a spline on the transmission input shaft is in the same place while you're pushing it forward.

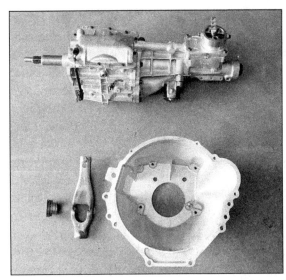

The T-5 transmission is by far the easiest manual OD conversion to perform. It requires minimal changes, presents the fewest issues in terms of packaging, and easily fits into the transmission tunnel. It's light yet strong enough even for moderately modified vehicles. In some cases you can retain the existing crossmember and driveshaft, although you have to add all of the clutch-pedal-related items.

In some cases the original transmission crossmember can be reused by simply drilling new holes in it because the transmission mount is only moved about an inch. This is acceptable if the power level hasn't been increased too much.

If your original crossmember doesn't work, there are plenty of aftermarket alternatives such as this one from MDL. It's intended for mounting a Tremec TKO in a 1967/1968 Mustang. The metal is thicker and a higher grade. These features plus the gusseted dual-shear design make for a very strong crossmember. The slots for the transmission mount are elongated to work with OEM/rubber mounts (shown) or stronger and safer polyurethane mounts. (Photo Courtesy Modern Driveline)

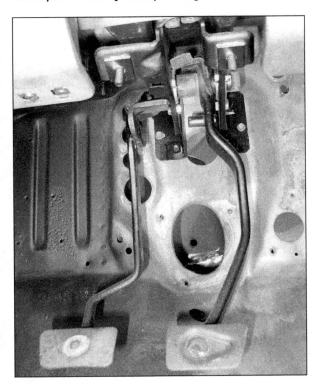

When converting from an automatic transmission to a manual transmission you must add a clutch pedal because the car doesn't come with one. You can get a used part from a salvage yard or buy just the pedal or as part of a kit. In either case, this is likely the most difficult part of the conversion because, unlike in this photo, there are a lot of other components near the area where the pedal must be mounted.

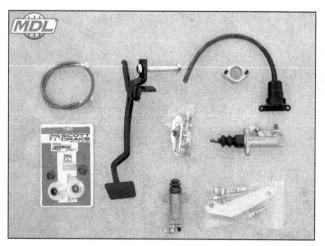

This kit from MDL includes a new clutch pedal along with a roller bearing upgrade for smoother clutch action and longer wear. It includes the components to install a complete hydraulic clutch actuation system. This is far superior to the OEM mechanical linkage and also provides several advantages (more exhaust and steering clearance, for example) when compared to cable-type systems. (Photo Courtesy Modern Driveline)

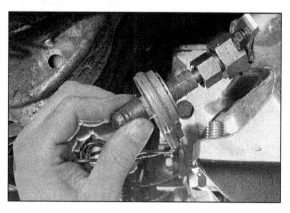

If you use electronic fuel injection (such as the Ford EEC-IV system) you should also install a vehicle speed sensor to provide the ECU with the signal it needs to function properly. If you don't provide the necessary signals, diagnostic trouble codes and erratic or unacceptable engine behavior is likely.

When upgrading to an OD transmission it's a good idea to go with a short-throw aftermarket shifter such as this T-5 unit from B&M. Most OEM shifters are relatively soft and vague. This B&M shifter reduces the shift throw (and thus the shift time) and provides a better, more precise feel with less play or sloppiness than OEM shifters. This B&M unit features special bias springs, which help to guide the handle during specific shifts to reduce missed shifts. The unit also has adjustable stop bolts to help prevent damage to the internal transmission parts during hard and fast shifts.

From Manual to Automatic

Converting a manual transmission car to an automatic is considerably simpler and less labor intensive. As mentioned, you don't need that third pedal anymore. You can either remove it (and its linkage) or just ignore it once it's been disconnected. It's better to take it all out to free up space, especially around the exhaust.

You may also need to rewire the clutch safety switch to work with the neutral safety switch on your automatic transmission or just bypass it. You can also wire it to a hidden/disguised switch to act as an anti-theft "kill switch."

You must remove your flywheel, pressure plate, clutch, etc., and replace them with the proper (in terms of size, number of ring gear teeth, balance, etc.) flex plate and torque converter.

Because most commonly used automatics have an integral bellhousing you need to remove the old manual transmission housing and likely install a different block plate. Depending on the specific combination you may have to modify or replace the crossmember and/or driveshaft. If you've increased the power significantly these changes become much more likely.

You need to install a new shifter, boot, and linkage (or cable), possibly along with some other changes. Depending on the new transmission you also have to adapt additional control cables (kickdown/TV cable), possibly hook up a vacuum line (for older transmissions), or use an electronic controller (for newer, electronic-shift transmissions).

If there were no transmission coolant lines (most likely) you must add sufficient cooling capacity via the transmission cooler in your radiator (if so equipped) or to a separate cooler that you install.

Finally, you must adapt the speedometer cable/gear as needed and hook up all electrical connections (backup lights, neutral safety switch, etc.).

The following photos show highlights of this process. This is not a step-by-step guide because there are too many differences among cars.

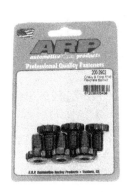

Use of the correct mounting bolts is critical. Some component combinations require special bolts with thinner heads and/or special washers to prevent problems. This can be further complicated when you use a stiffening plate. Always upgrade critical fasteners, such as flexplate and bellhousing bolts. These ARP fasteners are made from stronger materials using better manufacturing and quality-control methods. They have design features, such as smaller heads and special coatings, to ease their installation and improve their durability. ARP matches the fasteners precisely for their intended use and provides all washers.

After the transmission and clutch have been removed you need to replace the flywheel with a flex plate. This must have the correct diameter and correct number of ring gear teeth. It only mounts one way to ensure proper engine balance so you must be sure to use the proper balance spec to prevent vibration and potential damage. It's best to use an additional stiffener (the round steel plate under the flywheel bolts) as well as some threadlocker on the threads to prevent any engine oil that might get past a failing rear main seal from allowing the bolts to loosen. Remove the pilot bearing.

Newer automatic overdrive (AOD) transmissions tend to have a one-piece housing rather than the two-piece housing of older transmissions. This makes the transmission lighter and easier to install but can be a problem with high power levels and access to the converter.

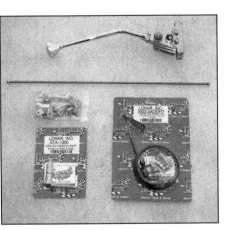

This shifter uses a rod-type direct linkage, but Lokar also offers cable shifters for direct mount to the transmission or the floor. Also shown are a kickdown cable and a new AOD selector shaft, which may be needed in some installations.

This Lokar shifter can be mounted directly to the transmission. It includes functions such as a neutral safety switch and a positive lockout for park and reverse. The knob perfectly matches the OEM shift pattern of the AOD.

This is a typical Lokar shifter cable installation. A special bracket mounts to the transmission pan to locate the cable directly in line with the shift lever. Adjustments can be made at the mounting bracket and at the rod end, which bolts to the shift lever. The cable is constructed from heat-resistant materials so there's no need for shielding.

Because your manual transmission didn't have any transmission cooling lines you have to add them. Short lengths of galvanized steel tubing with the correct fittings to attach to the bosses on the transmission will do. Hoses can then be run to similar lengths of steel tubing that have been installed in the cooler. This may be a cooler mounted in the radiator or a separate external cooler. The former is acceptable for a daily driver, especially in cooler areas. The latter is best for high-performance use.

This Lokar gas pedal with pad for 1965–1968 Mustangs is made of 6061 T6 aluminum. It's a direct replacement for the stock assembly and is ideally installed with the Lokar throttle cable and brackets. The spring-loaded gas pedal, Delrin bushings, and high-quality cables provide a much smoother and precise throttle actuation. The billet aluminum brake and clutch pedals with pads are also shown. (Photo Courtesy Lokar Performance Products)

Manual Transmission Upgrades

If you have a manual transmission in your daily driver there really isn't that much you need to do other than replace worn components and/or do some upgrades if you increase power significantly. If gas mileage, reduced wear, and noise reduction are priorities then you may want to install an OD manual transmission. The cost, however, usually isn't practical for a limited-budget daily driver unless you drive enough miles for the fuel savings to make up for it.

Clutch

The most cost-effective thing you can do is replace the bushings in the equalizer/Z-bar. There are replaceable parts on each end, which usually wear out. Installing new ones improves the action of your clutch significantly.

Similarly, the bushings on which the pedal assembly rotates are also prone to wear. These can be replaced with new bushings or, for a relatively minimal extra expense, roller bearings, which reduce play even more while making the clutch pedal movement smoother. They last a lot longer too. Even when properly maintained, these parts wear from movement and exposure to the elements.

This setup is adequate for many street cars but is usually not up to high-performance use. The pilot bearing in the crankshaft and the throwout bearing should be replaced if either is making noise, allows excessive movement of the input shaft, or is otherwise worn or damaged. Realistically, it's best to just replace them unless they're fairly new. They're relatively inexpensive parts but fairly labor intensive.

While you have access to the inside of the bellhousing you should ensure that all of the lubrication points (pivot ball, throwout bearing at the clips, etc.) are coated with a small amount of suitable grease. Do not put any lubricant on the input shaft splines. This causes clutch chatter from grease "slinging" onto the friction surfaces, and requires the clutch disc be replaced, again.

If the clutch disc is worn out you should replace it with one better than a direct-replacement version. An aftermarket disc may not cost any more but should last longer and be able to take more power. Make sure the output of the engine matches the clutch disc set when assembling a high-performance engine package. If you upgrade the clutch for this reason you should also upgrade the pressure plate. If your pressure plate is heat checked from a worn-out disc you may need to replace it anyway.

If you upgrade the pressure plate to one with significantly higher clamping pressure use an aftermarket Barillo Z-bar or similar unit that has roller bearings instead of bushings at its ends. This provides smoother clutch action and greatly improved life over the stock parts while being much less prone to bending with the higher load.

Likewise, if the flywheel is damaged it can usually be ground smooth enough to be reused. You probably don't need to spend the extra bucks

This "street" clutch disc from Advanced Clutch Technology is a better option than an OEM/ direct-replacement part for most daily drivers and vehicles with a moderate power increase. It takes more abuse and torque yet it doesn't cost much more than the OEM part. It has organic facings for smoother operation and a sprung hub and marcel layer between the facings to reduce shock loads on engagement. The metallic fibers in the facings help provide the greater holding power without the drawbacks of discs with facings made mostly or completely of metallic and/or ceramic materials. The facings are a bit thicker to provide longer wear and greater heat resistance. (Photo Courtesy Advanced Clutch Technology)

for a different flywheel; just make sure yours is in good shape. If you change the flywheel and/or pressure plate you may need to rebalance them as an assembly. The cost of doing this, however, can often tilt the decision in favor of simply buying new parts.

Mounts

If you plan to keep your transmission you might want to upgrade the shifter. You should also consider changing the engine and transmission mounts if they're worn out. They can cause shifting problems because the engine and transmission are moving all over the place. This causes the Z-bar to go out of position and not properly transmit the motion of the clutch pedal. In severe cases the clutch may not fully disengage.

For relatively unmodified vehicles new, direct-replacement rubber mounts are the cost-effective way to go. If you plan to make significantly more power and/or you like to beat on the car (i.e., "powershift" it) often, you may want to spend a bit extra now and upgrade to stronger polyurethane mounts such as those offered by Energy Suspension. These

The Energy Suspension safety interlock system offers an extra measure of safety. Even if all of the polyurethane fails the remaining metal parts continue to limit movement until the part can be replaced. This provides added safety and longer life compared to rubber parts. The movement of the engine and transmission mounts affects the operation of the clutch and/or shift linkages. Polyurethane parts better limit excessive movement. (Photo Courtesy Energy Suspension)

greatly reduce movement of the engine and transmission plus they also last much, much longer. The only real downside for a daily driver is they may transmit a bit more noise and vibration into the car. That's a small price to pay for making sure you don't have a sudden failure.

Energy Suspension's mounts also feature an integral safety interlock design so even if the polyurethane should fail, interlocking metal components prevent excessive movement.

Always check the condition of the roller pilot bearing whenever you can. Cars with automatic transmissions don't have one so you need to put a new one in when converting to a manual transmission. Inspect it to be sure it's not worn or damaged. The clutch fork must be properly installed and lubricated to avoid problems. There are spring clips where the throwout bearing attaches to the clutch fork and where the clutch fork attaches to the pivot ball of the bellhousing. It's critical to apply the correct amount of an appropriate grease wherever there's rubbing contact (such as between the clutch fork cup and the pivot ball).

Newer OD transmissions, such as the T-5 or the TKO, require the use of a different bellhousing than older transmissions. Adapter plates allow you to reuse the original bellhousing with the new transmission but are not preferable, especially with higher power levels. New OEM parts are a better fit, are very lightweight, and often have a cast-in boss (below the window for the clutch fork) to mount a clutch release cable, thus facilitating the conversion from an older mechanical linkage. (Photo Courtesy Tremec)

Fluid

You should upgrade the transmission fluid whenever you've had any significant increase in engine power. The forces on the internal parts increase, possibly beyond the point that a standard lubricant can provide adequate protection. This is especially true if the fluid is old or of unknown origin. If you're upgrading the clutch and/or you haven't changed the transmission fluid in a while it's best to do so.

There are proven benefits to using a synthetic product such as Synchromax from Royal Purple. It lasts much longer than regular fluid and it reduces internal friction so more power gets to the wheels while lowering transmission temperatures. It costs a bit more than regular fluids but the performance benefits far outweigh the cost, especially because it lasts so much longer.

Overdrives

A very popular upgrade for relatively unmodified, daily-driver vehicles with a manual transmission is to install a newer OD manual transmission to reduce engine speed on the highway. This reduces wear and noise while also improving fuel mileage. This can be practical, especially if you drive your car a lot.

For most daily drivers it's hard to beat the Borg-Warner/Tremec T-5 transmission. It comes in several variations but used ones from later Mustangs (1979–1993 Fox-Bodies in particular) are plentiful and not very expensive. These are 5-speed transmissions, which perform similarly to (yet better than) the older manual transmission through the first four gears with fourth still being 1:1. The benefit is that the T-5 gives you an OD fifth gear, usually with a .63:1 ratio, which reduces engine speed by 37 percent!

The T-5 is also pretty light (about 75 pounds), as is the OEM Fox-Body aluminum bellhousing that goes with it. Adapter plates allow you to keep your existing bellhousing and linkage. It's generally better to swap over to the newer stuff to save weight, avoid issues with the driveshaft and/or crossmember, and have smoother shifting.

Converting to a hydraulic clutch setup is the preferred way to go although even the cable conversion kits outperform mechanical linkages. The hydraulic setup is especially handy if you need headers and steering to get around. A stock T-5 out of a Fox-Body is usually good for about 300 ft-lbs or so, especially in a lighter first-generation Mustang that's going

If you use a T-5 transmission be aware that there are many variations of it. In addition to wanting greater torque capacity and smoother shifting, one of the easiest, and most critical, design features to look for is a steel input shaft/throwout bearing sleeve (shown). Some T-5s had an aluminum sleeve, which, besides being inherently weaker, also tends to wear out more quickly. Use only steel.

The clutch adjustment is usually made by turning the nuts on the link, which contacts the clutch fork to vary the distance between the Z-bar lever and the fork. Another nut on the other side of the Z-bar lever needs to be adjusted in kind to remove any slack, which results from the clutch adjustment. Proper adjustment is when the throwout bearing is just barely separated from the fingers on the pressure plate.

to be on relatively narrow street tires and hasn't been modified too much. In many cases, the T-5 goes in without any need to change the driveshaft, and the transmission crossmember can often be drilled to mate up with the T-5 mount (it's about an inch farther back).

To summarize, switching from your existing manual transmission to a newer T-5 involves:

- replacing the transmission and bellhousing with the newer parts (including the clutch, etc.)
- tossing the mechanical clutch linkage for a pull-type cable or push-type hydraulic system that's smoother and less affected by transmission movement
- getting a new transmission crossmember and/or driveshaft (though not usually)
- hooking up the various electrical and speedometer connections (at most, an adapter cable and perhaps a new electrical connector or two along with a new speedometer gear)

- installing a new shifter (usually comes with the transmission though you likely want to replace the OEM shifter with a short-throw aftermarket version) with a new handle

The high-performance street version gets up to about 400 hp or so; something of a domino effect occurs where modifications beget more modifications. This means going to a stronger version of the T-5 or using a Tremec TKO or T-56 instead. To some extent, the decision of which of these to use is determined by the year of your Mustang.

The 1964½–1966 models have a smaller transmission tunnel and thus the T-5 remains the best choice. However, if you need a stronger transmission with more torque capacity and/or you're willing to cut/modify the transmission tunnel, you can install a transmission with a larger case. These cars are also pretty limited in terms of tire size unless you enlarge the wheelwells; you probably don't need more than the T-5 anyway. You

can't usually get the extra power to the ground.

The FRPP World Class Z transmission (PN M-7003-Z) transmits up to about 500 hp and more than 400 ft-lbs of torque. It's conservatively rated at 330 but that's based on an extremely rigorous test procedure; many T-5s have successfully been used at more. It should be fine if you're not running slicks and doing a lot of clutch drop/drag race starts.

Modified T-5s and rebuild or upgrade kits are available from companies such as G-Force Transmissions and Astro Performance Warehouse, which claim to raise the capacity of a T-5 to as much as 600 hp and 500 ft-lbs in a 3,300-pound vehicle with the standard T-5 housing. You even can buy specially built T-5s with a proprietary housing and internal upgrades for significantly more torque capacity. Using a TKO is a better option unless you need a physically smaller T-5.

The TKO is not as easy to install as the T-5 because it requires a different bellhousing, clutch disc (usually must go from 10 to 26 splines), driveshaft yoke (31 versus 28 splines), and other parts.

Using a different bellhousing necessitates installing a new block plate as well, unless you're upgrading from a T-5. The stamped, lightweight OEM version should be sufficient. The overall length is also different and the shifter can be in a different place, so you need to resolve those issues. In addition, you may have to install a different crossmember, driveshaft (possibly), shift handle (the TKO has three possible shifter locations), and wiring adaptations.

These are common swaps and various companies have stepped up with components and/or kits to make it

A variation on hydraulic clutch actuation involves replacing the throwout bearing with a special unit that features the hydraulic mechanism integrated into it. This system from American Powertrain replaces the external cylinder and the clutch fork with a hydraulically actuated throwout bearing. This setup is very simple and compact but may not always be able to generate sufficient force if a very high-pressure plate is used. American Powertrain's prod-

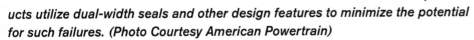

ucts utilize dual-width seals and other design features to minimize the potential for such failures. (Photo Courtesy American Powertrain)

For the higher power level of a street performance car the T-5 can be a viable choice, especially in the earlier/lighter cars. The World Class/Z version should be sufficient in terms of torque capacity for most of the vehicles in this category. It provides a dramatic drop in RPM at higher speeds, thus allowing a change to a higher numerical rear axle ratio for better acceleration, if so desired. For higher strength, upgrade kits can substantially increase the torque that a modified T-5 can handle. (Photo Courtesy Tremec)

One way to help compensate for the different shifter location(s) of the TKO is with a multi-position shifter such as this American Powertrain White Lightning. The ability to rotate the shift lever to one of 75 possible positions within a full 360-degree range provides additional flexibility to ensure it can be optimally located. This shifter also reduces the shift length (versus the OEM shifter) and provides user-adjustable shift biasing to facilitate faster, better shifting. (Photo Courtesy American Powertrain)

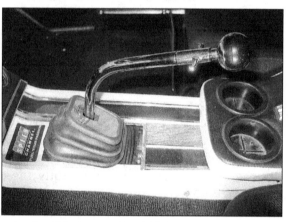

Various combinations of components can result in the shift handle not being where you want it to be. The shift ball also needs to be changed if you upgrade to a transmission with more gear ratios. Fortunately, a compatible shift lever from Mustangs Plus is available for just about any application. The choice is usually a tradeoff between the shift lever being closer to the driver and the shift lever being longer and increasing the shift length. In some cases the benefits of a short-throw shift can be offset by this.

easier. The TKO is rated at either 500 or 600 ft-lbs of torque and, in reality, can take more depending on vehicle weight, suspension design, tire choice, etc. It is a bigger transmission and it also weighs more (about 99 versus about 75 pounds for an unmodified T-5) but its shift quality isn't as smooth. It doesn't cost much more than the Z transmission and certainly is less than the modified T-5s.

There's not that much difference in the ratios between the T-5 and the TKO in that they both have first-gear ratios in the 2.87:1 to 3.27:1 range and fifth-gear ratios of .62:1 to .68:1. The only exception to this is a special close-ratio version of the 600-ft-lb TKO that has a ratio spread of 2.87:1 to .82:1 for potentially better performance when road racing. It's not very likely that a T-56 6-speed transmission would be considered for this type of vehicle due to its packaging, installation, and cost issues. (It's more justifiable for a high-performance street car.)

Clutch Disc Material

The transmission needs to provide smooth and precise shifting on the street for the high-performance street car but some smoothness may get sacrificed for higher torque capacity. A higher-pressure plate-clamping force and different clutch disc materials provide a firmer and sometimes more noticeable shift.

In some cases you can increase the clutch disc diameter to gain more capacity but this isn't always possible and it can slow engine response due to the higher rotational inertia of the larger disc. The more likely means of increasing capacity is through a change in the facing material. The three most commonly used facing materials are organic, Kevlar, and ceramic/metallic. Each may be used alone or in combination with another.

Organic facings are used on the vast majority of OEM clutches and on lower-cost lower-power aftermarket units. They're generally very smooth (minimal chatter) and wear reasonably well but have limited torque capacity. Other aspects of the clutch disc design (hub/springs, backing/marcel, etc.) can raise torque capacity but the "Achilles heal" of organic facings is they can't take higher heat.

One solution is to upgrade to Kevlar, which is superior in terms of resistance to heat plus it has much better wear characteristics. When used properly at relatively moderate power levels a disc with Kevlar on the sides can last indefinitely. Discs with an organic facing on one side and Kevlar on the other are also available as a lower-cost option that can be a bit smoother but the organic facing is still the weak link. This option may wear longer but the difference in torque capacity is significant.

It's generally better to use all Kevlar. Some companies advertise their discs as Kevlar when they only have a relatively small percentage (10 to 20) of Kevlar fiber in them. Reputable companies, such as Modern Driveline, however, offer discs that are almost 100-percent Kevlar and thus deliver its full benefits.

The choice of ceramic/metallic is relatively extreme and usually reserved for race vehicles. This is because these materials tend to have very abrupt engagement characteristics and they can cause greater wear on the flywheel and pressure plate surfaces.

These materials also are affected by temperature so there are very few situations where they may be suitable for street use, particularly in traffic and/or in colder weather. For the vast majority of cases in this performance category an organic and/or Kevlar disc with a sprung hub and a marcel (the wavy spring-like metal between the two clutch faces) along with the appropriate pressure plate is more than sufficient for the typical power level.

High-Performance Street Car

It's usually best to source individual components from a single sup-

The selection of suitable clutch components is widest for a high-performance street car due to its varying performance levels. These ACT products illustrate a few such options. A single-disc clutch is usually adequate. Clamping force levels can change as needed but the overall type of pressure plate is fairly constant. Flywheels, on the other hand, show more variation. Steel flywheels are generally preferred though the use of lighter-weight versions (second from the right, with the extra material removed near the ring gear) becomes more likely. Shown here is a progression from a street-oriented disc (next to the flywheel) to a full-race disc (at left). (Photo Courtesy Advanced Clutch Technology)

plier to ensure their compatibility. Most suppliers offer complete kits that include the clutch disc, pressure plate, throwout bearing, alignment tool, and sometimes even the pilot bearing. Different combinations are offered to suit various torque capacities, budgets, and intended purposes. Some can be supplied with a matching flywheel as well.

For this performance level there usually isn't much need to replace the flywheel unless the original can't be reused. If this is the case an option to consider is a lightened flywheel to gain better engine response. A reduc-

tion of about 20 to 40 percent in total weight is significant by itself but when most of the weight is reduced at the outer edge of the flywheel the effect on reducing rotational inertia can be much more significant.

For the small-block Ford, Advanced Clutch Technology (ACT) removes the maximum feasible amount of material from the outer edge of the flywheel without compromising support for the starter ring gear or the overall strength of the flywheel. The steel flywheel has enough weight to reduce engine pulsations and help prevent stalling without

The two discs on the right utilize smoother, more street-friendly organic facings with the main distinction between them being a solid versus a sprung hub. The latter is better suited to street use while the former can handle more torque and likely perform better at the track/strip. The disc on the left combines a sprung hub with a ceramic/metallic facing material to increase torque capacity while still trying to maintain reasonable street driving manners. (Photo Courtesy Advanced Clutch Technology)

This lightweight steel flywheel from ACT is a prime example of the type of flywheel best suited to the high-performance street car. It retains enough weight to make pulling away from a stop on the street fairly simple yet it still provides a meaningful reduction in inertia to improve engine response. (Photo Courtesy Advanced Clutch Technology)

This kit is intended for a heavier car and uses a flywheel with less weight reduction to help improve its launch. The clamping force of the pressure plate has been matched to the full Kevlar facing of the clutch disc. It includes a new throwout bearing, pilot bearing, and alignment tool. (Photo Courtesy Modern Driveline)

the need for special finesse in your footwork. This can be desirable on the street, especially in a heavier car.

The rest of the necessary modifications for the high-performance street car category mirror the "optional" modifications for the daily driver category. Polyurethane engine and transmission mounts, cable or hydraulic linkages, a short-throw shifter, a stronger/compatible crossmember, and so forth almost always need to be installed because of the increased power and the more aggressive use.

Unless you do a lot of drag racing you can probably get away with the OEM-style aluminum bellhousing and stock driveshaft/U-joints. If you're going to be seeing very high RPM and more than 400 hp you may want something safer, such as a QuickTime (QT) steel bellhousing and/or a stronger driveshaft.

Streetable Track-Day Car

The streetable track-day car sacrifices refinement during street use for durability and reliability under more-severe track conditions. With a lighter vehicle (such as a 1965/1966) a stronger T-5 may still be feasible if the power level is about 500 hp or so and the primary use is road courses, autocrosses, or open road races. In such situations the ease of packaging the T-5 and the limitations of the chassis in terms of wheel/tire size may make it a better choice than the TKO/T-56.

If the power level is higher and/or the primary use is drag racing, the T-5 may not be up to it. In such situations, it may be necessary to step up to the TKO and cut the transmission tunnel. The TKO fits the 1967–1973 cars and in my estimation is one of the most cost-effective options. It's also good for 600 ft-lbs or more depending on vehicle weight, tires, gear ratios, etc., which covers the vast majority of vehicles.

If even more torque capacity is needed you need to beef up the TKO or go with the T-56 Magnum. The latter is an improved version of the original T-56 and is good for more than 700 ft-lbs. It has been upgraded in terms of strength and shift feel to where it's not only much stronger than the TKO but also has smoother shifting. Unfortunately, it's also a much bigger transmission

and thus requires quite a few changes for it to go into an early Mustang. These include all of the items mentioned previously for the TKO (the crossmember/mount, yoke/driveshaft, bellhousing, clutch mechanism, shifter, clutch disc) plus the new speedometer and electrical connections. Modern Driveline and others offer complete kits to avoid any guesswork.

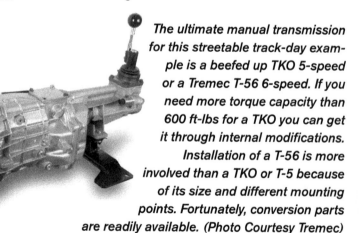

The ultimate manual transmission for this streetable track-day example is a beefed up TKO 5-speed or a Tremec T-56 6-speed. If you need more torque capacity than 600 ft-lbs for a TKO you can get it through internal modifications. Installation of a T-56 is more involved than a TKO or T-5 because of its size and different mounting points. Fortunately, conversion parts are readily available. (Photo Courtesy Tremec)

The conversion to a T-56 involves a few different items such as a different-length driveshaft and some different connections for the speedometer and wiring. The transmission crossmember likely also needs to be changed; a good idea anyway due to the increased power. Shifter and handle changes are similar to the TKO. (Photo Courtesy Tremec)

17 pounds), made from high-grade steel, and manufactured within very accurate tolerances for the best fit and quality. They're SFI compliant yet are totally suitable for street use in all but the harshest weather. They also use factory hardware (linkage, etc.).

Drag Racing

The clutch disc and pressure plate choice generally comes down to the torque capacity needed. If you can get by with a single-disc clutch you may want it to be as light as possible so the engine can rev more freely. An exception to this strategy may be in drag racing where you still need some flywheel weight to help launch the (usually heavier) car. Once your power level gets above 600 ft-lbs or so you probably want to use a twin-disc clutch to get the torque capacity you need without the extra rotational inertia that comes with a much larger/heavier disc.

A twin-disc clutch, by design, has four clutch facings instead of two so the clutch disc diameter can be

Because there's a much greater likelihood of higher RPM and power levels with the streetable track-day car it's prudent to use a steel "scattershield" for safety. In some forms of racing, particularly drag racing, this is a requirement anyway because compliance with SFI or similar specifications is mandatory once a certain elapsed time or trap/maximum speed is reached. Even if it's not a requirement it helps ensure you keep all

of your body parts in the event of a clutch explosion.

The solution is readily available in the form of a QT steel bellhousing and engine plate to replace the OEM aluminum parts. These are available for common transmission/engine combinations for a reasonable cost. Unlike older scattershields, which were large, heavy, and not very well made (huge flanges and loose bolts), these units are much lighter (about

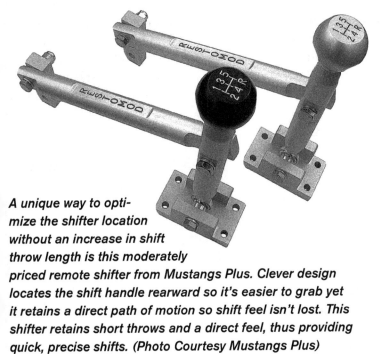

A unique way to optimize the shifter location without an increase in shift throw length is this moderately priced remote shifter from Mustangs Plus. Clever design locates the shift handle rearward so it's easier to grab yet it retains a direct path of motion so shift feel isn't lost. This shifter retains short throws and a direct feel, thus providing quick, precise shifts. (Photo Courtesy Mustangs Plus)

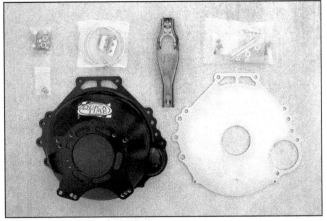

Higher forces and engine speeds require a stronger bellhousing. An OEM aluminum bellhousing doesn't provide enough protection so use of a steel "scattershield" type of bellhousing is warranted. QT parts use a higher-grade steel and superior manufacturing processes to keep the weight down while providing the needed protection in a smaller, better-fitting package.

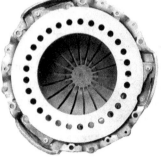
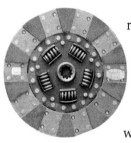

A lightened pressure plate helps provide maximum engine response. The strategic removal of material reduces the absolute weight of the pressure plate as well as the rotational inertia, thus allowing the engine to rev up more quickly. The clutch disc is very light because it uses a ceramic facing on the flywheel side with an organic facing on the other side. This, along with the sprung hub, provides high torque capacity yet retains smoother engagement.

The most significant means for improving engine response is the use of an aluminum flywheel. This results in a very dramatic reduction in weight and rotational inertia. This flywheel features a replaceable steel friction surface to provide acceptable durability and wear.

This exploded view of ACT's twin-disc clutch shows why this design is usually called for when torque levels are extremely high. Rather than using a single, large-diameter clutch disc (which is heavy and has much more rotational inertia) this design divides the total friction surface area over two smaller discs. (Photo Courtesy Advanced Clutch Technology)

reduced while still maintaining the surface area of the facing material needed for the torque level. Alternatively, it's also possible to use ceramic/metallic facings with a single disc but the result is usually a very abrupt engagement that would be a real handful in street use. Besides, the twin-disc design provides the greater torque capacity without this drastic deterioration in driveability. In fact, a twin-disc clutch can often be smoother than many single-disc clutches that don't even match its torque capacity.

The main drawback of the twin disc is its higher cost and small penalty in overall weight.

Once you get above 600 ft-lbs or so you're pretty much looking at the twin-disc setup if you still want to drive the car on the street without

major adjustments to your driving style. In a lighter car (1964½–1966) where you can't use that much power anyway (unless you've made some relatively radical modifications elsewhere) a lighter single Kevlar disc setup likely suffices.

The remainder of the related components can generally follow the lead of the street-performance car with the possible exceptions of the need to further beef up the crossmember, yokes, U-joints, and driveshaft based on the torque level. You may also want to consider using some form of torque strap, chain, or link between the engine and the frame to supplement the polyurethane mounts and further limit excess engine/transmission movement. This is particularly relevant in drag racing where the shock of shifting is more severe and can damage the polyurethane.

At this level you must ensure all of the small parts (such as fasteners) are up to the task as well. It doesn't do much good to have a strong transmission, clutch, and so forth if they're being held on by weak hardware. Upgrading to stronger, higher-quality fasteners such as those made by ARP ensure you have the strength you need and will, in many cases, improve the appearance of your ride and make subsequent removal easier.

Automatic Transmission Upgrades

In general, owners do not mate an automatic transmission to street or race engines with more than 700 hp. Most automatics are inherently weaker than the manual transmission that was available for the same vehicle. They tend to not have as high a torque rating and their gear

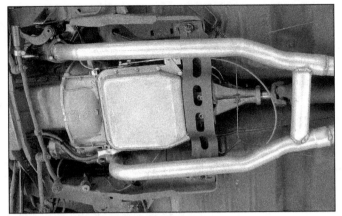

This completed AOD installation is in a 1968 Mustang. The transmission crossmember was moved back as far as it could go and new holes were drilled in it. There's not much clearance to the transmission pan but it's enough. (With a cast-aluminum pan this may not be feasible.) Even though the AOD is a bit larger there are no issues with the exhaust system or parking brake cable. The kickdown cable was mounted just in front of the transmission pan. The blue shifter cable hasn't been installed yet.

ratios are optimized for general street driving and fuel mileage.

Automatics can be an advantage in drag racing where their greater shifting consistency and torque multiplication are assets. On the street their primary appeal is convenience, particularly in heavy traffic.

In this section I discuss the common automatic transmission modifications for the three vehicle types. (I don't cover transmission brakes because they aren't for the street.) I give greater priority to driveability on the street over maximum torque capacity. These modifications are generic and apply mostly to strip use.

Initial Inspection

Replacing any worn mounts, properly adjusting all control cables and links, verifying the vacuum modulator (if so equipped) is functioning properly, etc., are all necessary steps before doing upgrades. A new transmission filter and the proper automatic transmission fluid should also be installed. The latter is particularly important to make sure the type of fluid (Type F, Mercon, etc.) is correct for the transmission. Failure to do so could cause improper shift behavior and expensive damage. Just use OEM-spec fluid unless you're making more power.

While the pan's off to change the filter/fluid, inspect inside the pan and the other transmission internals to make sure there aren't any signs of excessive wear of the friction materials (fine, dark sediment). If there are metal particles and/or the fluid has a burned odor you may be in for more work; a more in-depth inspection is needed.

If some freshening is required it is better to install a performance-oriented overhaul kit from a company such as TCI or B&M Racing rather than a standard rebuild kit. The aftermarket kits may cost a bit more but they give you better materials, which should hold up better under hard use. Most also allow you to tune your shift quality to some extent.

Shift Kit

If the transmission is okay, a desirable modification for a daily driver is the installation of a shift kit. This firms up the shifts for a performance feel and also helps prevent slippage under load.

A simple way to improve the performance of an original automatic transmission is to install a shift improver kit. These kits include the components necessary to make simple changes to the valve body so that shift pressure is raised. This provides firmer shifts while reducing slippage during shifts. When a more-serious level of modification is called for, a B&M Transpak (or similar) is the next step up. This kit includes all of the modifications in the shift improver kit plus the option of full manual shifting and further increases in-line pressure and shift firmness. (Photo Courtesy B&M Racing)

As an example, the B&M Racing Shift Improver Kit does a good job. It is inexpensive, require only hand tools, and can be installed in an afternoon.

Their Transpak adds full manual control to most applications. This allows you to downshift at any speed and hold the transmission in first

For a daily driver a relatively inexpensive performance shifter upgrade is this B&M Sport shifter. It's not a ratchet-style shifter so it's not ideal for drag racing, but it does have detents to prevent selection of the wrong gear plus classic T-handle and flat chrome stick styling to dress up your interior. (Photo Courtesy B&M Racing)

gear to whatever RPM you want without the transmission automatically upshifting. As you modify your vehicle more this allows you to realize the extra power you make at the top end.

Their TransKit is better suited to vehicle types other than a daily driver. B&M calls it "a transmission in a box" because it essentially allows you to rebuild your transmission/core to the same specs as their fully assembled transmissions.

Rebuild Kit

B&M and others offer full rebuild kits that can rehabilitate and improve just about any automatic transmission that hasn't been "ventilated" or otherwise suffered a catastrophic failure. These kits come in various levels, from street/strip to full racing, with the most robust materials.

If you've got the skills, experience, and a factory shop manual it can often be less costly to start with your own transmission and use the appropriate kit to rebuild it to the level you want. This is normally not the way to go for a daily driver with a tight budget.

A rebuilt or known, good used transmission is a less costly alternative if your existing transmission is shot but it can be the best choice if

you plan on keeping it as you further modify your vehicle. It's possible to rebuild a stock transmission to where it is suitable for a street-performance vehicle and possibly even for some street/strip/track-day cars.

Automatic Overdrive

A common upgrade for cars equipped with older automatics is to upgrade to a later OD transmission. The automatic overdrive (AOD) is the best choice for a daily driver based on its easy availability and low cost when purchased used or as a rebuild.

They're easy to modify and, best of all, they can often go right in where a C4 came out with little or no modification. They bolt right up to all Windsor small-blocks and some other engines. They can often use the same crossmember (the holes for the transmission mount may need redrilling) and, surprisingly, even the driveshaft. You may have to cut and slightly chamfer the driveshaft transmission yoke to prevent it from bottoming out in the AOD.

With a shift kit AODs are strong enough to be usable well into the street-performance category, at least until your modifications and torque level become fairly high. The biggest hassle with installing an AOD is the need to hook up the TV cable to the carburetor. You need a special adapter, available from many sources including Lokar. They also have flexible dipsticks and cable or tail-mount mechanical shifters (with boots, etc.) to further simplify your installation.

The AOD is a high-performance street transmission so there isn't much reason to keep your older C4 or C6 automatic transmission nor is

When a complete transmission rebuild is needed, full kits improve the shift behavior and also upgrade the internal components to withstand higher torque levels and abuse.

B&M's TransKit, for example, includes upgraded materials and components to essentially replicate the performance and capabilities you'd get if you bought a complete transmission from B&M. It allows you to build it yourself (or have someone do it) instead of buying it. (Photo Courtesy B&M Racing)

there any need, yet, to go with something more robust.

The AOD provides a huge reduction in RPM at higher speeds. Improvements in shift quality and (usually) lighter weight make up for the expense of switching. It certainly makes sense to do so if your older transmission needs an overhaul. The AOD with a shift kit suffices up to about 400 hp and 350 ft-lbs of torque, again depending on vehicle weight, power level, rear gear,

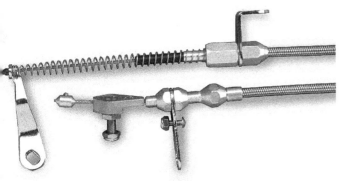

When installing an AOD into a car that had an older transmission you need to install a kickdown (or TV) cable because the other transmission probably had a vacuum modulator. Lokar's cables are ultra-high quality and provide super-smooth action while also being very appealing to the eye. In some cases it may be necessary to remove the shift lever and reposition it. This depends mainly on how things were positioned originally and whether you're also changing the shifter. (Photo Courtesy Lokar Performance Products)

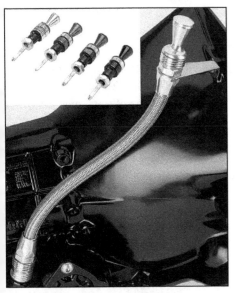

Lokar offers flexible dipsticks for most transmissions. They're braided steel with mounting brackets and locking tops. They are available in the various finishes shown and are an excellent way to flexibly accommodate the mounting of the dipstick with minimal concern for interference with other components. (Photo Courtesy Lokar Performance Products)

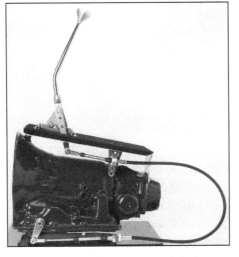

Another possibility is to use a tail-mount shifter. As the name suggests, they mount directly to the transmission and use a short, direct, mechanical linkage instead of a cable. (Photo Courtesy Lokar Performance Products)

tires, and so forth. The weak point of the standard AOD is the dual-input shaft; that's why going above these levels can be risky.

Upgraded AODs from companies such as TCI, B&M, and others are capable of much higher power levels (more than 600 hp) due to substantial design changes in the input shaft, valve body, and friction materials.

These transmissions are significantly more costly but they provide a way to stay with the AOD as your vehicle performance level increases well beyond what a standard AOD can handle. If you plan on going to higher power levels and want to stay with the AOD there's no real downside to going for one of these stronger transmissions from the start. There isn't any real difference in driveability if you use the same type of shift calibration; they are fine on the street yet can handle the strip. You won't have the expense of upgrading later.

AODs for higher outputs often omit the lockup feature of the converter because of changes to the valve body, etc. The loss of lockup may cost you a few MPG, mainly on the highway. Some say it's worth it because modified AODs with lockup can be a bit jerky at times. This isn't always the case, however, as it depends on the way the valve body and torque converter have been matched and your feel for such things. The difference in mileage is fairly small in any case.

This TCI StreetFighter is representative of a transmission best suited for street high-performance. This model is good for close to 600 hp and comes with a lockup or non-lockup torque converter. There's virtually no sacrifice in street driveability yet the shifts are firmer and reliability is far superior under aggressive use. (Photo Courtesy TCI)

Most other items (crossmember, mounts, driveshaft, control cables, etc.) are basically the same as in upgrading to an AOD in a daily driver unless, of course, you're at the higher power levels. Then you need to beef up these parts accordingly. Generally, you don't need to change the driveshaft or crossmember. You can also use the same control cables and other external connections. You want polyurethane mounts, a stronger/higher stall-speed torque converter, a better shifter, and high-performance transmission fluid with a supplementary fluid cooler. In the case of the latter, unless you live in a fairly cold climate it's better to cap off the cooler in the radiator and use an external cooler. It doesn't see the heat from the engine coolant and works better.

The main things to consider when choosing an AOD are the stall speed of the torque converter, whether or not you want lockup, and the type of shifter you want. The stall speed of the converter you choose depends on the torque curve of the engine, the weight of the car, the gears and tires used, and whether or not you're using any power adders (nitrous, supercharger, etc.). Transmission and converter manufacturers can help you make a final choice.

In general, the lower your engine's torque peak, the lower you want the stall speed of the converter to be. On a stock vehicle with a stock transmission and converter the stall speed is usually less than 2,000 rpm and is often in the 1,500-rpm range. This is mainly for fuel efficiency purposes; a "tighter" converter slips less and thus gives better MPG with less wear on the engine. A "looser" converter with a higher stall speed allows the engine to reach a higher RPM at launch, which (hopefully) puts it

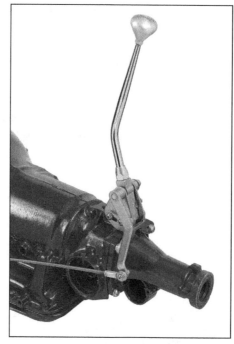

This is one of Lokar's "tail mount" shifters. Mounting directly to the transmission may be desirable in some cases where you have problems routing a cable or when you desire a more direct feel. (Photo Courtesy Lokar Performance Products)

closer to its torque peak and thus makes for a stronger launch.

This is another reason automatic transmissions aren't normally used

The inherent weak point of the standard AOD is the split-input shaft. It was used for providing lockup capability in top gear (OD) without having to redesign the entire transmission. It splits the torque from the engine along two different paths, which compromises the maximum torque the AOD can handle.

for track duty other than at a drag strip. The loose converter you need to get the most out of the engine would be problematic over the course of a longer race. Why? The inherent slippage of a higher stall speed converter is less efficient and creates more heat, which likely leads to durability issues in anything more than a fairly brief run.

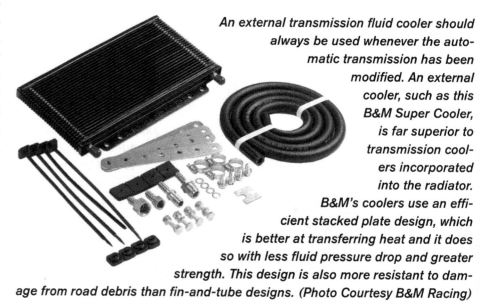

An external transmission fluid cooler should always be used whenever the automatic transmission has been modified. An external cooler, such as this B&M Super Cooler, is far superior to transmission coolers incorporated into the radiator. B&M's coolers use an efficient stacked plate design, which is better at transferring heat and it does so with less fluid pressure drop and greater strength. This design is also more resistant to damage from road debris than fin-and-tube designs. (Photo Courtesy B&M Racing)

Converter

It's necessary to distinguish between types of stall speed: "flash" (momentary) and "brake pedal" (continuous). Newer converter designs allow a brief, transient spike to a higher engine RPM before settling at the RPM the engine maintains while it is revved in gear with the brakes on. This can allow a better launch with less sacrifice in MPG and street driveability because the converter has something of a dual personality.

Under normal driving conditions it behaves as if it has a lower stall speed but at the strip it can briefly allow a higher effective stall speed at launch, especially if the engine is held at less than full throttle and full throttle is applied when the car launches. This requires some finesse in driving technique but it's worth it if you go to the strip often and don't want a loose converter on the street.

Some examples of stall speeds and compatible vehicle equipment are illustrated by TCI's range of street/strip high-performance converters. Their mildest version is the Breakaway series. These have stall speeds of about 2,200 to 2,400 rpm for small-blocks and 2,400 to 2,600 rpm for big-blocks (yes, the torque of the engine makes a difference). They are intended for vehicles with a 3.00:1 to 3.73:1 rear gear ratio and a camshaft duration of 265 to 280 degrees, which still have a relatively smooth idle and are only mildly modified. They increase stall speed about 1,000 rpm over stock while still emphasizing low-end performance and providing a harder launch and quicker acceleration.

The next step up is the StreetFighter series. These are for vehicles where the fuel system has been upgraded and the compression raised to the point where the idle is noticeably rough. This is due in large part to camshaft duration in the 280- to 300-degree range. The rear gear likely falls into the 3.55:1 to 4.56:1 range. The end result is stall speeds in the 3,000- to 3,400-rpm range for small-blocks and 3,400 to 3,600 rpm for big-blocks and roughly 1,500 more than stock. This allows even higher RPM launches with quicker reaction times and a greater emphasis on mid-range as well as low-end power.

The Super StreetFighter series is likely the most extreme level for the majority of high-performance street cars. Here you're talking about a car with cam duration in the 280- to 310-degree range. Thus the idle is clearly rough and there is a greater emphasis on top-end power with an even higher compression ratio and additional modifications. The rear gear is in the 3.73 to 4.88 range with the higher figures really only being usable with an OD transmission such as the AOD. The stall speed is about 2,000 rpm over stock or roughly 3,500 to 3,800 rpm for small-blocks and 3,800 to 4,000 rpm for big-blocks, thus providing even higher RPM launches and lower ETs.

The Ultimate StreetFighter series really isn't well suited for most street-driven vehicles and is better suited to streetable track-day cars. It's recommended for engines with more than 290 degrees of camshaft duration, a rear gear of 3.73:1 or more, and horsepower up to 750 (more than 1,000 with a power adder). The stall speed is about 2,000 rpm over stock (about 3,500 rpm for small- and big-blocks). This level of power and stall speed requires significant internal modifi- cation (hardened pre-ground pump hub, heavy-duty needle bearings, etc.) for the highest-RPM launches and greatest torque multiplication of these converters. This noticeably reduces ETs at the strip yet still allows limited use on the street, with more noise, wear, and lower MPG.

A TCI high-performance aftermarket torque converter features internal parts that have been furnace brazed for greater strength. Other reinforcements usually include the replacement of the thrust washers (for example, between the stator and the impeller) with heavy-duty needle bearings, the replacement of many components with new parts made from higher-strength steel, and the use of extra material (an "anti-ballooning" plate, for example) in critical areas to prevent flexing under high-stress conditions. (Photo Courtesy TCI)

Lockup

With the standard AOD either you have lockup or you don't because it's purely mechanical. This is a big plus when installing an AOD in an older car (no electronic controls). Because the lockup feature depends on the converter design and valve body the two must be compatible. A good rule is that lockup works better with fewer modifications, though, again, that statement depends on driver preference. The decision on lockup usually comes down to a tradeoff between driveability (perceived or not) and RPM/fuel economy.

If you have a relatively high threshold for shift quality you may make MPG with reduced engine noise and wear a priority. If you're more about smoothness and driveability you may decide against lockup. Differences in driveability and mileage are usually pretty small.

The tradeoff is also dependent on power level and the individual component manufacturer. Some manufacturers do a better job of balancing these tradeoffs than others. They're able to provide lockup with little, if any, effect on driveability. Most tend to delete lockup on AODs when you get into higher stall/torque capacity products due to the inherent weakness of the dual-input shaft. This is replaced by a solid, much stronger single shaft, which, by design, eliminates lockup.

Shifter

Choosing a shifter usually comes down to features and appearance. The functions you choose drive the appearance to some extent. If you want to have a reverse-lockout feature required by some sanctioning bodies, you likely have some form of lever or trigger. There are a few "stealth" designs that incorporate the feature (such as B&M's Quicksilver shifter) but most are more obvious about it.

Another consideration is how and where you want to mount the shifter and its compatibility with the transmission. If you have a reverse-

pattern valve body in the transmission it somewhat limits your shifter choices. A cable-shift mechanism gives you the most freedom to choose where you want to locate the shifter but it may not be the best choice if you shift very aggressively. A mechanical-linkage shifter, by design, must be attached to the trans-

For a street-performance car you probably want to go with a slightly more-sophisticated ratchet-type shifter. This B&M Quicksilver ratcheting shifter has the mechanism that allows you to make quicker, more dependable shifts in a drag race yet it lacks a visible lever/knob such shifters traditionally have. (Photo Courtesy B&M Racing)

The B&M Megashifter is not subtle; it's basically a Quicksilver shifter on steroids. It does away with the lift-to-operate system and replaces it with a visible lever to pull when you want to override the detents. It also sports a polished-aluminum T-handle rather than a ball, which you may find more attractive and/or easier to use at the strip. (Photo Courtesy B&M Racing)

If you happen to have a vehicle with a column shift (it happens) and want to convert to a floor shift, B&M offers the Unimatic shifter. It allows you to disconnect the column-shift mechanism and replace it with a smooth and reliable cable-shifting system. (Photo Courtesy B&M Racing)

mission, thus limiting its mounting options. It can take more abuse but it is much more dependent on the design of the specific transmission in order to get the best shift action.

Another thing to consider is whether you want a ratchet-style shifter (where there are detents, which allow you to simply move the shift lever without missing the gear you want). Also, you need to decide on having a neutral safety switch, backup light switch, and so forth.

AODE or 4R70W

For the streetable track-day car, more extensive upgrades are required. The AOD is marginally acceptable due to its torque limitations, unless it's been extensively modified. A better choice is the AODE or the 4R70W. These are successors to the AOD and eliminate most of its limitations. They're virtually identical in external dimensions so they fit virtually anywhere an AOD fits. They're rated for significantly higher torque levels (more than 1,000 hp when modified, and about 500 ft-lbs stock). They are electronically controlled so you don't have to make as many tradeoffs and you gain additional tuning capability. The main difference between the AODE and the 4R70W is that the latter has a wider ratio spread (that's what the "W" signifies).

The AOD and AODE have a 2.40:1 first gear with a 1.47:1 second and a .67:1 fourth while the 4R70W has a 2.84:1 first, a 1.55:1 second, and a .70:1 fourth (1:1 in third). This can be significant depending on vehicle weight and other factors. In general, if you have good traction at the line the 4R70W allows you leave a bit harder, whereas the AODE is a better bet if your car is traction limited due to weight, suspension, tires,

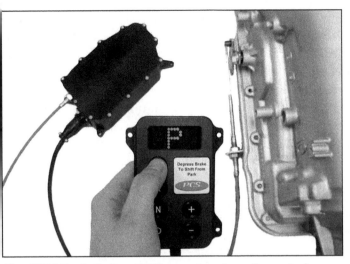

The GSM Push Button Shifter system from Powertrain Control Systems (PCS) replaces a column shifter or a floor shifter for most automatic transmissions. The control module can be mounted almost anywhere that's accessible to the driver, plus it features recessed and backlit buttons along with extra "+" and "-" buttons to allow for sequential shifts. (Photo Courtesy Powertrain Control Solutions)

When a modified AOD doesn't suit your needs, alternatives capable of handling more torque provide some very desirable additional features. The AODE/4R70W transmission is a newer, stronger version of the AOD, which eliminates most of the AOD's drawbacks while adding the benefit of electronic control. The latter provides far more flexibility in tuning the shift characteristics, plus it allows you to retain the lockup feature normally lost when the standard AOD is modified. It also allows you to use lockup in more situations. Another benefit of electronic control is you no longer need the external AOD TV cable. (Photo Courtesy Powertrain Control Solutions)

etc. The AODE also reduces engine revs a bit more on the highway and at top speed so that could be a factor for MPG, noise, and/or rear axle ratio choice.

With either version you must choose the right case because these transmissions were used mostly on 4.6L modular engines. The 5.0L and other small-block/Windsor versions are the cases you need to bolt up to an older engine. Most aftermarket suppliers can build the transmission the way you need it with the right case and internal modifications. You need a special AODE/4R70W torque converter (an AOD unit doesn't work). They are usually offered in similar variations. You should also use a stronger, SFI-compliant flex plate.

The main advantage of the AODE or the 4R70W is, of course, the electronic control. This allows you to choose and tune your shift points and shift firmness with much greater ease, flexibility, and accuracy compared to using a shift kit on an AOD. It also allows you to decide when (or not) to lock the converter. This eliminates the tradeoff of power versus lockup; you can have higher torque capacity and lockup. You can even have lockup in some other gears besides fourth if you want. This all requires an electronic controller. These transmissions came with one from the factory but it wasn't adjustable.

Shift Controller

Aftermarket products provide greater functionality with compatibility. An excellent example of this is the TCM-2300 Simple Shift controller from PCS. It uses simple rotary switches so no laptop is needed to make adjustments plus your passenger can do so while the car is moving. Built-in diagnostics indicate the gear and the lockup status. Each unit comes with a wiring harness specific to the transmission,

The PCS Simple Shift controller is far superior to OEM AODE/4R70W controllers. You can adjust shift firmness, shift points, and converter lockup (which you can't do with the OEM controller) plus you don't even need a computer. The LEDs on the unit act as indicators to confirm your adjustments and they provide a means to read the unit's built-in diagnostic trouble codes. Once you make your adjustments you can hide the controller. PCS offers complete kits for the AODE and 4R70W for EFI and carbureted (use their TPS kit) cars. (Photo Courtesy Powertrain Control Solutions)

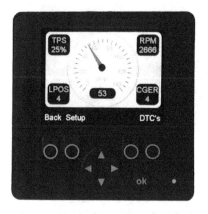

If you make adjustments often and/or you want to display what's going on while it's happening you can use the PCS Simple Shift Tuner. It can do your initial setup and then be removed or you can leave it connected to function as a datalogger and/or gauge, which can be configured to display live data. It also displays and clears trouble codes in a quick, user-friendly way. (Photo Courtesy Powertrain Control Solutions)

with the proper connecters, for easy installation.

PCS also offers the Simple Shift Tuner, which can remain connected and so the controller can be stored in a less-visible location. It allows you to do everything the rotary switches do in a more graphic and user-friendly format. It provides a gauge function that allows you to display live data for various parameters.

PCS also offers a software package for your laptop that allows you to view live data for the parameters and

The PCS D200 Dash Logger allows you to monitor data from their controller and add data from other sources into a single display. It can be configured to provide warnings based on your parameters, used as a large-screen tach with a built-in shift light, and communicate with external devices via RS-232 or CAN 2.0b protocols. (Photo Courtesy Powertrain Control Solutions)

diagnostic trouble codes. It adds a datalogging function with a monitor screen to help with tuning. The D200 stand-alone datalogger can combine the signals from the controller with inputs from other sensors. It can even act as a shift light!

Paddle Shifter

Once you have chosen the transmission, torque converter, and controller, another way to take advantage of the benefits of electronic control is with a paddle shifter mounted on the steering wheel. You can go F1 in your classic Mustang! The convenience of having the shift mechanism on the steering wheel lets you keep your hands on the wheel while shifting. This is safer and should also result in quicker, more consistent shifts and lower ETs. The electronic controller only works once the transmission is in gear so you need a manual shifter to go from park to drive or reverse, etc.

If you skip the paddle shifter, you should step up to a competition-type shifter. This can be a bit less convenient on the street but is more consistent and reliable at the strip. Companies, such as B&M Racing and Hurst, offer many variations.

Crossmember

At the high-torque levels of your high-powered streetable track-day car you may need an even stronger

transmission crossmember to prevent flexing and/or outright failure. Stronger steel units are available from many sources or can be fabricated.

Another option to consider is a billet aluminum X-Factor version from American Powertrain. It's plenty strong, it's lighter than a comparable steel unit, and it provides a lot of adjustability.

Cooler/Fan

At the power level of a streetable track-day car you should never use the cooler in the radiator tank. Instead, you should fit the largest, most efficient external cooler you can. Other than a small weight penalty and maybe some tighter packaging in some areas you really can't go too big.

Adding a small, high-flow fan is a good idea so cooling can continue after a run when the car is being driven back to the paddock or pit area. B&M Racing has a particularly efficient product in several sizes.

Blanket

Depending on how quick/fast your car runs, a transmission blanket may be required by the sanctioning body. A scattershield is required for a vehicle with a manual transmission. The purpose is identical: If the transmission blows this helps keep the flying parts from taking part of you with them.

The aluminum housings on OEM automatic transmissions were never intended to contain the internal parts in the event of a catastrophic failure. With a streetable track-day car's higher speeds, power levels, and forces it's possible "shrapnel" could come through the floorpan and injure you. A transmission blanket reduces that possibility and should be used at this level even if it's not a requirement.

DRIVELINE

Although the engine and transmission usually get the most attention the driveshaft and rear axle assembly are two essential parts of the equation. In this chapter I address the necessary compromises to be made when vehicles are used in different operating modes, under changing conditions, and with differing budgets. I concentrate primarily on the driveshaft, rear axle, and their various components (yokes, U-joints, gear ratios, differentials, axles, housings, etc.).

Driveshaft

In many cases the driveshaft transfers power from the engine/transmission to the rear axle/wheels and acts as a "fuse" because it can fail before other components when overloaded, the tires hook up, and the clutch doesn't slip, etc. The driveshaft often becomes the weakest link in the system. Therefore, a primary consideration in choosing a driveshaft is that it is strong and safe enough to not fail. Weight (total and rotating) is a secondary concern. Because there's little potential for parasitic/frictional loss the only other real considerations are reliability and serviceability.

Steel

For a vehicle primarily driven on the street that has only mild to moderate modification it's hard to beat a steel driveshaft. The original driveshaft is likely fine as long as it's not damaged and the U-joints are in good shape. Almost all first-generation Mustangs used a single-piece, steel driveshaft with an integral soundproofing liner on the inside surface of the tube. Tube diameters ranged from 2¾ to 3½ inches with various lengths and U-joint types. If your driveshaft is damaged or rusted just get a similar one from a salvage yard and put in new U-joints.

If a heavy-duty version (larger diameter and/or U-joints) was available for your car when it was fitted with a more powerful engine (yet it retained the same-style yokes on ends and is the correct length), you should be able to upgrade from a weaker standard OEM shaft to a stronger optional one. Just make sure the one you pick fits and is in good shape. Don't worry about the condition of the U-joints because you'll replace them.

The expense of a new steel driveshaft is rarely justified unless what you need isn't available from a salvage yard. There are a few inexpensive (under $300) aluminum ones

A direct-replacement aluminum driveshaft is usually the best solution for a street-driven car that's not too heavily modified. It's lighter and stronger than an OEM steel driveshaft. Here is an OEM steel driveshaft (top) from the 1968 coupe and a stronger and lighter aluminum driveshaft (bottom) from Inland Empire Driveline Services (IEDS). The original fit the C4 and 8-inch rear. It's 3 inches in diameter and weighs 19.1 pounds. The IEDS driveshaft is for an AOD and a 9-inch so the length was custom-made. Even though it's larger in diameter (3.5 inches with 1350s), and much stronger, it weighs only 14.7 pounds.

---

available from Ford Racing and others that make a good upgrade if they fit your car. They already come with new U-joints and a new slip yoke for the transmission. They may make sense if you need a new yoke and you want protection for future power increases. (Aluminum's reduced weight and inertia don't matter much in this case, unless you're seeing more power and/or RPM.)

Aluminum

For the vast majority of situations an aluminum driveshaft is best in terms of strength per pound per dollar. Used steel driveshafts are not always easy to find in the size and type you need plus the cost adds up quickly if you also need to buy a new slip yoke and new U-joints. For mild to moderate power one of the lower-priced, ready-made, direct-fit aluminum driveshafts cost little more than purchasing and refurbishing an OEM steel driveshaft.

A new steel driveshaft generally runs about $100 to $150 less than a better aluminum driveshaft. It is considerably heavier than aluminum and it may or may not be stronger. A steel shaft is likely more expensive than a basic, direct-fit aluminum shaft but it is less costly than an aluminum shaft designed for a high-performance application.

If you can't use an OEM steel driveshaft with new U-joints, etc., the best solution is usually a direct-fit aluminum driveshaft. If this basic aluminum shaft doesn't fit or lacks the necessary strength a stronger aluminum shaft with a larger diameter, thicker wall, larger U-joints, and/or stronger slip yoke may be best. Aluminum driveshafts capable of handling 600 hp or more can be purchased off the shelf for about $500 to $600. You can also have a driveshaft custom-made to fit your particular situation for about $600 to $1,000.

For my 1965 fastback I was lucky enough to find that a ready-made aluminum driveshaft from Ford Racing (intended to fit 1979–1993 Fox-Body Mustangs) was a perfect fit for the combination of small-block 302/5.0L with a T5 transmission and an 8-inch rear end. I will only be making about 450 hp so it can handle the power, and the slip yoke was a perfect fit because the T5 came in Fox-Body Mustangs. The 8-inch also had a compatible yoke and U-joints.

This Ford Racing aluminum shaft was the right length, saved a few pounds (and dollars), and still has some reserve strength if I decide to make more power. It also fit perfectly and worked just fine when I had an AOD in the car. The driveshaft in my 1968 coupe, however, had to be custom-made by Inland Empire Driveline Service (IEDS) because of all the parts I changed and the power I'm making. Changing out the stock C4 transmission for a TCI AODE resulted in the need to shorten the driveshaft slightly, as did the change from an 8-inch rear end to a much stronger 9-inch.

You need to pay attention to the overall length of the transmission you use and to whether or not the transmission output shaft sticks out past the shaft seal (as in the AOD) or is internal (as in the C4). This affects the location and length of the splines in the slip yoke, which must be correct to avoid failure of the slip yoke (too short) or having it hit or bind inside the transmission (too long).

Because I'm making around 600 hp with the 427 stroked Windsor I also wanted to go with bigger U-joints and a beefed-up slip yoke.

I provided IEDS with the necessary measurements and they were able to make a beautiful custom piece in about a week; the cost was quite reasonable ($600 to $700, depending on options).

Companies that specialize in driveline components are definitely the way to go if you can't use an off-the-shelf item. They can pretty much make whatever you need based on your parts and power level. In many cases they also have components on hand for some of the more common situations such as swapping an AOD or a T5 into a first-generation Mustang. They may also stock many of the small, oddball parts you might need such as special conversion U-joints, hard-to-find slip yokes, and similar items related to the driveshaft/driveline for most vehicles.

Composite

If your engine's power level is extremely high (over 1,000 hp or so) you may find that even an aluminum driveshaft is not up to the task. Some companies offer aluminum driveshafts that have been partially wrapped with carbon-fiber material to reinforce them. This certainly does gain you a bit more strength and safety versus aluminum alone. However, if you need maximum strength the answer is a composite driveshaft with a carbon-fiber (or similar) tube and metal (usually aluminum) end pieces.

A composite shaft can handle up to about 4,000 ft-lbs of torque and 14,000 rpm. They're much lighter than aluminum or steel, have a longer fatigue life, and are better at dampening (and withstanding) vibrations. Should a composite shaft fail it shreds itself rather than whipping around and beating up the

When the lightest possible weight, rotational inertia, and maximum strength are desired there's no substitute for a carbon-fiber composite driveshaft. This construction is also best at being able to tolerate extreme vibration levels and be most effective at dampening them. Their most significant benefit is the enhanced safety due to shredding on failure, rather than flailing about and causing damage.

vehicle (and/or driver). Composite shafts from IEDS further benefit from a wet-filament winding process, which contains no metal substrate so you have the lightest and strongest possible construction.

Composite shafts are almost always custom-made to spec so they normally cost upward of $1,000. If they're the only thing that can do the job for you they're well worth it.

Yokes and U-Joints

The benefits of having an upgraded driveshaft cannot be realized unless the connections at each end of it are also correct. Because the yokes are determined by the transmission and the rear axle assembly this becomes primarily a function of matching the U-joint size and type. The slip yoke at the front of the driveshaft must match the splines of the transmission output shaft and also be of the correct length. If you go to a more robust transmission you'll likely end up with a larger-diameter slip yoke. You also want to ensure you chose U-joints sufficiently strong for your power level.

Ford doesn't have many variations when it comes to slip yokes. Common ones are the 25-, 28-, and 31-spline versions. The smallest was generally found on the 6-cylinder, and the less-powerful small-block

V-8s were usually equipped with a 3-speed manual or small automatic transmission.

The 28-spline versions were commonly used on the more powerful small-blocks with 4-speed manual or C4 automatics as well as on some of the later transmissions such as the AOD and T5.

The largest yokes were reserved mainly for big-blocks, which came with a 4-speed Toploader or an FMX/C6 auto. The 31-spline yoke also fits some later transmissions such as the T45 and the Tremec TKO and T-56.

The point is that you should choose your transmission not only based on its capacity but also the ability to use a sufficiently strong slip yoke. You can also go with slip yokes that are forged/steel instead of the usual cast iron if you must use smaller transmission components.

At the other end of the driveshaft things are considerably simpler with the pinion yoke. This yoke size is basically determined by the diameter of the driveshaft tube and the size of the U-joints. You want to match the U-joint sizes at both ends of the driveshaft. This can be difficult some-

times because the rear axle may need something different. There are conversion U-joints to resolve this but they're not the most desirable option with higher power levels. In general, you should try to have the same-size U-joints all along the way. If it means having a different slip yoke or pinion yoke on the rear axle, it's preferable in terms of strength, reliability, and serviceability.

U-joints don't fail often if they're properly lubricated and maintained but you have an easier time finding a replacement when all the bearing caps are the same size. It's best to determine what the largest U-joint size is in the system and change all components to that size. Because there are only three main U-joint sizes (1310, 1330, and 1350) and the slip yoke usually determines what options you have, it's relatively simple.

The smallest U-joints (1310) are sufficient for street use

Regardless of what type of driveshaft you use you should consider using a driveshaft safety loop. It bolts to the floorpan to prevent the driveshaft from whipping around wildly in the event of a failure. This is especially important when drag racing, although rules for other types of racing may also require it. Generally, it should be mounted toward the front of the driveshaft with at least 2 inches of clearance at the extremes of the driveshaft's travel. For a street car be sure you have sufficient ground clearance.

with a mildly modified vehicle but not much more. After a few modifications, or if you take the car to the track, you're pushing it. In general it's better to have at least 1330 U-joints throughout the system. They are good for moderately to heavily modified vehicles when autocrossing or on a road course, and at least a moderately modified vehicle at the strip. You can get away with more when you're not at the drag strip because the shock loading of a road course or an autocross is much less. Similarly, an automatic transmission is less abusive than a manual transmission.

A 1330 U-joint is fine for the vast majority of cars still driven on the street and run mostly on street tires. A possible exception is the heavier 1971–1973 cars but these tend to not be modified as often.

Every car is different and you need to protect for what you have and what you're planning. Going from a 1310 to a 1330 U-joint shouldn't be very difficult or cost very much plus it provides more protection should you modify the vehicle further. The 1350 joints are normally only needed for heavily modified vehicles that spend a lot of time at the track. However, a powerful and/or heavier street car with grippy R-compound tires or drag radials may be enough reason to go with 1350s, just in case.

Bigger doesn't generally cost much more as long as you can make it work. I went with 1350 joints on my 1968 because I planned to use drag radials with 3.70:1 gears and a torquey 427W. It was no problem making them work with the AOD transmission and 9-inch rear.

Be sure to buy permanently lubricated U-joints because they're stronger (a grease fitting creates a weak point) and use better materials (such

The differences among the three common U-joint sizes are illustrated here. The 1310 joint (left) is the smallest in size and strength with the smallest bearing caps and trunnion (the "cross" the bearing assemblies rest on). The 1330 (center) uses the same basic bearing cap as the 1310 but does so with a larger and stronger trunnion. The 1350 joint (right) is the strongest because it beefs up the footprint of the 1330 with larger (and longer) bearing/cap assemblies coupled with an even thicker trunnion section. Material, design, and construction differences among brands affect strength but the dimensions are the same. These three are permanent-lube types.

as silicone or polyurethane) for the seals. Use a high-grade iron or steel for the main body/trunnion. A lifetime heavy-duty U-joint doesn't cost much more than a basic version but it gives you more strength and protection. Keep the insides of the bearing caps clean and properly lubricated with an appropriate grease. If you don't check before final assembly, it's too late.

Rear Axle

Early Mustangs came with three types of rear axle assemblies: 7.5-, 8-, and 9-inch. The 8.8-inch axles found in later Mustangs and other vehicles can also be used but it requires some fabrication to retrofit them. For a performance vehicle the 7.5-inch unit isn't up to the

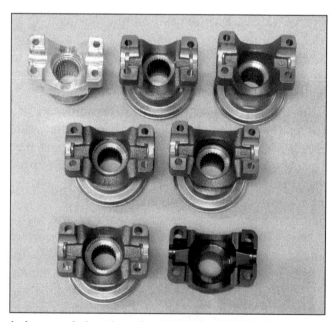

The pinion yoke on the axle assembly is usually the same type as on the downstream end of the driveshaft. There are conversion U-joints available to match different joint sizes but it's better to avoid using them by using the same U-joint sizes. Pinion yokes can be made of aluminum, gray or nodular iron, or forged steel. The 1310 and 1330 styles also come in long and short lengths. Yokes for 1350 joints are all short but there can be differences in the internal spline size and count.

Quick-release bearing caps are an option for the pinion yokes. Compared to standard steel straps (right) they are easier and quicker to remove plus they spread the load more evenly over the surface of the bearing. They can be made from several different metals, although aluminum *(lighter weight with adequate strength) and steel (maximum strength) are most common. All are far superior to OEM straps.*

task and is not discussed here. The 8-inch, contrary to some opinions, can prove to be quite acceptable for most street-driven vehicles and even many vehicles taken to the track (but not the drag strip). The 9-inch is the choice of many racers and high-performance vehicle owners and is the best option when performance levels rise significantly beyond stock. Even the 9-inch requires upgrades for extreme power.

There are several pinion yoke options for each type of rear axle assembly. Different yokes are needed for the various U-joint types (1310, 1330, and 1350). All except the 1350 come in long and short versions, depending on the original vehicle. The original factory parts were usually made from cast iron. Aftermarket examples available from rear axle specialists (such as Currie Enterprises) can be made from aluminum (for less weight and rotational inertia), nodular iron (stronger than OEM), or forged steel (strongest). It's generally preferable to use the short style because it's lighter and stronger. This is easily accommodated if you're having a custom driveshaft made; just be sure you specify the correct

dimensions. It may also be possible if you use a pre-made shaft.

The 8- and 9-inch have removable center sections but the 8.8-inch does not; it simply has a rear cover to allow access to the internals. The 9-inch is the high-performance rear axle of choice.

Housing

There can be significant differences in the basic strength of the housing. Some have swedged (narrowed) axle tubes, which considerably reduces the strength of the housing. Most do not have any reinforcement from the center section to the tubes; some do.

The size of the axle tubes can vary; bigger is generally better. Likewise, the size of the bearings at the end of the tube can vary from early small bearings to the later, large Torino size. The latter is preferable in most cases.

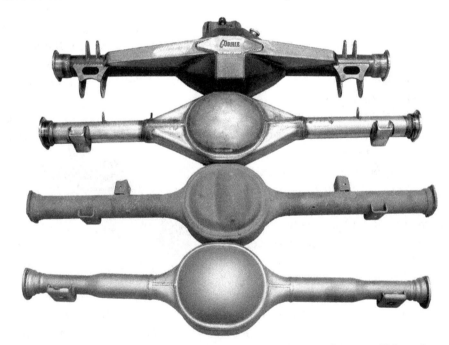

Ford rear axle housings come in many different sizes and types. Although differences between an 8-inch unit and a 9-inch unit are to be expected, there are many possible differences even within the same axle type. There are differences in the diameter of the axle tubes and the amount of reinforcement around the center section. Larger, uniformly straight tubes (third from top) are more desirable than swedged tubes (bottom). Similarly, large tubes can allow for the use of larger, stronger bearings. An OEM housing can be reinforced (second from top) or a fully fabricated aftermarket assembly (top) can be used when maximum strength is needed.

A fabricated aftermarket housing (this one is from Currie Enterprises) can be much stronger than even a reinforced OEM housing. All components are made from thicker, superior metals. Extra reinforcement such as the plate, which braces the end of the axle tube to the rest of the housing, makes the whole assembly far stronger and more rigid. Full welds replace partial welds and/or press fits. The design of the housing is stronger due to its shape, which better spreads out the forces and reduces weak spots.

The 8-inch bearing (left) is only available in a fairly limited number of variations. The 9-inch bearing (middle) is not only larger and stronger than the 8-inch, it's also available in many different styles from ball bearing to roller bearing, etc. It can be had with external O-rings (shown), plus other special designs. The Torino bearing (right) is strongest and has the most options.

The difference in bearing size makes a significant contribution to the overall strength of the assembly. The small bearing of an 8-inch housing (left) is fine for most street use or light track use with a light, mildly modified car. Once the power level rises appreciably and/or the vehicle weight and track use increase you should at least go to a "small" 9-inch bearing (middle). This is a major step up from the 8-inch case, plus you get all of the other benefits of the 9-inch axle. The larger 9-inch bearing (right) is often referred to as the Torino bearing because it was standard on that vehicle (the Mustang generally got the "small" 9-inch bearing).

Center Section

The heart of any rear axle assembly is the center section. This is where the most critical components (gear set and differential) are located. Other components such as axles, bearings, etc., are also important in the respect that they must be able to perform without failure but they don't directly affect performance. The choice of gear ratio and the type of differential clearly do.

The main function of the center section casting is to hold these components precisely in place and not deflect under load. Different options do this to varying degrees. The design features of the casting (or billet/forging) such as extra ribs, the use of larger and stronger bearings and gears, and other associated components all vary. This is one of the main advantages of the 9-inch over the 8-inch; everything is just bigger and stronger.

When one bearing at each axle end isn't enough you can upgrade to two by doing a full-floating axle conversion such as this one from Baer. This divides the forces at the end of the axle so the weight of the vehicle is supported by one bearing and the cornering forces are handled by the other bearing. This is necessary in cases where extremely high cornering loads can cause axle bowing/bending, which, in turn, causes the wheel flange to deflect a small amount. (Axle bearing life is greatly reduced under extreme use.) This deflection, though relatively small, is enough to push the brake pads slightly back into the calipers. (Photo Courtesy Baer Racing)

The 9-inch axle is the most widely used for performance purposes but many concepts I discuss also apply to the 8-inch, and some even to the 8.8-inch.

I went to the driveline experts at Currie Enterprises for some specific details on these axles. Some of the obvious visual differences include strengthening the ribs, machining for weight reduction, using different pinion bearing options, and using a different casting material. These differences vary depending on the specific center section type and the manufacturer.

The 8-inch center section casting (left) is made from regular iron with some strengthening ribs. It's hindered by the relatively small pinion bearing, as well as other areas where weight and cost were prioritized over strength. The standard OEM-style 9-inch casting (left middle) has a larger pinion bearing as well as deeper (though fewer) ribs. This style is good for up to about 450 hp.

The Sportsman casting (right middle) has superior ribbing and is made of stronger nodular iron, as indicated by the "N" cast above the pinion bearing housing. It is significantly stronger due to the material used and other design features such as the larger Daytona inner pinion. This is good for about 650 hp. The Currie 9+ casting (right) has the larger, 3.25-inch carrier bearings (thus is able to use 35- to 40-spline axles) and nodular material. It incorporates the larger and stronger NASCAR pinion bearing. A steel pinion yoke is also evident, as is the billet aluminum pinion support that supports 850 hp.

An extremely critical area of the center section to consider is the carrier bearing cap design. The casting on the left uses a machined bearing retainer instead of a simple stamping while also using a shorter, stronger cap screw and tab to constrain it. It has much thicker bearing caps, both around the bearing and under the bolts, for much greater strength. The stamped, longer tab of the casting on the right is weaker due to the material used and the greater length. It also has a less-precise fit with the bearing retainer, allowing more movement. The bearing cap is thinner over the bearing plus the location of the retaining tab bolt creates a significant weak point in terms of possible cracking around the bolt hole; it's clearly less strong and less stable.

The 8-inch pinion support (left) uses the smallest bearings and has the smallest as-cast ribs. The OEM-style 9-inch (left middle) is clearly stronger by virtue of the larger pinion bearing and the thicker as-cast ribs. The support made from billet aluminum (right middle) also uses the larger bearing and has significantly more material around the bearing for reinforcement. Even though it is lighter than the OEM-style 9-inch it is still stronger. The forged steel example (right) is the strongest. It has the largest NASCAR bearing and maximum reinforcement/material.

If you want a factory/OEM appearance and a stronger center section, manufacturers such as Currie Enterprises, Moser, and Strange offer factory replica castings. Made from stronger nodular material this Currie example slots between the Sportsman and the 9+, so it's able to handle approximately 700 to 750 hp while still retaining an accurate OEM look.

Other, less common, variations on center-section castings include lightweight versions, such as this. The front face was cast thinner to save weight. This reduces strength, though not by much. Castings may be selectively milled or otherwise machined to remove weight from specific areas. Different metals may also be used.

An important feature to look for when choosing a center section is the additional support around the inner pinion bearing. The casting on the left covers the pinion bearing much more completely and it has much more material cast into the area tying it into the rest of the casting. This greatly increases the stability of the pinion gear under load, which is critical to avoiding failure and achieving good service life. The casting on the right is also shallower next to the carrier bearing. The bearing cap designs of these two examples are also different.

Gear Set

The first decision to make regarding your gear set is what ratio to use. The ratio you choose depends on your priorities. What's available varies by the rear axle type but it's safe to say the 9-inch has far more options than the others. In general, ratios of 3.00:1 or less are not used for performance purposes, except perhaps where a higher top speed or better fuel mileage is the priority. Most street-driven vehicles intended for performance use have a ratio in the range of 3.25:1 to 4.10:1 with the higher numbers being best suited for drag racing.

The transmission also affects the choice of gear set because the use of an OD transmission such as an AOD or a T5 allows the use of a numerically higher gear without the penalty of higher engine RPM on the highway. A higher numerical ratio generally provides better acceleration while the lower numbers, theoretically at least, offer the potential of a higher top speed and/or better fuel mileage. You can be sure the latter reduces engine RPM at any given vehicle speed.

Ratios over 6.00:1 are available for the 9-inch axle though such extremes are only appropriate for drag racing and other specialized uses; they're not suitable for vehicles driven on the street.

An OD transmission and/or one with more ratios (5- or 6-speed versus 4-speed) and a wider ratio spread provides more flexibility. There's not much difference in the cost of the gears in terms of the ratio chosen, except perhaps for the really high (over 5.00:1) ratios. The cost of the gears is more dependent on the material and any special finishing operations (lightening, polishing, linecoating, heat treating, cryogenics, etc.).

For low to moderate performance levels and ratios, new factory/OEM gears are commonly thought to have the best wear and noise characteristics. Even used OEM gears can be better than some aftermarket brands if they're not too worn or otherwise damaged (pitting, chipping, scoring, heat checking, etc.). You should never use any set of used gears that shows any sign of damage or wear. The possibility of a catastrophic failure does not justify the risk.

Limited-Slip Differential

The gear ratio determines how well you match the engine's RPM and torque characteristics to the way the vehicle is used. The carrier/differential determines how the torque gets transmitted to the tires. You need to have a powerful engine with the proper transmission and the correct rear-end ratios in a limited-slip differential (LSD).

The most common type of LSD on early Mustangs with an 8- or 9-inch axle is the Traction-Lok type, which uses the same concept as the Eaton Positraction (Posi) and others. This design is far superior to the Ford LSD found in most smaller rear ends,

Most high-performance street cars use the ring-and-pinion gear set as is, right out of the box. If you desire greater performance and/or durability you can also choose from many different surface treatments, coatings, and manufacturing processes, including different heat treatments and even cryogenic treatments. This gear set has been lightened by removing material from around the back face of the ring gear. Both gears have also been micropolished to reduce friction and wear. The extra cost of such options may be justified or necessary in competition or with extreme loads.

including the 8-inch, which were neither strong enough nor durable enough for serious performance use.

This rear design uses a series of steel plates with corresponding friction plates sandwiched between them to keep the wheels spinning. It relies on a preloaded spring setup to keep the plates together when going straight yet the springs allow for differential action when turning.

Older units were prone to wear though newer versions of the Eaton Posi feature carbon-friction technology along with precision-forged gears for greater durability and strength. These units are rebuildable, if necessary, and relatively inexpensive. They operate automatically so they are a good all-around unit for a mildly to moderately modified vehicle. Their main disadvantage is they're not always smooth and may cause tire squeal or gear chatter when going around tight corners. They also change their characteristics as they wear. Still, they're very robust and economical.

The 9-inch axle type is able to accommodate much larger, stronger axles with up to 40 splines, whereas smaller axles types may be limited to 31- or 33-spline axles, which may not be strong enough. You must match the splines of the carrier/differential to those of the axles, which further affects your number of options.

It's best to do all rear axle upgrades at the same time, if possible, because there are many interdependencies among parts and you avoid disassembling the rear axle more than once.

For higher-output heavier vehicles and/or more severe use, the Eaton Detroit Locker is an excellent solution, especially on the drag strip. This design was intended mainly for racing use only, though it could be

bought over-the-counter at a Ford dealer (for the 9-inch). It operates on the same basic principle as the Posi but replaces the plate arrangement with a couple of very strong ratcheting "dog ring" gears that are constantly meshed together when going straight. There's no potential for slippage as there is with the Posi.

When turning, the gears separate by sliding along their splines and the teeth on their sides ratchet (jump) over one another for differentiation. This results in a very audible clunking sound and a harsh action, which is really not suitable for street use. This style is available for the 8.8-inch axles with C-clips and even the 7.5-inch axles so it may be a viable solution in cases where the ultimate in strength and durability is needed.

An interesting variation on the Detroit Locker is the Eaton ELocker, which is most commonly used with 8.8-inch axles. This differential allows the driver to lock or unlock it at will via a pushbutton connected to built-in electromagnets. The Detroit Locker is ultimately stronger but the ELocker comes close and spares you the harshness. The ELocker is maintenance free though it's serviceable if necessary.

Versions using air instead of electricity are called Air Lockers. They essentially give you an open differential for the street (smoother, no chatter/clunking) but allow you to have a no-slip LSD when you get to the track/strip. While originally

TrueTrac (TT) differentials don't require any maintenance and are very durable. Their torque-bias ratio, in fact, stays virtually constant over the life of the differential. This type is quickly becoming the most common for OEM use in performance vehicles. The TT is offered for 8-, 8.8-, and 9-inch rears; even those with 33-spline axles.

intended for all-wheel-drive and off-road vehicles they have been adopted by performance-oriented drivers because they provide smooth operation on the street with tremendous strength in competition.

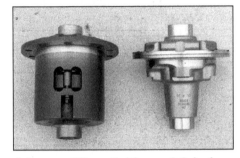

A Torsen differential for an 8.8-inch C-clip axle (left), compared with a TrueTrac differential for a 9-inch (right) illustrates the difference in size when C-clips are used. They are less desirable in performance applications because the clips can fail and result in the loss of an axle. The Torsen differential reduces the likelihood of this by employing a robust retention system (the forged-steel block in the access window) along with a very stout locking bolt. They're available in several versions (including the T2-R with serviceable clutch packs for racing) for many Ford axle applications, especially the 8.8-inch rear. They're virtually indestructible plus they're also maintenance free (except the T-2R race version).

FORD MUSTANG: HOW TO BUILD AND MODIFY 1964½–1973   97

The Eaton Detroit TrueTrac (TT) helical gear-style differential is an excellent all-around choice for a vehicle driven on the street; it is also aggressively used on the track/strip. This design is by far the simplest and most effective for the street. It's also more expensive due to the precision needed during its manufacture. They are torque-sensing rather than speed-sensing differentials.

Their biasing and differentiation functions are constantly working, regardless of speed, in a fully automatic manner. The transfer of torque from one axle to another is totally consistent and seamless. There is no locking/unlocking, which can destabilize the vehicle and break traction in a turn. Helical differentials are the smoothest, quietest, and most progressive design, which makes them the best choice for street, road course, and autocross use.

TTs work great on the drag strip and are a better choice than any of the other differentials unless you're dealing with extremepower, slicks, and a heavy car with a manual transmission. In other words, they are for anything but the "worst case" scenario and/or where the budget is limited. These units are extremely strong and are suitable for all but the most extreme power levels when used on the drag strip. In almost any other use there virtually is no power limit because something else is likely to break first.

The original helical gear differential was the Torsen. It adds to the features of the TrueTrac by being available in several different styles (T-1, T-2, T-2R, etc.), which have different bias ratios ranging from about 1.5:1 to over 3.0:1 (up to 5.0:1 in the T-1) to better suit different situations. Their design is also better able to handle the highest torque levels with minimal chance of failure. Torsen differentials were available as an option on the 2013 and newer Boss 302 Mustang (standard on the Laguna Seca model) and were also included in Ford's factory road race cars such as the FR500S with winning results.

The T-2R race version incorporates serviceable friction plates to supplement the helical gears to "tune" performance and provide a higher bias ratio under the most severe conditions. It also makes the unit compatible with electronic traction control.

Rear Axle Assembly

Always use the appropriate factory manual and/or manufacturer's instructions when assembling a rear axle. It's also extremely important to keep everything as clean as possible and ensure your torque wrench is properly calibrated. Failure to properly torque the fasteners for the bearing caps and other items will almost surely cause a problem of some kind if not outright epic failure.

The following photos are highlights of installing a rear axle at Currie Enterprises, where they have the benefit of specialized fixtures and tools to make the process easier and quicker. This is not a step-by-step guide because there are too many differences among cars.

The assembly of the rear axle begins with the installation of the pinion support and pinion gear. Install the inner bearing into the center section casting and then assemble the pinion bearings, pinion yoke, and seal onto the pinion gear and pinion support using a hydraulic press and a seal installer. This is a very precise operation and must be done correctly to avoid excessive play or preloading of the bearings as well as damage to the seal. Install the pinion gear/support/yoke assembly into the center section using the correct torque for the bolts but no gasket or sealant.

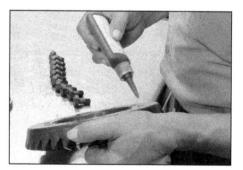

Prepare the ring gear for assembly onto the differential by putting some threadlocker on the threads of these very highly torqued bolts and into the bolt holes of the ring gear. This is an absolutely critical and mandatory step to prevent loosening due to the extreme and constant vibration these parts are subjected to.

After the carrier bearings have been pressed on, the ring gear can be installed. The ring gear has a very close fit with the differential so you need to get the bolts started and then go around the ring gear sequentially and evenly to pull up the ring gear to meet the differential. The key is to not cock the gear so that any metal gets shaved off. The gear must be brought up smoothly and evenly before the final torquing.

Once the differential and ring gear assembly have been mounted in the center section, check and set the side play of the carrier bearings. This is critical because you are setting the final location of these parts relative to the pinion gear as well as the amount of preload in the bearings. Obviously, the differential must spin freely but side play must also be minimized. Several adjustments are usually needed to set this.

With the pinion gear and the carrier bearing side/retaining plates in their preliminary location (note the retaining straps and bolts are missing here), check the gear mesh pattern. You do this by applying a special white grease to the ring gear teeth and then spinning the pinion gear (a drill and socket on the pinion gear retaining nut works fine if you go slowly to prevent slinging off the grease). This distributes the grease over the ring gear so its pattern can be observed to see if more adjustment is needed.

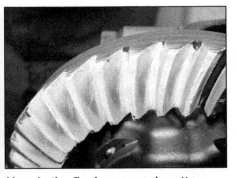

Here is the final gear mesh pattern. The area where the grease is thinnest is centered both horizontally and vertically on the face of each gear tooth. This may not be the case on your first check. If the pattern is not centered vertically you may need to place a shim under the pinion bearing support to slightly move it away from the ring gear, thus achieving the desired pattern. If the pattern is off in the horizontal direction you have to readjust the carrier bearing location by turning the side retaining plates until you get what you need.

Once you achieve the proper gear mesh pattern the side-plate retaining straps can be installed and the bearing cap bolts can be brought to their final torques. Here I've used one of the strongest combinations of the center section casting (note the reinforced inner pinion support) and bearing caps (thicker caps with ribs and the side locking strap/bolt). There's no need to remove the grease on the gear.

Currie Enterprises offers a unique option for carrier bearing races. Instead of having to get a new center section casting if you want to move up in axle size, Currie offers these adapters that allow you to initially use smaller axles (with their corresponding differential) in a center section with the larger carrier bearing opening normally needed for larger axles. When you're ready to upgrade to the larger axles and differential you only need to replace them and the bearings/races; you can keep the center section casting you have. This reduces cost and allows greater interchangeability.

The final steps in the assembly process involve the installation of the center section into the axle housing, and then the installation of the axles with their bearings and seals. Other than choosing the correct axles the main thing to consider is what type of axle bearing to use (ball, tapered, etc.) as determined by the size of the bearing pocket in the axle housing and the intended use

Once the axle assembly is complete you may still have to address the installation of brake lines, suspension brackets, brake hardware, and so forth before you install the whole assembly in the car. Before the axle is finally installed you must also fill it up with the appropriate amount and type of gear oil.

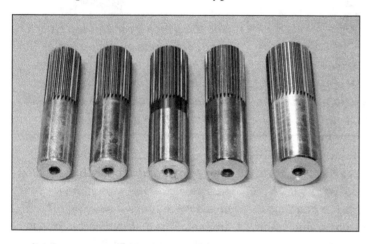

From left to right are 28-, 31-, 33-, 35-, and 40-spline axles. The 28-splines are acceptable for street and mild performance applications. You want to move up to the 31-spline versions for a vehicle that's been modified, especially if you intend to drag race. The 33-spline axles are reserved for pretty serious power levels and generally aren't needed for the type of vehicles discussed in this book. Differential options become much more limited when you go beyond 31-spline axles. Eaton offers a 33-spline TrueTrac differential for the 8.8-inch axle. Street-driven vehicles almost never need anything bigger.

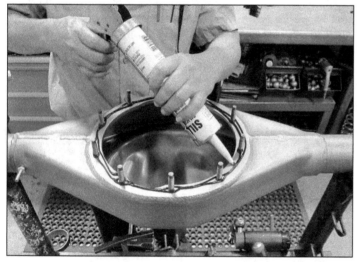

Before the finished center section is placed into the housing apply some RTV (or similar) sealant to prevent leaks. Notice that there are two separate beads, one on each side of the studs. The use of sealant without a gasket is preferable because a gasket is not as stable under load, which could, potentially, alter the relationship between the differential and the axles. Increasing wear, friction, and/or noise plus a greater risk of failure could result. Currie also epoxies a strong magnet to the bottom of the axle housing before the center section is installed to catch any stray metal particles.

This mostly finished rear axle assembly is a beauty. I'm confident I have more than enough strength for my powertrain. The use of the TrueTrac differential and a 3.70:1 gear ratio provides very good streetability with the TCI AODE transmission. All that's left before I paint it is to weld on a few tabs for the upper control arms of the Ridetech suspension. Then it gets installed in the car where I finish it off with the parking brake cables and side-to-side brake hard lines.

BRAKES

A high-performance Mustang needs high-performance brakes. Better stopping capability allows you to travel at a higher speed for a longer distance and/or period of time because you can quickly slow the car enough to negotiate a turn without spinning out.

On the street, brakes are used very often even though they may not be used very hard. Certain changes to optimize a brake system for the street (longer wear with less dust, for example) conflict with those for the track but most characteristics that make a good track system also make a good street system. It generally comes down to what's necessary for the intended purpose and the most cost-effective way to get it. Aesthetics and wheel clearance also figure in but they're easy to accommodate.

Early Mustangs used antiquated disc and drum brake systems. They are not up to performance use, or even regular street use, by today's standards. This is due in part to the suspension design where, for example, deterioration and wear of the strut rod bushings can drastically affect brake performance and/or cause the car to dart to one side under heavy braking.

Another big factor reducing braking capability is the prevalence of drum brakes. (I operate under the premise that nobody reading this book and wanting to improve the performance of their early Mustang considers keeping drum brakes on their car so I don't discuss them. They simply aren't up to the task nor are they the best when so many low-cost disc conversions exist.) Similarly, older OEM front disc brakes are not advisable, even the four-piston variety. The total capacity of these setups is limited by their piston sizes, rotor sizes, materials, and other properties. Furthermore, they're not inexpensive or easy to find.

Aftermarket systems offer better performance at lower cost. In this chapter I discuss some options for upgrading your braking system to the level you need. I begin by discussing individual components in a typical brake system and what can be done to improve them for various situations.

Master Cylinders and Power Boosters

The first brake system component you run into beyond the firewall is the master cylinder or the power brake booster (if you have power brakes). For any vehicle that's driven

Brembo ceramic rotors are beyond the needs (and budget) of most readers of this book but they do represent the ultimate in terms of stopping power and low weight. Such rotors can be used on the street although they tend to perform poorly until warmed up. Once warm, they have incredible stopping power and fade resistance. Special pads and calipers are required due to the higher heat and pressure.

on the street you almost always want power brakes simply because of the fatigue factor. On a long trip, or even in heavy traffic on a long commute, power brakes reduce driver strain and can thus improve alertness. Power brakes generally also ensure you're able to achieve line pressures high enough to obtain the shortest braking distances, even with excessive pedal pressure.

On the downside, power brakes add complexity, cost, weight, and take up room in the engine compartment. For racers and those who often drive their cars very aggressively power brakes can reduce pedal feel and modulation. This hinders the driver from braking consistently and with confidence. Most race cars lack power assist to provide the best possible pedal feel and modulation while also avoiding the extra complexity and weight. Power brakes are usually used in racing in longer, endurance-type races where the issue of driver fatigue is a concern. For all but the most extreme street vehicles a proper power brake system is the best choice for comfort and less fatigue on public roads with minimal loss of feel and/or control.

Master Cylinder

More than a few early Mustangs came equipped with manual (non-power) brakes and a single-chamber master cylinder. From a performance and a safety standpoint this configuration leaves a lot to be desired and should never be considered for performance use.

A dual-chamber master cylinder is the only way to go and care must be taken to properly match the piston bore sizes inside the master cylinder to the brake hardware. A drum-brake master cylinder can almost never be used when converting to discs, for example. Depending on how many pistons there are in the calipers and what their dimensions are, there likely needs to be a change in the bore size. There's no way to predict what may be needed in a given combination but, in general, the final parts must ensure the required line pressures are achieved in the front and rear brake circuits.

Line pressure should be checked with an appropriate gauge, not only when the system is first used but also periodically to help spot signs of a drop due to seal wear or other factors. Monitoring line pressure improves performance and safety because it can indicate the potential for a failure well before one actually occurs.

Power Booster

Under normal circumstances it's not particularly difficult to find a suitable power booster if the car didn't come with power brakes. Most OEM boosters provide sufficient assist for normal street use and most track use. Other than perhaps some heat shielding you need little else when installing a compatible booster.

When a very aggressive camshaft is used, there may not be sufficient engine vacuum available to provide sufficient power assist. There are several ways to resolve this with the easiest and most reliable being to use an electrically powered vacuum pump. Such devices are powered by the vehicle's electrical system/alternator and automatically switch on when the brake booster vacuum is below a certain level. The pump runs until a specific level is reached and then shuts off.

The pump cycles on and off automatically as dictated by the use of the braking system and other factors such as temperature and altitude. If engine compartment space is not available to fit a power booster and/or extremely high line pressures are required, there's another alternative: hydraulic assist.

Companies such as Power Brake Service have developed conversion kits based on the Bosch Hydro-Boost system used on many late-model vehicles. These systems are able to achieve the extremely high line pressures (1,200 to 2,000 psi at the calipers) needed when using four-wheel-disc brakes in heavier vehicles. They use the power steering pump to generate the pressure assist so no engine vacuum or external vacuum pump is needed. This reduces complexity and frees up significant underhood space.

The booster unit is remarkably compact, even smaller than the small-diameter vacuum boosters used in many special applications. The hydroboost unit is modest in circumference plus it's short enough to mount between the master cylinder and the firewall.

The cost of these systems is reasonable even if their unique capabilities are not considered, usually on the same order as the small-diameter/

With limited underhood space this style of brake booster is one solution. It's longer and narrower than the standard unit so it may fit where the latter can't. Unless you have a very aggressive cam with low vacuum this may be a practical choice.

When underhood space is really at a premium and/or very high brake line pressures are needed, a hydroboost unit is best. Sold by Power Brake Service, it has a very small "footprint" so it can fit where most other options can't. It is relatively short and narrow. Because it uses pressure from the power steering pump to generate its assist it's also not affected by low engine vacuum nor does it require wiring. (Photo Courtesy Power Brake Service)

racing vacuum booster kits. Hydroboost systems are immune from vacuum fluctuations, provide the most additional room underhood, and achieve the highest line pressures for master cylinders with bore diameters between 15/16 and 1⅜ inches.

Brake Lines and Valves

Getting the brake fluid and pressure from the master cylinder to the calipers is done through a network of hard lines. These are usually made from galvanized steel. Companies such as Classic Tube offer kits for most early Mustangs made out of stainless steel, which look better and last longer; they can even be lighter.

At the end of each hard line there is a flexible hose, which extends from the car body to the brake caliper. Because this hose must be able to move with the wheel it usually has some extra slack, which translates to a little extra fluid volume. Furthermore, because OEM hoses are made from reinforced rubber they tend to expand when pressure is applied.

These and other factors combine to delay the caliper's response to pedal pressure, especially when high line pressures are experienced. This reduces the ability of the driver to get the best performance out of the brakes and could lead to premature hose failure. The solution is to use reinforced steel braided hoses instead of the OEM parts.

Such hoses exhibit virtually no expansion under pressure and thus provide a noticeable improvement in braking response while also providing much greater protection from potential damage and leaks caused by road debris, heat from headers/exhaust,

etc. Most disc conversion kits include them. They're also available from a wide variety of sources.

The proportioning valve is responsible for taking the fluid and pressure output from each chamber of the master cylinder and directing it to the appropriate calipers. It also acts as a safety valve in that it provides the driver with a warning if the pressure in one brake circuit falls out of balance with the other. This valve is required for virtually any all-disc system and is the same design as those found on production vehicles.

When changing from drums to discs or even changing the existing disc system it's critical to use the correct proportioning valve for your hardware. Otherwise, you might end up with a very unbalanced system that locks up too easily or quickly or otherwise doesn't perform properly. OEM components can often be used in most instances, though many aftermarket brake kits include new, superior valving products.

Between the proportioning valve and the caliper there may be a brake bias valve and/or a residual pressure check valve. The former is used to adjust the line pressure going to

Differences in brake hardware, tire/wheel combination, and even tire pressure can greatly affect the front-to-rear brake balance. Excessive nose dive under braking and the burning off of fuel can be very significant on the track. This Baer adjustable brake-balance valve can compensate for this on the fly to get optimum balance. It's spliced into the rear brake line, ideally, within reach of the driver. (Photo Courtesy Baer Racing)

The choice of brake fluid in a performance vehicle is critical. Unless you go through brake fluid quickly, buy the kind that comes in a metal can. Plastic bottles don't protect from moisture as well. A bottle that's been on the shelf for a while may not meet the required specs for DOT 4 (the only type you should use). A higher dry-boiling point is better when new. A higher wet-boiling point performs better as the fluid ages and absorbs water from the air. Do not use DOT 5/silicone fluid. (Photo Courtesy ATE)

the rear brakes to help prevent their premature lockup. This can occur when the rear of the vehicle becomes unloaded during hard braking, especially if there are significant differences in the caliper, rotor, piston, tire, and wheel sizes. Such valves are manually adjusted as necessary and can even be used to compensate for tire wear and other factors during an event if they're readily accessible to the driver or crew.

In some cases a residual pressure check valve may also be installed in the brake line to help prevent excessive pedal travel due to fluid draining back by gravity to a low-mounted master cylinder. By ensuring the line is "primed" the brakes respond more quickly to pedal inputs and are easier for the driver to modulate. The valves for disc-brake systems are rated very low, about 2 pounds, because calipers are not subject to return spring pressure.

Front Calipers

For the most part, the calipers in an OEM front disc-brake package aren't up to high-performance driving. The single-piston caliper versions are fine for a daily driver that occasionally sees some enthusiastic driving. Their sliding-piston design is inherently less stable plus the rotors usually aren't big enough for extreme use. Upgrading the rear brakes to discs provides a similar improvement in braking performance, especially in the wet. Still, the nose-heavy design of the Mustang coupled with lots of forward weight transfer under braking can overwhelm the stock front brakes while the rears unload and are unable to work with maximum effectiveness.

A somewhat rare option found on early Mustangs is OEM four-piston front brakes. This is a significant improvement over the normal front disc option because it's a fixed (not sliding/floating) design. Also there are four pistons (instead of one) to better distribute the higher clamping pressure over the pads.

A fixed-caliper design is superior to a floating/sliding single-piston caliper because the brake pads are pushed more squarely and evenly against sides of the rotor. This design can make for very quick pad changes because only two easily accessible bolts (or clips) need to be removed. These brakes are suitable for mild track use with the proper pads and brake fluid. They're a relatively rare option and not really something you'd want to convert to or pay extra for.

An aftermarket four-piston caliper is a much better choice than the original/OEM versions. This SSBC product also has a quick-change pad feature, which utilizes simple clips instead of bolts, thus eliminating the need for a tool. It is also much easier to find pads in a variety of compounds compared to older/OEM parts. A system such as this is clearly a superior choice for regular street use as well as being able to handle frequent, yet moderate, track use.

When the most extreme track use (short of competitive/pro racing) is anticipated it is likely to be necessary to go with an even more robust caliper. This eight-piston SSBC example can provide extreme stopping power because of the extra clamping force provided by the additional pistons and the size of the pads. Such calipers are bulkier, and they benefit by having additional thermal mass to absorb more heat. The downside is a weight penalty and the need to use a larger-diameter wheel.

Aftermarket front brake kits generally follow the same basic design as OEM four-piston calipers. Unlike OEM parts, however, aftermarket

As piston forces and piston quantity increase to meet extreme braking needs you must ensure the additional pressure is properly distributed across the pads. The necessarily larger pads tend to wear unevenly due to their size and the higher loads unless a staggered-piston arrangement similar to this Baer caliper is used. This design distributes the piston forces across the pad to prevent it from becoming misaligned with the rotor, thus resulting in uneven wear. This can significantly improve braking performance and pad life under the most severe conditions. This approach is fine for street use but its extra cost doesn't make it practical in most cases unless it is really needed on the track. (Photo Courtesy Baer Racing)

kits are offered with larger pistons in stronger calipers, which act on larger rotors with other features to improve performance. Kits intended for more-extreme use include calipers with six or even eight pistons in much larger, reinforced calipers, which may be a "monoblock" design machined from a single block of metal. Many even have pistons, which are staggered in size to help ensure more uniform pad wear.

Any of the components for high-performance driving are inevitably much, much stronger and lighter than their OEM counterparts while providing incredibly better braking performance due to their superior designs, materials, and manufacturing processes. Pad choice is critical to achieving this improved performance.

Rear Calipers and Parking Brakes

The situation for the rear is less complicated than for the front because the back of the car plays less of a role in braking, especially on a street-driven car. It's rare to see calipers with more than one or two pistons each at the rear. Furthermore, the need for a parking brake on a street-driven vehicle can make more than two pistons less practical from a packaging and cost perspective.

In any event, converting from drums to discs almost always requires the removal of the axles,

though some kits may include a split mounting flange to avoid this. The rear brake setup tends to be a simplified and scaled-down setup compared to the front with the primary difference being the parking brake.

Several popular designs of parking brakes are available. Each has its own pros and cons. All follow the OEM approach of adding a cable-controlled actuation system to supplement the hydraulic actuation. With a sliding/floating caliper it's simple to have the cable action pull on the sliding portion of the caliper. There are internal and external designs to do this with the former being simpler while the latter tends to provide greater clamping force at the expense of added complexity and a less-straightforward installation/adjustment process. Either works well enough if the kit is properly designed and installed.

A new approach has recently become popular primarily due to its ability to provide even greater holding power while keeping the caliper design simple. This approach removes the parking brake function from the caliper entirely and instead incorporates a small drum-style brake into the rotor. This allows a standard caliper to be used instead of one that's more complicated and likely less effective due to the integral parking brake. By separating the parking brake function from the caliper it can

The differences between the OEM rear drum brake setup and a high-quality aftermarket disc conversion kit by Currie Enterprises are obvious. The disc kit (top) is far less complex with fewer parts and less need for adjustments over time. The Currie kit (bottom) uses rebuilt and/or modified OEM components (in this case from a 1990s Thunderbird application) to provide superior braking while still being able to fit inside the stock 14- or 15-inch wheels. This is a far better option than the Granada setup because of its better performance and easy access to replacement pads.

be optimized. The downside is there are extra components, cost, and a unique rotor design.

A final consideration is the interface/compatibility with the OEM parking brake cable. If you're converting from drums you need new cables because the ends don't match. Most kits include new cables if they're needed. Companies such as Lokar offer a wide variety of model-specific and universal products.

The Currie disc conversion kit uses an OEM/Ford caliper and rotor from a late-model Thunderbird. This makes replacement pads very easy to find. The caliper is very low in profile and fits inside 14- and 15-inch wheels. The axles must come out to install the main mounting plate (new axle seals are included) but the rest of the mounting brackets are simple bolt-ons once this is done. This kit uses a single-piston sliding caliper over a vented rotor, which is fine for daily-driver and mild strip/track use.

A key step when converting from drums to discs is to ensure the new rotors are properly centered on the axle. You cannot depend on the wheel studs for this, and you must use the correct centering ring. This ring sits between the rotor and the axle flange while also just fitting over the hub in the middle of the axle. The outside diameter just fits inside the center bore of the new rotor. This results in a "hub-centric" positioning of the rotor, which does a much better job of minimizing differences between the rotor and axle centers (rotor runout).

This Currie kit is fairly discreet, especially when used under wheels such as the steel GT variety, which have more of a masking effect on the underlying components. If you want the benefits of converting from drums to discs at the rear axle, and want to do so in as subtle and reliable a manner as is possible, it is hard to beat this kit.

When converting from drums to discs, or even when upgrading discs already on the vehicle, you often have to make some kind of adaptation for the parking brake cables. This is a cable style where the end of the cable has a metal ball that engages a cast-in cup with an access slot. The body of the cable passes through a hole in another cast tab.

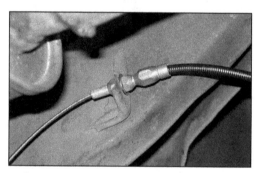

This is an example of a universal kit where the OEM spring clip or C-clip is replaced by a Lokar threaded collar and nut arrangement that's much more secure and stable. Different ends and cable lengths are available to suit any need. This is particularly convenient when the OEM configuration uses unequal-length cables and/ or when multiple cable sections are used to get around various undercar parts.

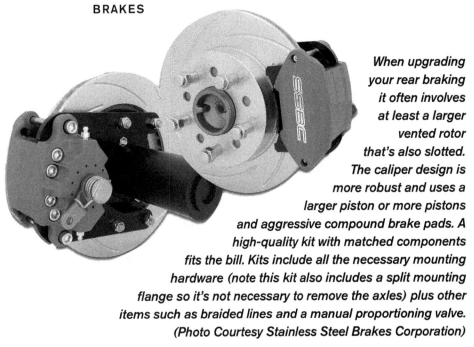

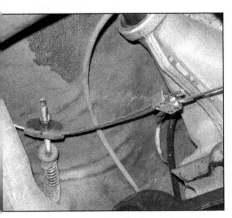

To make universal cables work it's sometimes necessary to splice them to each other or to the original factory forward cable. Here, the very long factory cable was replaced by two shorter cables that have been spliced together. This approach allows you to route the cables through the factory guides.

When upgrading your rear braking it often involves at least a larger vented rotor that's also slotted. The caliper design is more robust and uses a larger piston or more pistons and aggressive compound brake pads. A high-quality kit with matched components fits the bill. Kits include all the necessary mounting hardware (note this kit also includes a split mounting flange so it's not necessary to remove the axles) plus other items such as braided lines and a manual proportioning valve. (Photo Courtesy Stainless Steel Brakes Corporation)

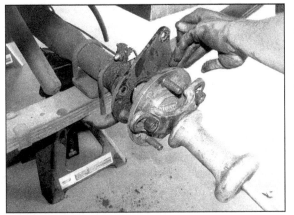

The majority of rear disc brake kits require removal of the rear axles to install the caliper mounting plates. A few (such as the SSBC kit) do not require this. Other than as a matter of convenience there's little difference in the performance of either type. In general, kits designed for extreme braking are inevitably single-piece designs to obtain the greatest strength with minimal weight. If you remove the axles it's always best to inspect and/or replace the axle seals and bearings.

This style of parking brake is an internal drum design. Ironically, one area where drum brakes are often superior to discs is as a parking brake. This is due to the drum's larger working area, thus requiring less pressure from the pedal or lever to actuate so you don't have to be a bodybuilder to stop the car from rolling down a hill, for example. You still have a disc brake to do the main stopping work but the small, internal drum does a better job as a parking brake. A unique rotor is required because the drum is part of the rotor "hat" design.

Rotors and Pads

Disc-brake rotors have improved dramatically over the years primarily as a result of much better materials and greatly improved manufacturing techniques. Make sure you're getting high-quality rotors from a reputable US manufacturer (Baer, SSBC, Hawk, Stop Tech, Performance Friction, Raybestos, Bendix, etc.), not an inexpensive copy that can cost you more in the end. Premium foreign brands (such as Brembo, Alcon, and Disc Brakes Australia) have proven themselves in the market and on the track.

Rotor Diameter

Besides basic compatibility with your vehicle you need to consider rotor diameter. A larger-diameter rotor provides more swept area/ braking surface and thus more ultimate braking capability (all things being equal).

However, you can go too big and increase weight and cost for no benefit. This may be for aesthetic purposes (such as with a larger wheel) but it's impractical from a functional standpoint. You should only get as large a brake as is necessary, no bigger.

Brake Thickness

Thinner, solid brakes may be acceptable on the rear (only) of a daily driver but should never be considered for use on the front or with any higher-performance vehicle. They simply can't take the heat of extreme use.

Thicker, vented rotors allow cooling air to pass through the rotor to reduce temperatures and provide more "thermal mass." This allows them to absorb heat at a greater rate over a longer period of time before their temperature becomes excessive. Virtually all pro/racing rotors (except for drag racing and a few others) are vented because they work better.

Only vented rotors should be considered for any high-performance application. Solid rear discs may be okay when converting from drums.

Crossdrilling or Slotting

The next thing to consider is whether you want plain rotors or those with slots and/or holes. These should only be considered when the rotor is of known, good quality because these machining operations can cause problems with inferior rotors. Cracks tend to form around the machined areas unless the correct material and manufacturing processes (heat treatment, surface treatment, etc.) are used.

Crossdrilled holes have been used on production vehicles. They help evacuate the gases formed from the pads reaching higher temperatures. On a solid rotor these gases can build up between the pad and the rotor, thus reducing braking power.

Slotting performs the same function as crossdrilling yet it does so with less structural weakening. The gases can still escape, though not as easily. Slotting does, however,

provide even more initial "bite" than crossdrilling. Slots have sharp edges (versus the radii of holes) that grab the pad more aggressively and make the brakes easier and quicker to modulate under hard-driving conditions.

The two styles have other pros and cons, not to mention their appeal (or lack thereof) from an aesthetic standpoint. One way to resolve this quandary is to use a mix of both. The slots give you initial bite while the holes evacuate the gases, save a little weight, and even help cooling if you run brake ducts to the rotors.

Rotor Construction

Less-expensive rotors tend to be single-piece units, like most OEM rotors. Racing and high-performance rotors tend to be two-piece or multi-piece designs. Using a separate center section allows a lighter material such as aluminum to replace the iron of a single-piece rotor. This saves a significant amount of unsprung weight, which can aid wheel control and improve handling.

A floating-style disc is even better at compensating for the expansion of the rotor as it heats up. This design allows the disc to grow with less restriction imposed by the center "hat," thus helping to reduce distortion and warping. This keeps the whole rotor more dimensionally stable, which in turn, enhances the overall braking capability. This design is more expensive to produce but the advantages are clear if you need very extreme braking power. The rotors and/or hats must be properly treated/plated to

prevent corrosion (for aesthetics) and to prevent rust from getting on the brake pads.

Pad Grip

In general, pad choice is a compromise between long life and high grip. Softer pads deliver better performance and shorter life than hard pads. The balance you choose depends on how you use the vehicle.

Owners of street and track cars often have a set of street pads and a set of track pads. You want to be able to take full advantage of the sticky tires you may be installing when you run at the track. You don't get the extra braking power the sticky tires can provide if you don't have pads capable of locking up the tires. You need to have this extra braking power to get the best performance. It's up to the driver to use this power properly but you can't "threshold brake" if you can't reach the threshold!

The initial step up from an OEM replacement rotor is something along the lines of the Baer DecelaRotor. It's made from a high-quality material that's plated for superior corrosion resistance. It's vented, drilled, and slotted with the hole design and locations optimized to reduce the possibility of cracking while also maximizing the ability to evacuate the gases produced during hard braking. Such designs provide better initial bite and more even pad wear compared to unslotted OEM rotors. (Photo Courtesy Baer Racing)

New discs may have differences in hub thickness and/or other components (steering knuckles, for example), which result in the hub surface moving. Similarly, larger brake calipers may require wheels with a different offset, which may also move the tire laterally. One way to restore the correct location is through the use of wheel spacers such as these made by Baer. They're usually available in thicknesses from about 1/4 to 1 inch with various bolt patterns. (Photo Courtesy Baer Racing)

Early Mustangs didn't come with anti-lock brakes and it's not feasible to add them. The driver needs brakes that act quickly and smoothly, yet are easy to modulate and can achieve enough stopping power for the situation. Brake pads are available from many companies but few offer as complete a selection as does Hawk Performance.

Vehicle Type 1: Daily Driver

For a daily driver the emphasis is on lower cost, reliability, and a mild performance increase over stock. Because the OEM system on these cars is much older technology this isn't hard to accomplish.

The front rotors should be a single-piece type of about 11 to 12 inches in diameter with a single- or dual-piston caliper. Many such systems exist for very reasonable cost; some don't even require that you change the front spindles. Such a system generally allows you to keep using the OEM 14- or 15-inch wheels, if you like, and provides a very significant increase in braking power with great reliability, long wear, and easily obtainable replacement pads.

The improvements in materials and processes plus the conversion to discs are significant benefits. When combined with larger rotors and better pads you see a big improvement in braking, especially with grippy tires.

At the rear you should go with an OEM single-piston sliding caliper that is low in profile with a 10- or 11-inch (preferably vented) rotor.

A Currie Enterprises kit, for example, takes the OEM rear disc brake system from an early 1990s Thunderbird and adapts it to an 8- or 9-inch axle. You get the benefit of a proven OEM system with easily found replacement pads for a relatively low cost. Currie includes new axle bearings, wheel studs, hub spacers, and parking brake cables to make the job easier. Combined with an upgraded front setup, this Currie rear kit helps dramatically improve braking performance while providing long life and smooth operation.

With a combination like that, a Hawk Premium Ceramic/OES pad or similar is the recommended choice. It provides better stopping power than OEM pads with very low dusting and low wear. These pads are designed to minimize brake noise and wear plus they carry a lifetime warranty. You can drive the car every day yet still take it to an autocross event or short-duration track day without having brake issues or swapping in other pads.

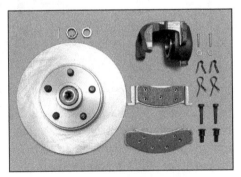

For a daily driver the OEM-style single-piston sliding calipers with an appropriate rotor are fine. New rotors and calipers provide a significant benefit over the original parts. This is even more true when converting from drums. Here you can see the difference in size between a front pad (bottom) and a typical rear pad for a disc-conversion kit (top). The rear rotors are smaller.

This Currie rear-disc conversion kit is a perfect solution for upgrading a daily driver with stock drum brakes. Everything you need, including new axle seals, parking brake cables, and the correct centering rings, is included. The calipers are OEM Ford parts and come loaded with pads suited for street use. The cost is reasonable and installation is pretty straightforward.

Vehicle Type 2: High-Performance Street Car

This car is driven more aggressively (but not necessarily as often) on the street while also seeing occasional track-day events. This requires changes to the size and type of brake components.

At the front the common choice is an aftermarket four-piston fixed caliper on a one- or two-piece rotor of about 11 or 12 inches in diameter. It's desirable to go with slotted rotors for a better bite with some extra cooling/outgasing relief. Power brakes are strongly recommended, as are braided-steel brake lines. A manually adjustable brake bias valve is also highly desirable because it allows you to better optimize the brake balance at the track yet return it to normal for the drive home.

The SSBC Force 10 is a high-performance street system. This is a complete kit that includes a manual brake-bias valve, a brake-line pressure gauge, and a new master cylinder (necessary when converting from drums). The vented rotors are up-sized a bit and feature slots and plating. The fixed front calipers allow for quick removal of the included pads.

The rear brakes aren't much different from those on a daily driver except that the rotors are likely a bit larger (11 or 12 inches) and the rear calipers are more likely fixed instead of sliding. The use of proper hub-centering rings is just as important here as it is with the other vehicle

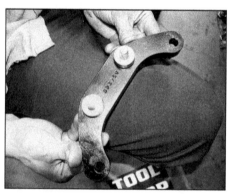

Because the SSBC four-piston front calipers are a fixed/opposed piston design their mounting must be very precise. The mounting brackets include spacers and shims, which must be used to properly adjust the caliper mounting location relative to the rotor. The gap between the pads and the rotor should be equal on both sides plus the pads must be perfectly parallel to the rotor surface. Shims are used to achieve this during the initial installation. These should not need to be changed once the initial caliper location is properly set.

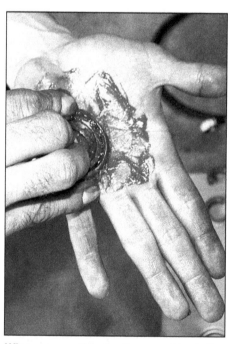

When converting to discs and installing a new spindle it's necessary to ensure the wheel bearings have been properly packed with an appropriate grease. A premium synthetic grease (such as Red Line or Royal Purple) with high water resistance works best.

When mounting the rotors it's critical that the wheel bearing preload be property set. The kit manufacturer generally provides the necessary information for this. Some general guidelines are that the rotor spins freely and smoothly, there is virtually no visible play or movement if the rotor is rocked back and forth (with hands grasping the rotor 180 degrees apart and moving in opposite directions), and the slots (if any) are positioned correctly (the inner/leading edge of the slot contacting the pad first).

types: to ensure the rotor is correctly located with minimal runout.

The common pad choice is a Hawk HPS for the street and even some of the more moderate track uses. It provides considerably higher friction levels with only a minor increase in dusting, wear, and noise. Wear is still quite good for the

pad and the rotor while the OEM-style noise dampening features are retained. They cost a bit more but are well worth it and can realistically be used for the street and on the track if the car isn't too extreme.

When conditions dictate, HP Plus pads (or similar) can be used all around at the track or just on the

front if the rear brakes aren't very heavily loaded. These pads provide even more stopping power while still being usable on the street. They aren't very well suited for prolonged street use, however, because they tend to dust noticeably more, wear faster, and are noisier than the HPS versions. They also need more grippy tires.

When combining components from different manufacturers, it may be necessary to make a few adjustments. For example you need to know whether the centering ring for an OEM Ford axle works with an aftermarket axle (such as this one by Currie).

There may be times when a special centering ring or similar component needs to be specially made/matched to the combination of components being used.

The split mounting flange of the SSBC kit simplifies installation because there's no need to remove the axles. The use of a sliding-style caliper eliminates the need to use shims to precisely locate the caliper relative to the rotor. The two alignment pins (shown) locate the caliper the correct distance from the axle centerline and keep it parallel to the rotor while still allowing it to move to grip the rotor.

The SSBC kit includes larger-diameter, thicker rotors to handle more extreme use than an OEM-level conversion kit. The upgraded rotors have more thermal mass so they're able to absorb more heat energy. Also, their enhanced internal cooling vanes help dissipate the heat more quickly. This allows SSBC to use a more-aggressive pad compound, which then provides more braking power with a smaller, lighter rotor.

Vehicle Type 3: Streetable Track-Day/Drag Strip Car

This vehicle type is a Jekyll and Hyde; it turns into a beast at the track/strip. Tires and brake pads are swapped, suspension settings are changed, some weight may be removed, maybe the engine gets a different tune; you get the idea. You can still drive to the event but not the way the car is normally set up:

you optimize it for the event.

You want a braking system that performs as needed on the street yet has the reserve capacity to handle extreme (though not professional level) use at the track. For the front most owners go with at least a 12- or 13-inch two-piece slotted, cross-drilled, and vented rotor with a

fixed caliper boasting four or more pistons. The optimum combination depends on many factors such as vehicle weight, degree of suspension modification, and type of duty the car will see.

You also want to plumb a manual brake-bias valve into the cockpit so you can adjust brake balance on the

Vehicle Type 3: Streetable Track-Day/Drag Strip Car *continued*

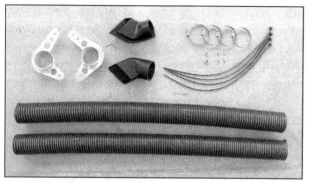

With an extreme high-performance brake system, you install brake cooling ducts from openings on the front of the car (usually low on the front, just above the spoiler or splitter to get the most pressure) to the center of the rotors. This requires special brackets that mount to the spindle to accept the ducting/hose and properly aim it at the rotors so the air flows from the center outward. Use zip ties to keep the ducting away from tires, sway bars, etc.

fly during the event. A hydroboost brake booster is a prime candidate for this scenario because of its high line pressures, compact size, and independence from engine vacuum. You need to use a racing-grade DOT4 brake fluid with a sufficiently high temperature rating. You surely want to consider running cooling ducts from the front of the car to the center of the front rotors to keep them from overheating on the track.

The rear setup should most likely feature a fixed four-piston caliper on at least an 11- or 12-inch two-piece vented, slotted, and crossdrilled rotor. A bigger rear rotor may be feasible in a heavier car if the suspension minimizes dive under braking and the tires can support it.

The parking brake is critical because the pads likely have less grip when cold even though they're better when hot. Therefore, one of the inner drum-type parking brakes is best but other types can also be acceptable depending on how much you use the parking brake, the weight of the car, whether you park on hills, etc.

For this vehicle type the pad choice is more critical and more flexible. Due to the extremely high heat this setup can generate only an HP Plus pad or a race compound, such as the DTC-30 (or possibly something even more aggressive), should be the choice on the track. You can keep the HP Plus pads all the time if you don't drive the car that often and you don't mind the extra dust, noise, and (potential) wear. The HP Plus needs to operate in warmer weather and is not suited for colder climates. If you don't use extreme braking on the street you can use the HPS for minimal dusting, longer wear, and less noise.

When you go to the drag strip other changes may be appropriate at this level. Because repeated stops are not part of the drag-strip duty cycle, the brake setup can be lighter and less dependent on cooling under extreme conditions. If the vehicle is still used on the street, however, the guiding principle becomes maximum performance on the street with the reserve capacity necessary for high-speed stops with lots of time for cooling at the strip.

A four-piston fixed caliper in the front and the back (or maybe

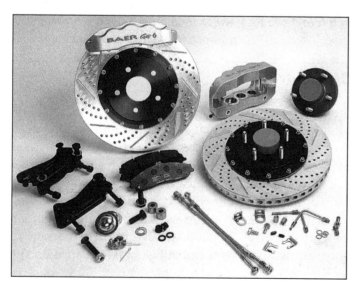

The Baer Pro Plus system is suitable for a street/track car. It comes with "only" 13- or 14-inch two-piece rotors with all the essentials: 1-inch-thick, vented, enhanced internal cooling vanes, drilled, slotted, plated, etc.

The 6P calipers are six pistons in a staggered arrangement to minimize pad taper, machined billet two-piece body with stainless steel pistons and hardware, dual DOT-compliant seals, and a choice of three standard colors or the custom color of your choice. Braided steel lines and special hubs are also included.

The ExtremePlus with a 14- or 15-inch rotor and a 6S one-piece forged monoblock caliper is usable on the street but it's more of a racing system. The cost and capabilities aren't easily justified for street use. (Photo Courtesy Baer Racing)

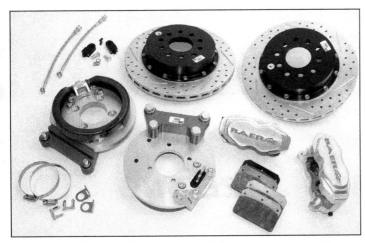

The 13-inch rotors are the maximum for this setup. They incorporate the effective "drum-in-hat" parking brake. The four-piston fixed calipers feature stainless steel pistons and hardware along with dual DOT-compliant seals and the same color options as the front. Many older Mustangs don't need this much capability. (Photo Courtesy Baer Racing)

The drum-in-hat system may require the removal of the axles to mount the billet backing plate. The clearance between the axle flange/wheel studs, the backing plate, and its studs must be checked against the spec provided by Baer to make sure it is enough to avoid any problem with contact. The larger hole in the axle flange allows access to the backing plate nuts so they can be tightened.

even a smaller one in the rear if you don't need much brake on the street) should work well. The rotors should be the vented two-piece type with slots and drilling, though their diameter likely does not need to be as large as for a high-performance street car.

Pad choice can be a bit more extreme for the strip where you may want to use a dedicated race pad if the HP Plus or DTC-30 doesn't heat up fast enough. The race pads can be swapped in at the track or you can drive to the track with them already installed. Just remember to take them out when you get back home or you'll see a lot of dust plus you may damage the rotors.

Some drag racers use minimal front brakes and a dual-caliper setup at the rear when they have huge rear tires, a parachute, and wheelie bars. It may also be a requirement in certain classes to have a dual-caliper brake setup on the rear axle, especially when a transmission brake is used to hold/launch the car. Such a setup isn't advisable or necessary on the street and only benefits extremely modified cars on the strip.

Here the brake shoe has been installed. The clearance to the axle flange must be sufficient to compensate for the lateral movement of the axle under hard cornering. This is particularly true with C-clip-style axles (such as in the 8.8-inch).

As with the front fixed calipers, these at the rear also require shims to ensure the calipers are properly centered over the rotors. Here, a shim has been placed between the black caliper mount and the aluminum parking brake backing plate. Care must be taken to ensure the gap on both sides of the rotor is equal and uniform.

Keep the gap on each side of the rotor as close to equal as possible when using a fixed caliper. (This is not required when using a sliding/floating caliper due to the way it operates.) Once you've ensured the pads are parallel to the rotors and the rotor spins freely you're ready for some track time.

SUSPENSION AND STEERING

Because power is useless without control you need to understand how the suspension helps the force at the tires be transformed into motion while the steering (for the most part) determines what direction the motion is in. This chapter concentrates on street and highway (including high-speed events) use and covers some road course applications. A pure drag race suspension isn't well suited to street use so I briefly address it in the high-performance street and streetable track-day sections. I also cover steering options for the three vehicle types.

Suspension Upgrades

The daily driver focuses on minor modifications with a limited budget based on the factory-style suspension. The high-performance street car takes things up a notch by using upgraded components at the front and eliminating the leaf springs at the rear. The track-day car utilizes a more-robust design at the front and rear plus more radical options when there are no budgetary or other constraints. In each section I consider the tradeoffs among cost, handling, ride comfort, installation, streetability, and reliability.

Vehicle Type 1: Daily Driver

In its time the suspension of the first-generation Mustang was as advanced as any pony or muscle car suspension from Detroit. The double-stamped control arm, coil springs, and shock suspension provided good road-holding and handling characteristics for its day, but it is certainly antiquated by today's standards and must be replaced to reach modern high-performance standards. The live-axle rear suspension with shocks and leaf springs also provided competent traction and damping duties, and certainly was much better than the single-leaf rear suspension on the Camaro, which had tramping and wheel-hop problems.

Although the ride and handling were not very refined, it was a capable suspension. With some modifications, however, the basic design even proved to be race worthy. The basic suspension was developed and refined for use in SCCA Trans-Am road racing. In 1970 Parnelli Jones took the Boss 302 to the Trans-Am Championship. The suspension is crude by today's standards but it had pretty high limits and capability. It was very strong too.

Because making any major changes to the stock design of my project car would inevitably exceed my budget, I profile certain targeted upgrades that yield the biggest performance increase for a reasonable investment.

I try to do so in a way that also helps make up for 40 or more years of wear and aging by replacing worn or damaged parts with cost-effective upgrades rather than installing direct-replacement parts. The majority of these upgrades involves eliminating excessive compliance/play in the suspension so that the movement of the parts is limited to a smaller range and is thus more predictable.

Ride Comfort

When you upgrade the suspension there is generally a very small tradeoff in a slightly harsher ride and the possibility of a feeling bit more vibration in the cabin but the improvement in dynamic response

Vehicle Type 1: Daily Driver *continued*

compensates for it. The cost of most of the parts is relatively low plus their durability usually exceeds that of the OEM parts. The lower control arm with a strut rod has some pretty large (and soft) rubber bushings. Like any OEM suspension design, the rubber is intended to improve ride comfort plus reduce vibration and road noise. Unfortunately, these bushings tend to allow too much unwanted movement and, over time, they fail.

Perhaps the worst offender of the many rubber bushings in the stock suspension are those for the strut rods. These are also where the most improvement is possible, mainly because they play such a major role under hard braking. The elimination of excess movement/compliance stabilizes the lower arm and greatly improves vehicle handling, braking, and stability.

The stock rear suspension is a model of simplicity but soft rubber bushings produce greater compliance. Because there are far fewer of these bushings their effect is less.

Using leaf springs also introduces some unique issues. A harsher ride is one of them plus things like spring wrap-up also come into play. Still, there are a few things you can do to the stock suspension to improve it enough for street and moderate performance use. (For extreme/track use more radical modifications are needed.)

Upper Control Arm

The front suspension design of first-generation Mustangs didn't change much. It consisted of an upper control arm, a lower control arm, and a strut rod on each side combined with an anti-sway bar,

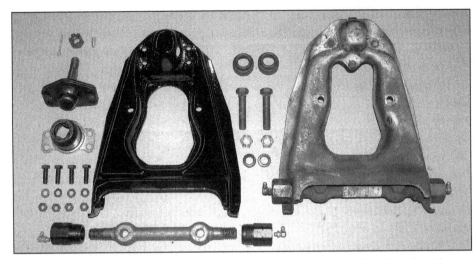

The stock upper control arms are generally suitable for a daily driver but they still can benefit from a few modifications. These Global West arms are the stronger four-bolt variety plus they utilize a revised bushing design with harder durometer rubber to reduce excessive and unwanted movement of the arm.

springs, shocks, etc. You can upgrade the parts and make substantial improvements in performance.

The stock upper control arm is adequate for many high-performance street applications and does not need much improvement. However, you can install four-bolt ball joints and not drill new mounting holes 1 inch lower in the shock towers for a Shelby mod. Global West Suspension, Mustangs Plus, and others make upgraded upper arms that are stronger and have revised geometry to take advantage of a dropped location.

Global West offers negative-roll components for road racing; those optimized for drag racing are fine for street use. These OEM-style arms feature slightly revised mounting nuts and cross shafts to reduce play via more precise threads. Harder bushings help minimize slight fore and aft movement. Tubular, non-OEM arms are also available.

The OEM design utilizes a spring perch that positions the spring on

the upper control arm. A centering ring inside the shock tower locates the top end of the spring while the shock absorber passes through the center of it and the spring. A special mount secures the top of the shock. The spring and shock capably handle the suspension loads but it's not optimal because most of the load is placed on the upper control arm. In addition the OEM spring perch uses a relatively compliant rubber bushing, which isn't the best for performance or durability.

An easy and inexpensive way to fix this is to replace the OEM perches with ones using polyurethane. This significantly reduces the amount of unwanted movement while providing some cushioning. For maximum performance and handling, perches with roller bearings virtually eliminate all play and friction. They can even improve the ride due to less initial impact friction ("stiction").

Koni offers a line of "classic" shocks that are an excellent choice

Vehicle Type 1: Daily Driver *continued*

A quick and relatively easy way to remove some of the squishiness of the stock suspension is to replace the OEM rubber-bushed spring perches. Polyurethane perches cushion the ride, allow less movement, and last longer. Perches using bearings instead of bushings provide the maximum reduction in unwanted movement. They don't compress to any noticeable degree and they reduce friction and impact harshness.

for a simple, non-adjustable shock likely to be used in a daily driver. There are many more sophisticated and expensive options, which may be adjustable, but they are not really needed at this level of modification or its cost criteria.

Global West, Total Control Products, and others offer direct-replacement springs with various rates and ride heights to suit various situations. When combined with the better arms, bushings, shocks, etc., they very noticeably improve the dynamics of the vehicle.

When going to a higher spring rate it's also advisable to replace the OEM rubber spring isolators with polyurethane components from Energy Suspension or a similar manufacturer. These better tolerate higher spring rates and further reduce unwanted compliance.

Lower Control Arm

Upgraded aftermarket lower control arms provide significant performance improvement over stock. Global West offers a significantly reinforced stock-type lower arm that is "boxed" on the underside to greatly improve strength. Spherical bearings replace the OEM rubber bushings, provide lower stiction, and virtually eliminate unwanted compliance. They accept all other OEM components and are a very good choice for drag race vehicles where the need for lighter weight is more important than the need to handle higher cornering. To get the full benefit of them you should also replace the OEM eccentric "cam" bolts with Global West's lockout kit.

These stronger square plates are held in place by the factory flanges and don't move out of adjustment under heavy loading as the OEM cam bolts often do. They have six settings covering a wider adjustment range than the OEM bolts. This is a simple and inexpensive way to improve the stability and consistency of suspension alignment.

Strut Rods

The strut rods are an often overlooked component in the front suspension. They greatly affect the stability of the car, especially under hard braking. In addition to locating the lower control arm front-to-back, strut rods are responsible for absorbing the majority of the braking forces transferred to the suspension.

If the strut rods are improperly adjusted the wheel alignment may be off and there can be a high possibility of the car pulling to one side under braking or acceleration. If a strut rod bushing fails you can be sure that happens, severely and quickly. A worn/failing bushing usually causes the car to pull to one side when trying to drive straight. It's a good idea to replace OEM strut rod bushings on any vehicle with high mileage because rubber deteriorates over time, even if the car has been sitting.

For a daily driver that sees lots of potholes and other road hazards it's best to use rubber bushings. You can inexpensively upgrade to a higher durometer/stiffer rubber to reduce movement yet still have cushioning so the benefits are significant.

First-generation Mustangs were equipped with mundane hydraulic shocks at the factory, which faded after severe acceleration, hard braking, and aggressive cornering. These twin-tube, steel-bodied, gas-charged Koni Sport shocks provide excellent damping and are an affordable alternative to high-end aluminum-bodied shocks. These shocks provide a significant dampening improvement over the stock shocks and more consistent dampening at high speeds while providing decent levels of comfort. A Mustang's cornering ability is improved while body roll is limited. (Photo Courtesy Koni)

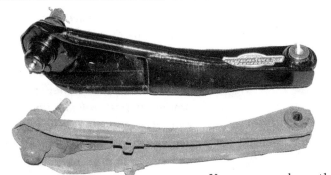

Upgrading the lower control arms follows the same theme as the uppers but takes things a bit further. The reinforcement of this Global West arm (top) is more obvious because it is boxed to significantly improve strength while keeping weight and cost fairly low. It eliminates the OEM rubber bushing in favor of a spherical bearing. This almost fully eliminates any compliance or friction while helping to reinforce the mounting box.

Eliminating compliance and flexing of the lower arm is of little benefit if the arm is not kept in proper alignment/ adjustment. The stock eccentric adjusters can loosen and/or shift under hard use, thus causing the alignment to be out of spec. Replacing them with thicker, square lockout plates eliminates this possibility because they are held firmly in place yet still allow for a wide range of adjustment (in six steps versus continuously).

Polyurethane should never be used for a street car because it can restrict and bind the arc of suspension travel. A sudden suspension jolt or impact can cause the strut rod to bend (or even break off) at the base of the threads.

Bars and Braces

Most remaining front suspension components can also be cost-effectively upgraded in a daily driver to provide very noticeable benefits.

You can replace the various bushings associated with the anti-sway bars (end links, mounts) with high-quality polyurethane parts, such as those from Energy Suspension. This provides increased firmness for high-performance applications.

To avoid potential noise and squeaks over time Energy Suspension includes grease fittings to allow for additional lubrication as necessary. The anti-sway bars themselves can also be upgraded with thicker/stiffer parts to reduce body roll. This isn't necessary in a drag race situation where the front bar may be removed (at least at the strip) to reduce weight. Even on a road course car a stiffer bar may not always be best if it throws the handling balance off, especially with lighter small-blocks.

No suspension system can work to its full potential unless it's connected to a stable platform/vehicle. Early Mustangs were never known for having great torsional strength or chassis rigidity. Like many other cars that rolled out of Detroit the Mustang is a unibody car and, unless the body and suspension have been recently restored, time has most likely taken its toll. These cars tend to sag a bit due to a combination of metal fatigue, corrosion, rust, loose or missing fasteners, and broken welds.

The most common example is that the shock towers tend to bend inward toward the engine. The Mustang had this issue from the beginning so "export braces" and Monte Carlo bars were offered. An export brace bolts between the firewall and the shock towers to brace them under hard cornering. A Monte Carlo bar provides additional support by connecting to the shock towers across the engine bay to further reduce their movement relative to each other.

The OEM parts aren't very strong so it's best to use good aftermarket components

The strut bar bushings are an area where great improvement is possible. For a daily driver the most cost-effective thing to do is to replace the existing bushings with firmer/higher durometer versions such as these available through Global West. They significantly reduce the amount of movement yet still provide some isolation from noise and vibration, etc. Do not use polyurethane bushings here; they can cause strut rod failure. Replace or upgrade the strut rods if they're bent.

Vehicle Type 1: Daily Driver *continued*

such as those sold by Mustangs Plus and Global West. The best export brace designs have thick flanges and welded joints to minimize movement. They're non-adjustable and may require some effort to install because every car ages and moves differently.

Versions that provide greater adjustability are easier to install but do not provide as much torsional rigidity once they're in. The best Monte Carlo bar designs use thick, straight tubing with thick brackets and adjustable rod ends with opposing threads to allow adjustment by simply rotating the bar (versus having to adjust each side separately). A curved bar may be necessary to clear a larger distributor or other obstruction but these are not as strong unless they use thicker-wall tubes.

Subframe Connectors

One of most effective and affordable methods for improving chassis strength and ridgity is to use subframe connectors. When building a high-performance or restomod Mustang, installing subframe connectors is an absolute must. These tie the front subframe to the rear frame rails

to supplement the stiffness provided by the body and the floorpan. Bolt-in designs are generally not as effective as weld-in designs but welding them after they're bolted in usually helps.

The best designs have fully welded tubes and large, thick attachment brackets that contact the frame stubs on three sides. Even for cars not driven aggressively the installation of subframe connectors with an export brace and a Monte Carlo bar stiffen the car so that squeaks and rattles are greatly reduced.

A simple, inexpensive upgrade is to replace the OEM anti-sway bar bushings and links with polyurethane-based parts such as these from Energy Suspension. They reduce the amount of body roll and improve the overall response of the suspension. They do, however, require periodic lubrication to prevent noise.

Other than cost, the only possible negative to subframe connectors is the potential loss of ground clearance, especially with a lowered car, and maybe a small weight increase.

Leaf Springs

For a daily driver the factory leaf spring-style suspension is usually retained. This is somewhat of a performance limitation but there is no inexpensive alternative. Having said that, the stock leaf-spring suspension can be vastly improved, even to the point where it is acceptable for daily use as well as limited track use.

As with the front, the goal is the minimization of unwanted compliance/movement along with general spring and shock firming. The starting point is the elimination of the stock rubber spring eye and shackle bushings because they're probably worn out anyway. Using direct-fit polyurethane bushings is okay if you want to keep costs to a minimum. They reduce movement and provide more cushioning compared to their rubber counterparts but they can squeak if not greased.

A better solution is to use Del-A-Lum bushings from Global West. Although these cost more than rubber bushings, they substantially improve performance. Their design is

A front bar with a different torsional stiffness is usually included in a sway-bar kit to better balance the front and rear roll stiffness. Such bars may be smaller or larger in diameter than the stock bar depending on differences in materials, design (solid versus hollow), shape, and adjustability (extra holes, etc.). You can't always judge stiffness by its appearance.

This front suspension uses reinforced stock-type control arms and strut rods and upgraded bushings. The springs and shocks have been replaced with more performance-oriented parts plus the spring perches were replaced with polyurethane parts. Even though much more radical (and costly) options are available, this simple level of upgrading still makes a dramatic improvement in vehicle performance.

Early Mustangs benefit greatly from a Monte Carlo bar (the straight, adjustable bar between the shock towers) and an export brace (the fixed bars running between the firewall and the shock towers). These can be adapted to work with most engine swaps such as this 5.0L EFI engine. They should both be used whenever possible.

Perhaps the most common method of stiffening up the body is to use subframe connectors, such as these weld-in units from Global West. The design of these components is critical if they are to provide any noticeable benefit and not have ground-clearance issues.

unique in that the spring and shackle bolts ride inside a plated steel sleeve that is inside precisely machined cylindrical Delrin bushings. These bushings rest inside anodized aluminum housings, which are inserted into the spring and/or frame rail. This construction accomplishes several things.

First, there is virtually no compliance in any direction. The springs cannot move sideways to any degree, thus enhancing stability while allowing for slightly more effective tire clearance and/or wider tires.

Second, because there are no bushings that compress, the springs only rotate in the vertical plane; they don't twist or cock at an angle under

load. Again, there is better leaf stability due to more precise, consistent, and restrained motion.

Finally, because this design has such inherently low internal friction there is a reduction in impact harshness and an improved ability for the spring to move through the desired range of motion. Extra strong, plated, steel shackles and Delrin side bushings further ensure accurate movement of each spring. Grease fittings for each Del-A-Lum bushing ensure they can stay properly lubricated throughout their very long life.

The springs themselves are available in various configurations and rates to suit different needs.

Once you determine the correct spring rate you can finalize the type of spring to determine the rear ride height. Global West offers normal, reverse-eye, and mid-eye springs, which can drop the rear of the vehicle up to 1½ to 2 inches below stock while preserving the correct spring shape/arc (some others alter the spring shape).

The guidelines for the front apply to shock absorbers: Stick with a premium brand such as Koni (Classic line) for simple and non-adjustable versions. There's little point in upgrading to a more expensive, adjustable shock in a daily driver unless you intend to stay with leaf springs for the foreseeable future.

Vehicle Type 1: Daily Driver *continued*

Global West advises against using anti-sway bars when their complete suspension system is used. They claim it's not necessary due to their choice of springs, shocks, and geometry. In higher-performance situations a rear bar may prove to be beneficial if it helps balance the car but this probably isn't an issue with a daily driver.

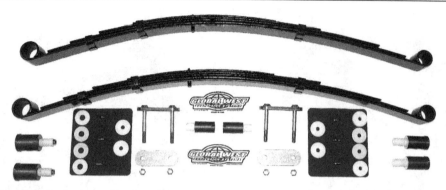

The rear spring eye receives the same type of Del-A-Lum bushing and enjoys the same benefits. In addition, the frame bushing is also replaced with a Del-A-Lum bushing to eliminate another source of unwanted compliance and instability. This firming up of the leaf spring mounts requires stronger shackles to ensure the springs stay properly located.

The simple design of leaf springs doesn't offer many possibilities for change but they provide very dramatic results. The springs can be replaced with others having a different spring rate and revised construction, which can alter the vehicle height. These reverse-eye springs lower the car (at the same spring rate). Global West's Del-A-Lum bushings replace the OEM rubber bushings and eliminate unwanted movement, compliance, and friction by keeping the springs properly and consistently located. The spring shackles are also reinforced.

Del-A-Lum bushings fit where the OEM rubber mounts go. Side-to-side movement is almost completely eliminated through the use of Delrin thrust surfaces. The internal structure of these bushings is such that the spring eye can only rotate around the mounting bolt; it cannot cock sideways or move back and forth as is possible with a compressible bushing. This greatly stabilizes the spring and produces much more accurate, consistent, and limited motion.

Vehicle Type 2: High-Performance Street Car

To take handling performance to the next level, be sure the subframe and the suspension are strong and sound. This is because high-performance applications place greater loads on the car, which means that achieving greater torsional rigidity in the frame and suspension is imperative.

Reinforcements

For the daily driver you can reinforce the basic body structure to provide a more stable foundation for the suspension. For this vehicle type, the chassis should receive additional stiffening for higher cornering forces.

Each shock tower should be fully welded along each seam to enhance their overall strength. Even higher spring loads and cornering forces place a greater load on the body and chassis and cracks tend to develop in the thin sheet metal of the towers. This degrades performance and destabilizes the car under hard cor-

nering and braking. In extreme cases, enough cracks can lead to suspension failure, which obviously is dangerous.

Another modification is to supplement the existing subframe connectors with side rails that extend out to the sills to further stiffen the floorpan. The increase in weight is minimal plus it's located low and centrally in the car, thus helping to improve handling. The real benefit, however, is the greatly improved stiffness and torsional bending. The front and

Vehicle Type 2: High-Performance Street Car *continued*

The design of the Del-A-Lum frame bushing eliminates the potential for any significant lateral movement (while only allowing the rotation of the mounting bolt) but not its movement in other directions.

rear suspensions are tied together so the chassis and suspension system respond as a single unit.

The extra rails also can provide a more convenient jacking point for lowered cars.

Hybrid Front Suspension

To keep the overall cost down for this level of build, a "hybrid" front suspension keeps the stock suspension layout and geometry but uses many high-performance upgraded parts. This configuration is well suited as a transition from a daily driver because the main components are completely suitable for daily street use yet allow maximum performance when additional upgrades are installed.

You need to install tubular upper control arms as the first step in this upgrade. Global West offers top-quality chrome-moly tubular arms that provide superior strength and torsional rigidity over the stock stamped-steel arms. These arms also offer several degrees of positive caster adjustment for improved handling characteristics and specialized suspension setups. The caster is adjusted on the strut rods that have jam nuts.

These are not only much, much stronger than OEM arms but they also incorporate revised geometry and use Del-A-Lum bushings instead of rubber or polyurethane on the cross shaft. This greatly reduces friction and virtually eliminates unwanted movement. These arms can use the stock spring perches, etc., or a simple, bolt-on coil-over kit.

Coil-Overs

The Total Control Products (TCP) Econo Bolt-On Coil-Over spring and shock combination is a great way to upgrade the stock front suspension. The shocks provide 7½ inches of travel. These coil-overs easily replace the existing springs, perches, and shocks with simple, modular units that provide far greater tunability and adjustment potential. They simply bolt onto the existing factory or aftermarket (preferred) upper arms and require only minimal adaptation on top of the shock towers. Single/16-step and double/256 combination shocks are available along with numerous spring rates. The ease of replacement makes it feasible to have extra springs to swap as needed for different uses.

Various upper mounts are available to lower the front ride height as much as 2 inches even before the adjustability of the coil-over is considered. These units are lighter than stock parts, require minimal maintenance (just a grease fitting on top), and provide virtually the same adjustability as more-expensive systems with easier installation.

The lower arms also should be upgraded to stronger tubular units for this application. Global West again has the answer with their extremely strong tubular arms. They feature the same spherical bearings as the boxed OEM arms while providing far more strength and an extra mounting point for the strut rods.

Combining Global West's upper and lower tubular control arms virtually eliminates friction over the entire range of movement. You can easily and smoothly move either one through its full arc with just your fingers after it's been installed.

To achieve the ultimate in front-suspension performance while still retaining the factory shock towers

If you change the leaf springs and/ or the rear axle assembly make sure to use compatible parts that locate and retain the springs on the axle. Incompatible designs could result in the locating peg on the springs not reaching the corresponding hole on the axle mounting plate. When an axle assembly with a recessed locating hole is used special metal inserts such as these from Global West are likely to be needed. They simply drop in but can also be epoxied.

Vehicle Type 2: High-Performance Street Car *continued*

This upgraded daily driver rear suspension doesn't look much different than the original suspension unless you look closely. The upgraded Koni shocks are obvious but the better springs and Del-A-Lum bushings don't stand out very much. The difference they make in terms of vehicle performance, however, is extremely obvious.

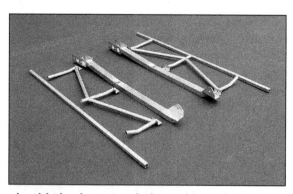

These Global West tubular upper control arms are stout enough to handle even the most extreme loads. They can come with revised geometry to further improve handling in street or road race use. They allow use of all stock components but, realistically, these parts should also be upgraded to achieve the best result. Note the use of Del-A-Lum bushings (no rubber), the reinforced spring perch mounts, and the extra bar.

One way to help ensure proper handling balance for a given vehicle is to source all components from a single supplier as a matched kit for a particular type of driving. This kit from Chris Alston's Chassisworks is one example. Kits from other suppliers can include new rear springs and/or other components as well. (Photo Courtesy Chris Alston's Chassisworks)

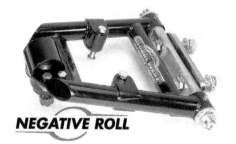

NEGATIVE ROLL

These direct-bolt-in Varishock coil-over shocks from TCP provide easily adjustable ride height and shock valving with the OEM front suspension design. They are also lighter than the components they replace. These can be used with stock or aftermarket upper control arms, though the latter is really best. (Photo Courtesy Global West Suspension)

a full coil-over conversion system is necessary. This relocates the mounting point of the coil-over assembly to the lower control arm to better distribute forces. In addition, it provides even more beneficial geometry while still using the basic OEM design.

Such designs are more costly than a hybrid setup yet they can provide a bit better performance under the most demanding conditions. They provide at least as much tunability with superior geometry plus they're still far less costly than a full Mustang II subframe system.

Leaf Springs versus Coil Springs

Leaf springs serve their purpose well as a good, simple, safe, durable, and relatively inexpensive form of rear suspension when using a solid axle. You cannot precisely tune spring rate for the best compromise between road holding and ride comfort.

For a high-performance application a higher spring rate is needed and this produces a harsher ride and fails to maintain as stable a total rear tire contact patch. This is mainly due to the inherent friction between the leaves of each spring along with the more-random motion of each spring (and thus the axle and tires) due to bushing compliance, spring wrap up, etc.

Coil springs lack the internal friction of leaf springs. Well-tuned shocks are able to dampen the springs and thus the loads placed on a coil-over suspension are easier to control and distribute and are more consistently dampened.

You rarely see leaf springs on new cars. The ride and behavior on rough surfaces and/or with high loading is simply better and more predictable and consistent with coil springs, even in drag racing.

Air Springs

Air springs are able to change damping characteristics on demand for increased ground clearance and performance at various speeds and applications. However, they have a higher cost and progressive "spring" rate. They also are much more complicated to install (and tune) due to the need for an air compressor, tank, lines, etc. Air springs add weight and take up space.

Three- and Four-Links

Straight four-link and some three-link designs are often low in cost and relatively easy to install. They suffer from having a panhard rod that creates lateral movement of the rear axle due to the arc the panhard rod swings through. Panhard rods can be advantageous in some situations where most of the turns on a track are in the same direction. In most cases a Watt's linkage offers

superior performance but costs more. Lower-cost systems tend to use polyurethane bushings and other less-costly components to keep the price down. They're usually bolt-in designs, which may be fine on the street but often are not suited to more extreme use. In most cases, however, such systems can still outperform OEM leaf springs.

G-Links

TCP's "g-link" system is a canted four-link design. It's typical of similar mid-priced and more-capable systems. Based on 1979–2004 Mustangs, it's a direct bolt-in with only minimal welding required. TCP offers this particular system in three types: polyurethane bushings, spherical bearings, and billet aluminum arms with spherical bearings. All have the same basic geometry and installation. The polyurethane version has a little more compliance than the others but may require a bit more maintenance in terms of lubrication but it's also less costly.

The mid-priced g-link system has steel lower links versus the lighter, more-obvious, and more-costly billet aluminum links of the highest-cost system but it is otherwise identical. Three different versions of coil-over shock are also available for each configuration: 16-step single-adjustable (bump and rebound together), 16-step dual-adjustable (bump and rebound independently), and 16-step four-way adjustable (bump and rebound independently adjustable at high- and low-piston speed settings) with remote reservoirs for optimal performance.

The TCP system has high-quality components, a modular design, and

many adjustments, so you can set it up for high-performance street use or for a day at the track. The upper and lower links can be installed in multiple positions and are also adjustable in length. This provides firm or soft roll control. Instead of having to change the length of a link you may just need to change to a different hole.

Similarly, ride height can be changed by adjusting the collars on the shocks or by moving the upper shock mount to a different hole in the cradle. This added flexibility can be very convenient plus it can be a competitive advantage with quicker adjustments.

Provisions are made for all the optional features TCP offers for these

These tubular lower control arms from Global West provide exceptional strength and performance for a stock-style front suspension. The extra reinforcement is obvious at the end where the tubes come together at the chassis mount, across the tubes, and even right up to the ball joint. The OEM rubber bushing has been replaced with a spherical bearing. These arms offer additional strut rod mounting holes plus revised geometry for potentially better performance, especially when used as part of a complete negative-roll kit. The anti-sway bar bushing mounts are even radiused for stability and durability! (Photo Courtesy Global West Suspension)

Vehicle Type 2: High-Performance Street Car *continued*

systems. Whether you go with no rear anti-sway bar, a sliding-link solid bar, or a splined tubular bar it bolts right up to the g-link system whether you're using the OEM axle or one of TCP's FAB9 axle housings.

A final feature of the g-link is its exceptional provision for ongoing maintenance. All spherical bearings have grease fittings and are capable of being readjusted and even rebuilt if necessary. A simple adjustment ring and set screw provide the ability to compensate for any excess wear by reducing the internal clearances.

Strut Bars

The far greater handling and braking forces of high-performance use require a significant redesign of the strut bars. A rubber bushing is no

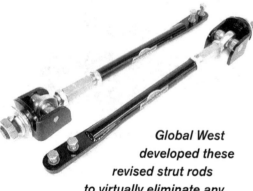

Global West developed these revised strut rods to virtually eliminate any movement along the centerline of the rod, thus maintaining a much more consistent rod location/alignment and minimizing the effects of hard braking and cornering. By using adjustable-length rods with rod ends that index to the frame (to ensure proper alignment) these strut rods also provide additional adjustment capability for a more precise alignment. Friction and wear are greatly reduced so they last longer. The ride can be a bit harsher. (Photo Courtesy Global West Suspension)

longer suitable for such use and must be eliminated. A rod end or spherical bearing is normally used in place of the rubber bushing, along with a much stronger and adjustable rod.

These designs completely eliminate any excessive for-and-aft movement of the strut rod while greatly reducing friction and strength. The location of the true pivot point is held stable and constant (it moves around with rubber), thus minimizing random variations in the caster change throughout the full arc of movement.

Anti-Sway Bar

Further front anti-sway bar modifications may not be needed if you already did some. Generally, when you make significant changes to the springs and/or shocks you also need to change, or at least readjust, the anti-sway bar(s). Remember, the suspension is a system, not just a combination of parts. Everything needs to be compatible to get the best result.

For a high-performance street car, you probably don't need adjustable anti-sway bars. You still must, how-

Underbody subframe connectors can be supplemented for higher-performance use. Adding additional bars and tying them into the side sills reinforces the main tubes of the subframe connectors and the floorpan. The loads are also more widely distributed, minimizing concentrations, which can cause problems at weak spots. The new bars also make great jacking points.

ever, ensure the bar(s) is matched to the rest of the suspension. It's a question of achieving the proper balance. You probably won't be changing the parts out much so you just need to get things right at first and then you can rely on shock settings, tire pressures, and so on for any tuning you might need to do.

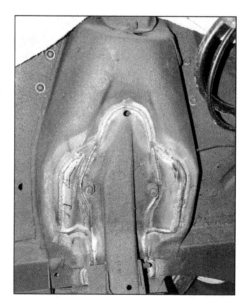

When the additional loads of high-performance driving are to be the norm, additional strengthening measures are needed for the body structure. A simple but critical upgrade is to fully weld the shock towers. The majority of the front suspension loads are imposed on the shock towers yet they're only partially welded from the factory. Over time even normal loads can lead to cracks in the towers. Full welds do a much better job of distributing these loads across the entirety of the shock tower, thus avoiding the concentrated stress that causes cracks.

Vehicle Type 3: Streetable Track-Day Car

A vehicle in this category sees a lot of extreme use so it needs even more chassis stiffening than the other types. I discuss roll bars and cages in Chapter 12 but there are other modifications you can make to the basic body structure. Mustangs Plus offers a chassis-strengthening kit that provides weld-on reinforcement panels primarily for the floorpan area. These panels box off the bottom of the car while better tying together and reinforcing the major structures. This involves significant cost and complexity including some major modification of the basic vehicle. If much higher power levels and cornering loads will be generated such modifications are likely necessary.

When combined with a proper roll bar/roll cage structure you have as stable (and safe) a platform as possible (without a full tube chassis) when starting with an early Mustang body. Some upgrades may also be required by sanctioning bodies and/or event organizers before they let you run.

The suspension solution for this vehicle type builds on the high-performance street type and it's basically an upgrade with greater emphasis on strength and tunability: a coil-over system from Ridetech. Ridetech offers

An elaborate (and costly) strut rod design is from TCP. The concentric-pivot assembly utilizes two pre-loaded Delrin bushings inside billet aluminum housings to relocate the effective pivot point farther forward, thus effectively lengthening the strut rod while also eliminating unwanted compliance/movement. The longer rod reduces the alignment change throughout the range of travel, thus allowing less of a compromise in setting the caster, etc. (Photo Courtesy Total Control Products)

With this Global West complete coil-over conversion system, the OEM spring/shock setup is replaced by a coil-over setup, which mounts to the revised lower control arm to better direct/distribute the spring forces. This geometry is inherently superior to the OEM design for a number of reasons yet the same basic control arms and strut rods can be used. An adapter is added to the lower arm to accept the bottom mount of the coil-over unit. The upper arms are modified to allow the coil-over to pass through plus there is a special mounting scheme for the coil-over to the shock tower.

three levels of coil-over, or Shock-Wave/air-spring, configurations.

The Level 1 system comes with non-adjustable shocks and no front anti-sway bar. The Level 2 coil-over system is the same except for the shocks (single adjustable for rebound) and the inclusion of the optional MUSCLEbar with PosiLinks front anti-sway bar. The Level 3 system includes the front bar along with the best shocks (single adjustment for rebound with dual-stage high- and low-speed adjustments for compression, plus remote reservoirs) and is the preferred choice for this vehicle type.

Steering Upgrades

No suspension system is of much value if your steering system also isn't up to the task. The steering is responsible for the cornering loads the suspension has to deal with but, more importantly, it takes you where you want to go (most of the time). The standard steering systems on early

Mustangs left quite a bit to be desired. Even right off the showroom floor they were vague, void of any real communication from the road, and not very responsive to inputs. They were usable enough and safe enough for normal street use but, other than perhaps in drag racing, they were not really feasible for use during any type of high-speed high-performance driving.

The main reason is their complexity. The use of a hydraulic cylinder/ram to provide power assist wasn't a very elegant solution; it introduced many more joints where excess wear and play could develop. The system weighed more and was prone to leaks. It presented a challenge for packaging when you wanted to install headers.

Ridetech Level 2 Coil-Over Front Suspension

The Ridetech front suspension differs from other designs primarily because the lower control arm is essentially a one-piece A-arm rather than a two-piece lower arm/strut rod design. The strut rod has been integrated into the lower arm to form a single unit. This is stronger and lighter plus it allows for revised geometry, which dramatically improves handling due to more-desirable caster and camber curves. The OEM rubber strut rod bushing is replaced by a spherical bearing precisely held in place by aluminum retainers to ensure proper, stable geometry.

The upper arms are similarly robust in their design through the incorporation of rod ends. They replace the factory bushings, improved geometry, and a dropped cross shaft for a better camber curve.

The top mount of the coil-over units is very strong and precise. It properly locates and centers the coil-over unit at the correct mounting angle. The adjustment knob for each coil-over is readily accessible for quick adjustments. There's no need to drill new holes for the upper arms so the potential for error is eliminated and greater strength is ensured. Adjustment shims are provided for the upper arms for greater adjustment range.

In some situations (such as when a much-wider engine is used) it is necessary to go beyond simply upgrading the OEM-style front suspension. In such cases a more radical approach resulting in significantly higher cost and installation complexity may be needed. The rewards can be great when the limitations of the stock mounting points and design are eliminated.

The following is an installation overview, not a step-by-step guide because there are too many differences among cars. ■

With this coil-over conversion from TCP, the upper control arm mount already incorporates the dropped position so no additional holes need to be drilled. The upper arms are adjustable to provide greater flexibility in terms of alignment at some sacrifice in ultimate strength. These upper arms replace the OEM rubber bushings with rod ends for strength and a more-stable/consistent location. TCP includes its unique strut rods and lower arms plus a lower mount for the coil-over unit. The upper mount has revised geometry. (Photo Courtesy Total Control Products)

A different front anti-sway bar is needed to compensate for most upgrades in suspension design, spring rate, etc. An adjustable bar may not always be necessary but it can be a benefit when going between street and track use. The bushings and end links should at least be upgraded to polyurethane. The higher loads encountered in high-performance driving apply greater stress to virtually every part of the suspension. TCP's billet anti-sway bar mounts (shown) are much better able to tolerate higher forces without flexing or the risk of failure. (Photo Courtesy Total Control Products)

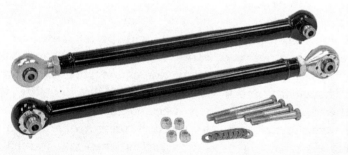

These lower links show the adjustability, strength, lower friction, and serviceability of the TCP design. The elimination of rubber bushings provides many benefits while adding strength to the torque boxes. The spherical bearings can be readjusted throughout their life to maintain proper internal clearances. Provisions are also made for periodic lubrication as needed. (Photo Courtesy Total Control Products)

When frequent track use is to be the norm and street use is minimal, even further reinforcement of the body is both feasible and advisable, to the extent allowed by rules and/or budgets. This Chassis Strengthening Kit from Mustangs Plus is a panel reinforcement option, which can be very effective. It greatly improves the overall stiffness of the floorpan by creating boxed sections to reduce flexing and bending. (Photo Courtesy Mustangs Plus)

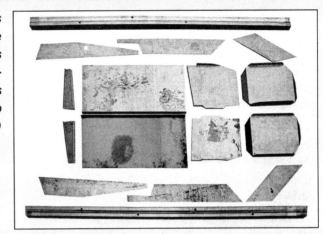

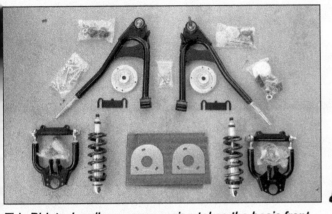

This Ridetech coil-over suspension takes the basic front suspension concept as far as it can go without completely removing the shock towers. The main improvement is integrating the lower control arm and strut rod into single-piece A-arms, which are inherently stronger and provide better geometry than the OEM design. This system uses an upper arm design similar to the coil-over conversion with a dropped mounting location already built into the arm (no extra holes) along with adjustability and rod ends (versus bushings). Adjustment shims are included if needed. Upper and lower coil-over are non-compliant to improve responsiveness and strength while offering multiple offsets for different ride heights. Shock tower reinforcement plates strengthen them to better handle the higher forces they see while also providing a unique look.

A further improvement can be had by combining the Monte Carlo bar and export brace into a single, welded assembly when possible. Clearance issues with the intake manifold or a large distributor cap, etc., may preclude doing so. Be sure to account for changes necessary to accommodate new upper shock mounts, etc.

Dirt and road debris tend to accumulate underneath the upper arms due to the drain holes frequently getting clogged. This causes a buildup, which can retain moisture and result in severe rusting. All dirt and debris should be removed and the surfaces cleaned of any rust before they're sealed.

Ridetech's ingenious upper mount design combines upper and lower plates, which sandwich and reinforce the shock tower upper surface while positively locating the upper coil-over mount. This greatly strengthens and stabilizes the upper mounting point as well as the shock tower. Any possible flexing is reduced to an absolute minimum (short of installing a full tube chassis setup). Shock adjustments are easily made with the turn of a knob (or two). The support plates for the combination Monte Carlo bar and export brace can still be installed in place.

Ridetech Level 2 Coil-Over Rear Suspension

The Ridetech rear suspension is a canted four-link setup. There are some significant features that make it well suited for a streetable track-day car. First, the system is designed for maximum strength. This required elimination of some of adjustability. Because this system was developed with frequent track use in mind there are fewer provisions for switching between "street mode" and "track mode" to ensure maximum strength. This can be seen in how the upper cradle only provides a single mounting option for the upper links and the coil-over units. Multiple mounting options are still retained for the lower links. The idea here is to make adjustments primarily through the coil-over units rather than worrying about more variables and potential weaker points.

Furthermore, the coil-over units have solider mounting points (aluminum spacers with rod ends versus polyurethane bushings) and greater adjustment range. The design of the upper cradle still allows bolt-in installation but is a stronger single weldment, which is more suitable for welding than a cradle consisting of multiple parts. All miscellaneous brackets are made from thicker steel to again ensure maximum strength and simplicity. While the upper links retain their adjustability by necessity (for setting proper pinion angle and/or axle preload), the lower links are not adjustable for the sake of simplicity and greater strength.

If this were an all-out race solution the few polyurethane bushings could also be replaced by spherical bearings or something similar to a Del-A-Lum bushing. This would increase cost, noise and the perception of vibration because there would then be virtually no cushioning left.

The following is an installation overview, not a step-by-step guide because there are too many differences among cars. ■

The method Ridetech uses to secure the strut rod/lower control arm bearing is as robust as it gets. The bearing is held in place by machined billet aluminum retainers connected with three Allen bolts instead of a threaded sleeve and nut arrangement. This requires three holes to be precisely drilled in the OEM metal bushing retainer so the bolts line up. You definitely want to "measure/center punch twice and drill once" to avoid problems with assembly. The locknut on the threaded end of the arm, combined with the supplied spacer and washer, takes up any slack.

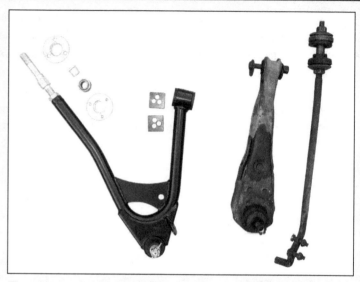

The change from a two-piece setup to a one-piece setup is the most obvious difference from the OEM design. These gusseted tubular arms are much stronger than the stock arms plus they're better located by the square plates (similar to Global West's lockout kit) shown rather than by eccentric bolts to minimize the potential for falling out of adjustment. The geometry has been revised to improve caster and camber over the full range of motion. The elimination of rubber strut rod bushings eliminates unwanted compliance and movement. It also allows the lower arm to essentially function like an A-arm, mimicking a dual-wishbone setup.

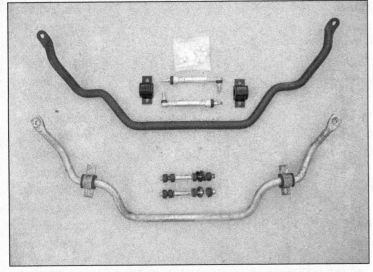

A new front anti-sway bar is inevitably required to balance the new springs and shocks. The key to success is overall handling balance. Bigger is not always better. The best option is to go tubular to save weight if you need a really stiff bar. This Ridetech system came with the optional MUSCLEbar with PosiLinks, which effectively turns the Level 2 system into a Level 3 system without the better (and more costly) remote-reservoir coil-overs. The bar is matched to the rest of the system so there's no provision for adjustment. The end link design is especially good; it uses durable sealed-metal ball joints instead of more-compliant bushings.

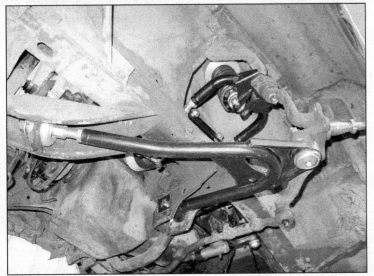

In concept, the Ridetech system remains similar to the OEM design. Attention to detail, however, is where it far exceeds the OEM setup in performance, adjustability, strength, and durability. Unwanted movement from bushings is virtually eliminated, as is friction. Geometry and stiffness are greatly enhanced. This dramatically improves system response and stability for a more-consistent caster/camber curve and better feel for the driver.

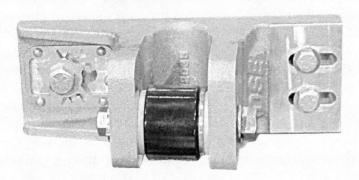

This closeup of the DSE Speed-LIGN system shows how the unique approach works. Aluminum castings supporting the suspension-mounting points are allowed to slide front-to-back and side-to-side when their respective mounting bolts are loosened. On one opposing face of each casting there is a star-shaped washer used to set the adjustment. The casting is moved to where the desired settings are reached and then the mounting bolts are tightened to retain the settings. If a change is needed the bolts can be loosened and the casting can be moved, this time using the markings on the star wheel for reference, to obtain a new setting before the bolts are again tightened. This allows for very quick, repeatable, and accurate changes in caster or camber without the need for special tools or an alignment setup.

Ridetech Level 2 Coil-Over Rear Suspension *CONTINUED*

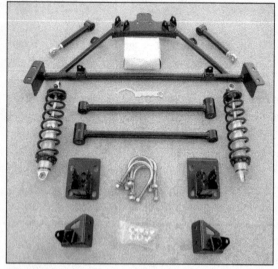

The Ridetech rear suspension is similar to that in the high-performance street car but with some significant differences. First, the upper cradle is a single weldment that's straighter and simpler in design. It's inherently stronger than the curved and complex multi-piece assembly, especially if it's welded and bolted in. The canted four-link design is similar but there are differences in the bushings and in the amount of adjustability. This system has some polyurethane bushings to provide cushioning and isolation from noise and vibration. The coil-over units have bearings instead of bushings and thus are stiffer and more responsive. Adjustment options are fewer because only the lower links have multiple mounting holes.

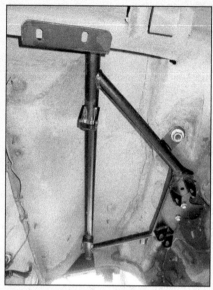

Here is the upper cradle after it's been bolted in. The main bar serves as a mount for the top of the coil-overs and it significantly braces/reinforces the frame rails. The rest of the assembly is held in by very large bolts on the side struts (these go to the original upper shock mounts) and four smaller bolts at the pinion snubber contact pad. Loads are well distributed and the triangular shape adds a lot of strength.

Vehicle Type 1: Daily Driver

For a daily driver that sees mostly street use and a minimal modification budget it's only practical to minimally repair the stock system to the extent it's necessary. Tie rod ends, ball joints, and so forth aren't especially expensive and should be the first things to get replaced if they're worn or damaged with excessive play.

Another prime candidate for replacement is the rag joint between the steering column and the steering box. Even if this looks okay it's a good idea to replace it if it's been on for a long time because the rubber deteriorates over time, thus creating more play and slower steering response. In some cases the joint

could actually fail under extreme use. Even though you likely won't lose steering altogether you'll probably end up someplace you don't want to, fast. Replacing the rag joint is cheap insurance against that. The steering box usually doesn't need much attention other than perhaps a slight adjustment of the worm gear clearance if it's excessive. This is easily done by loosening the locknut on the steering box and adjusting the screw per factory instructions. In extreme cases and/or where the box is leaking or otherwise damaged you can have it rebuilt or buy one that already has been rebuilt. If the cost of doing this proves to be too high

you can perform an upgrade instead.

The power steering pump rarely has any problems other than perhaps a leaking seal or hose. These should be replaced unless you plan on upgrading. The problem with these systems is usually the hydraulic ram/cylinder and/or the associated control valve. They tend to leak due to wear of the seals. Their rubber bushings at the frame rail mount also tend to disintegrate over time, thus allowing the ram to move more than it should. This quickly makes the steering more vague and slow.

Inexpensive rebuild kits with superior materials reduce the tendency for leaks or excessive play after

Vehicle Type 1: Daily Driver *continued*

the rebuild. If the various rubber components are cracked or otherwise deteriorated they too can be replaced for little cost. Rebuilt rams are available, though they're not cheap. If you're thinking of buying a complete replacement you probably should just save your money and upgrade to a better system instead. If you have no need to keep the original components for judging at a show, for example, it just doesn't pay to keep the stock system unless it's in good shape and you don't want to put much money into a daily driver. Basically, keep the stock system healthy until you can afford to toss it. Otherwise, wait to upgrade it.

Vehicle Type 2: High-Performance Street Car

For any type of high-performance use you should toss the original steering system and replace it with a modern and effective solution. A prime example of this is the integral power steering conversion kit from Borgeson Universal. Kits are available for the 1964½–1970 models whether they came with manual or power steering. There may be clearance issues if you're using the factory Z-bar on a manual transmission car; you may need to change to a cable or hydraulic clutch release system to make things work.

The Borgeson system completely eliminates the hydraulic ram/cylinder and control valve because all of their functionality has been incorporated into the new steering box. A higher-output pump is required so one is supplied with the necessary mounting bracket, hoses, steering link adaptor (if needed), and even a new rag joint. You may need to modify the stock steering column a bit but it's a small price to pay for the

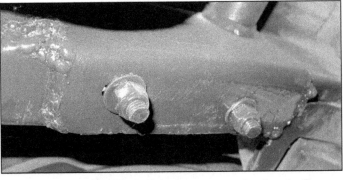

To make things even stronger, you can weld the mounting plates wherever you can get to them. This further reduces flexing and adds strength by tying much of the rear of the car together to absorb the suspension loads. Proper weld penetration is critical. (These welds aren't pretty but they're deep enough and don't show.)

The installation of the upper links is by far the most difficult aspect of installing this suspension. The reason is the tabs to be welded to the axle housing must be precisely located to ensure the axle is properly located in all directions. These tabs are critical for setting proper pinion angle. The upper links are adjustable in length to allow the proper setting to be reached but this may not be possible if the tabs are not located properly. If the cradle and axle tabs are properly placed the length of the upper links should be nearly identical. Be sure to paint all welds.

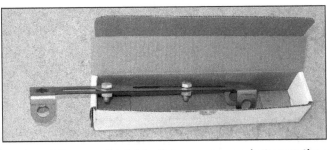

Ridetech provides these fixtures to help ensure the axle tabs are welded in the right place. After the axle has been verified as being correctly located and centered these adjustable fixtures are run between the axle and the upper link mounts on the cradle. The tabs to be welded are bolted to the other end before the fixtures are adjusted to rest the tabs in the proper place for welding. The tabs almost surely need to be trimmed a bit before welding to minimize gaps between the tabs and the housing. Once the tabs have been welded on and painted, the fixtures can be removed and replaced by the upper links.

Vehicle Type 2: High-Performance Street Car *continued*

benefits you receive. The steering is much more direct and responsive while also being much more durable and reliable with minimal risk of leaks.

Considering all the new parts you get, this is one of the best upgrades you can make for the money. You experience better steering every time you drive the car. If your old/OEM system needs any significant amount of investment for your daily driver or high-performance street car this Borgeson setup is the better way to go. It's also fine for a street/strip car that just drag races.

The following is an installation overview of a Borgeson power-steering conversion. It is not a step-by-step guide because there are too many differences among cars.

The mounting brackets for the lower links are simple to bolt on because they are located by the spring pad pegs on the axle. Ensure the nuts on the U-bolts are evenly tightened and not over-tightened to the point of warping the flanges. Some of the provided locknuts are fairly thin so it's easy to strip them; thicker ones are easy to find.

The finished installation shows these coil-overs, which allow the usual adjustment to ride height and valving (via the adjustment knobs at the top of each coil-over). Non-adjustable and double-adjustable versions plus other springs are available. The lower links can be mounted in any of three locations to optimize the geometry for different purposes.

Vehicle Type 3: Streetable Track-Day Car

For a streetable track-day car that sees more that just the drag strip you want to take things a bit further for maximum performance. This means converting to a rack-and-pinion steering system. The advantages of doing so are many, whether you go power or manual. The system is simpler, and there are a lot fewer joints. You simply have the rack and a means for mounting tie rods and U-joints plus a means for connecting to the steering column. It almost always weighs less than a regular system when you consider all the links, joints, and so forth it doesn't have.

In a powered system you also need a pump and hoses because the power assist is usually integral to the rack, if you want it to be. Manual racks are sometimes preferable, however, where light weight is a priority and high cornering (or parking) forces are rarely, if ever, encountered. Think drag racing.

Add-on electric power assist kits can significantly reduce steering effort on just about any vehicle and do so without the need for a pump or hoses. They are usually installed under the dash, either with a new steering column or through modifications to the existing steering column. Some units integrate the assist motor directly onto the rack, though that can be a packaging problem. Electric-assist systems generally don't have the same direct feel as a hydraulic system. If you don't need that last bit of communication with the road this may be an acceptable option, though not necessarily an inexpensive or easily installed one.

Better rack-and-pinion systems such as the TCP conversion kit mount the rack in such a way that it's not bearing any load other than that of the steering forces. Designs that allow the rack to be loaded in other ways can be prone to premature wear, sticking, resistance while moving, and even the risk of failure. Those that remove the tubular factory crossmember and replace it with an unbraced/unreinforced rack can be problematic. Those with proper reinforcement, however, can actually

Vehicle Type 3: Streetable Track-Day Car *continued*

help stiffen the lower control arm mounts and the frame rails in general, thus providing some handling benefit.

Look for a system that uses existing factory mounting points for installation and has a vehicle-specific mounting bracket to ensure proper fit and clearance with the road and oil pan. The mounting location should also minimize the need for any corrective measures such as the installation of a bump steer kit or making exhaust modifications.

The TCP kit meets all these criteria while also having an exceptionally quick ratio (three turns lock-to-lock versus four or more for OEM racks), straight-cut gears, a large-diameter rack for strength, and the correct geometry. TCP includes specific mounting hardware for each car.

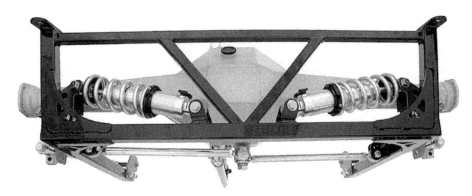

An interesting and effective rear suspension upgrade for early Mustangs is from TCP. This torque-arm/pushrod system does an incredible job of improving handling performance and traction under acceleration and braking. The long torque arm mounted directly to the front of the axle housing (and also to the body near the transmission) uses the axle forces generated to help plant the tires under acceleration and greatly reduce dive under braking. A Watt's linkage virtually eliminates lateral movement (versus the inherent arcing path of panhard rods). The support cradle is reinforced by gussets and links, which extend forward to attach to the original leaf-spring mounts. The cradle may interfere with large exhausts. (Photo Courtesy Total Control Products)

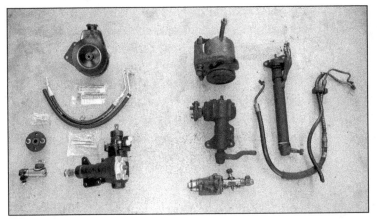

A very effective and reasonably priced way to dramatically improve steering performance is to replace it with a more contemporary system such as this one from Borgeson (left). It has far fewer system components. More importantly, the integration of the power assist directly into the steering box greatly improves steering feel and response. Weight and the number of potential leaks are also reduced plus additional header clearance is provided. This setup is absolutely the minimum that should be considered for any kind of performance driving and even for strip use if you're drag racing.

Installation of a new steering box is pretty simple; it's a direct bolt-in. Its larger size, however, requires some modification of the steering shaft. For 1968 and later models with a collapsible column (shown) the column can simply be "persuaded" back into the firewall with a suitable mallet. In some cases you may need to further trim the column housing. For earlier cars you need to cut the column and use the included shorter, solid shaft.

WHEELS AND TIRES

When it comes to overall vehicle performance potential the tire is the most important single component. The tires, with help from the wheels and suspension, are responsible for putting the power to the ground, cornering, stopping, ride quality, and even less obvious things such as fuel economy and interior noise.

In this chapter I cover the most popular wheel and tire options for a first-generation Mustang. I focus on performance, comfort, wear, life, and cost. I can't cover every possible combination so I provide useful guidelines and recommendations for the three vehicle types (daily driver, performance street car, and streetable track-day car). I also discuss tire pressure monitors.

Wheel Sizes

In general, wheels tend to be more of an aesthetic choice than a consideration for performance. But a wheel and tire upgrade is necessary to extract the maximum performance from the vehicle.

There are 14-, 15-, or 16-inch reproduction-style wheels to fit your car that are easy to find. Most are steel reproductions, although there are some aluminum wheels in these sizes as well.

This 1967 Shelby Magstar replica wheel is a hybrid construction in that it combines a CNC-machined aluminum center section with a chromed, spun-steel outer rim. This allows for a lighter wheel with sharper distinct features than if it were an all-steel wheel. The machined edges on the center section enhance the effect of the black paint while also providing more visual depth and character. Because this is a replica wheel it is only available in the original 15 x 7 size but there are many other examples of wheels with similar construction and/or features in this and other sizes. (Photo Courtesy Specialty Wheel)

This 1968/1969 GT Rallye styled steel wheel, for example, is available in sizes from 14 x 6 to 15 x 8. The 14 x 6 size is optionally available with the choice of a black outer rim and polished stainless steel trim rings. It comes in a triple chrome finish; a special argent silver wheel center is available as a special order. This meets or exceeds the Ford Motor Company specification. (Photo Courtesy Specialty Wheel)

If you wish to keep a relatively stock look and size wheel on your car there are numerous sources for virtually any original-style wheel in a 14- or 15-inch size. This Ford replica wheel from Specialty Wheel is just one of the 10 or so classic styles they offer with the correct bolt pattern and backspacing. Some of them are also available in larger diameters. These wheels are manufactured with dies, which have closer tolerances and sharper edges (plus CNC-machining, etc.) than the original wheels and also benefit from better, more-durable materials and finishes. (Photo Courtesy Specialty Wheel)

If you plan on a more steady diet of track days and longer duration events you want to go up to at least a 17-inch rim to allow for the use of even larger brakes and to further reduce the sidewall height. This still allows for mostly street use though the ride tends to be a bit stiffer due to the lower sidewall. You also need to pay more attention to potholes, etc., though the risk of a bent rim should still remain low.

There are many 17-inch wheels, mostly of the one-piece cast variety, with a very broad range of widths and backspacings to fit first-gens of all types.

Vintage Wheel Works is a favorite of many who see regular track use because they offer several classic racing styles (such as the Minilite look of this Vintage 48 wheel) in a relatively light and inexpensive package. Their wheels meet US DOT specifications as well as the requirements of most sanctioning bodies. They are generally a two-piece design made from T6 heat-treated 356 aluminum centers with spun 6061 aluminum rims so they are very light and very strong, yet not overly expensive. Their many offerings range from 15 to 18 inches in diameter with widths up to 11 inches plus a very broad selection of backspacings suitable for use on early Mustangs.

If you want to introduce the style of a later-model Mustang to your project there are many possibilities. This is a 16-inch 5 Star/Pony wheel from a Fox-Body. These are available with the proper five-lug bolt pattern (the Fox originally used a four-lug pattern) and offset for the early cars. The upgrade to 16 inches not only changes the look of the car but can also allow for slightly wider tires. The larger diameter reduces potential interference with the front ball joints, thus allowing the wheel to tuck in more. They are easy to find in a 7- or 8-inch width plus many other sizes, diameters, and offsets. Alternative finishes such as chrome, black, or even white are also offered, though with fewer size options.

The jump to 16 inches also allows many larger disc brake packages to be used. Tire widths of 225 front and 245 rear should fit a 1964½–1966 with no problem on 8-inch rims with a 4.5-inch backspacing. Later cars can go considerably larger in width and diameter. A package such as this is ideal for relatively comfortable street use and can also be used in autocross, open road, drag strip, and brief track events with little risk.

17-Inch Wheels

Wheels larger than 17 inches offer a larger contact patch for increased performance but this may create fitment and clearance issues with the bodywork. A 17-inch wheel has enough sidewall height to provide good ride comfort while the lower sidewall (versus a 16-inch or smaller wheel) provides improved steering response and feel. You should still be able to use a 45 or 50 aspect ratio tire with a 17-inch rim.

Single-piece aluminum or billet wheels can provide excellent strength and design flexibility (for plenty of style options) at very reasonable prices. While they aren't as light as

These Vintage 48 wheels and Toyo R888 tires are significantly wider than 16-inch wheels yet their overall diameter and rolling circumference (and thus the speedometer calibration and/or VSS signal) are virtually identical.

The even larger brakes necessitate even higher backspacing. This moves the wheel farther toward the center of the car, thus providing more clearance to the fender yet even less possible interference with the upper ball joint. You still want to roll the inner fender lip and make sure the tires don't rub the inner wheelwell/frame at full steering lock.

two- and three-piece wheels they are stronger and resist damage from potholes or flexing under extreme cornering. Special casting technologies are used with two- and three-piece designs, some using a steel outer ring for extra strength.

Vintage Wheel Works offers wheels for early Mustangs. They carry classic styles and have a variety of finishes and other appearance options (center caps, color combination, etc.). Forged wheels in 17-inch size offer exceptional strength for their weight but they are typically $500 per wheel or more. They are offered in one-, two- or three-piece versions and have a limited selection in available styles. Those offering minimal weight may also not be as well suited to dealing with the impacts encountered in street use.

In general, unless you'll be seeing quite a bit of track time (and have the suspension modifications to make best use of it) the case for going all out with a relatively more

costly forging is usually not all that compelling at the 17-inch wheel size.

18-Inch Wheels

An 18-inch wheel provides maximum track-day performance and some degree of streetability. This rim gives you the lowest practical sidewall height without making the wheel too weak or too heavy. The early Mustangs, particularly 1965/1966 cars, are better suited to this wheel because they typically clear the suspension and allow the use of a wider wheel with more favorable backspacing. A 17-inch rim also does this to some extent but the 18-inch wheel provides more clearance for a larger brake caliper.

Cast, composite, and forged wheels are available. Castings tend to be on the heavy side and the composites can be less suitable for the extreme and uneven impact forces from potholes, etc.

Care still must be taken, however, when making the final choice because

For frequent track use an upgrade to 18-inch wheels is desired. This allows the use of the largest brake packages while further reducing the sidewall height to the lowest practical amount for optimum steering response. On early Mustangs in particular, performance is not gained by going above 18 inches in diameter.

This Weld Racing RT-S wheel for early Mustangs can be used on the track as well as on the street. It's a super-light two-piece forging available in several simple styles and finishes, yet which can be had in a very wide range of fitments. These wheels have several unique features such as a choice of three different spoke profiles (to ensure optimum clearance to the brakes) plus the use of finite element analysis and other advanced techniques during their design and production to minimize PMOI and weight without losing strength. This significantly improves braking and acceleration.

When mounted on the vehicle the lower sidewall height of the 18-inch wheel is fairly obvious. Another issue to consider, while not a problem here, is that a larger diameter also creates more space around the rotor/drum. If you've upgraded the brakes it's usually not a problem from a visual perspective. However, if you go with a significantly larger wheel without installing larger brakes the space between the rotor and the rim will, at some point, not look very good. The small rotor tends to get "lost" in the larger rim. The more open the wheel design, the greater the problem. Not a look that says "performance" or "stopping power."

some 18-inch forgings are rather fragile. A simple design, such as basic five-spoke, split five-spoke, mesh-pattern, etc., typically offers the best balance of weight and strength.

20-Inch and Larger Wheels

Wheel diameters of more than 18 inches are best thought of as being used primarily for their looks, not for performance. Although some (such as the 20-inch Weld RT-S) can be suitable for performance and track use they still suffer from certain compromises relative to an 18-inch counterpart. When comparing similar 18- and 20-inch wheels the latter is heavier, more expensive, inherently less strong unless extra material is added to compensate, less able to tolerate impacts such as potholes (due to the lower sidewall tire it must use), and provides a harsher ride.

Other factors such as tire wear and noise are often also negatively affected. Other than appearance, about the only thing that can be considered to be an improvement in performance is steering response, due mostly to the lower sidewall tire. If a heavier wheel (such as a casting) is chosen to reduce cost the polar moment of inertia (PMOI) likely increases significantly, thus requiring a brake upgrade (more cost and weight, etc.) just to maintain equal stopping power.

From an aesthetic perspective, there's also the potential for the brakes to get "lost" in the much larger wheel due to the increased gap between the rotor/drum and the inside of the rim. A larger rotor (bigger drums are hard to come by) is pretty much a given to avoid having such an unsightly gap. The bottom line is that unless you've done some very extensive suspension and braking modifications to your early Mustang it's very unlikely you'd see any performance gain by going over 18 inches in diameter.

You will, however, have more cost, more weight, and several other negatives to contend with including the fact that most of these larger wheels are not exactly "classic" in their styling. With few exceptions (such as the Weld RT-S) fitment options are also limited unless you're willing to cut the bodywork—seems like a lot of trouble just for a certain look with less-than-maximum performance.

When you change to a much larger, wider wheel, fit is a critical factor. Backspacing becomes much more important and brake caliper clearance is a prime consideration. Likewise, when fitting larger brakes you need to be sure the calipers clear the spokes as well as the inside of the rim.

Weld Racing offers high-end forged wheels in the RT-S series for early Mustangs. These forged wheels offer an excellent balance of weight and strength plus Weld also makes an extra effort to ensure proper strength for street use with little, if any, weight gain. Furthermore, Weld also prioritizes the reduction of PMOI, often referred to as the "flywheel effect."

This side-by-side comparison gives you an idea of the differences in wheel diameter versus sidewall height. These tires do not have the exact same overall diameter but they're pretty close. The way they look on the car is what matters and the later, larger cars can use a larger-diameter wheel because of their larger wheelwells and because the large wheel is more proportionally correct for their size. They also need a wider tire, which is easier to accommodate with the larger rim. When wheel diameter and/or width is increased significantly you should upgrade the brakes to fill the visual gap and to compensate for the increased rotational inertia (and braking distance) of larger-diameter wheel/ tire combinations.

PMOI has a greater impact on performance than does weight alone. By carefully using finite element analysis plus other design and manufacturing techniques, Weld is able to put material where it does the most good for strength without increasing PMOI. This provides improved acceleration and braking, especially under transient conditions.

Perhaps the best feature of the Weld RT-S wheels is that they are offered in a wide range of offsets, widths (4 to 18 inches), and diameters (15, 17, 18, and 20 inches) plus three different pad heights, which provide clearance for even the largest aftermarket brakes. This wide variety and fitment flexibility is possible because Weld makes the RT-S wheels by precisely welding together two forged rim shells (which can easily be varied in size) with a forged center (which can have different styling, sizing, and pad heights) into a very strong, yet relatively light, assembly. They fit virtually any combination of brake and suspension parts you may

put on your early Mustang without the need for doing costly bodywork to avoid rubs.

If you decide to go over 18 inches you need to seriously consider an upgrade to larger brakes as well.

Wheel Fitment Guidelines

Regardless of what size wheel you decide to use there are certain guidelines you can follow to help ensure there aren't any fitment problems. These come from shops such as Mustangs Plus and wheel manufacturers such as Weld Racing that have decades of experience selling and installing various components on stock and modified first-generation Mustangs. They often include information in their catalog and on their website to help customers make decisions and are, of course, also available by phone and email to answer more specific questions. Also be sure to ask around and look on Internet forums to find what's worked for others with a setup similar to what you have.

Here are a few general guidelines for fitment considerations:

Backspacing

First you need to decide if you're going to make the wheels fit the car or modify the car to fit the look of the wheels. Do you absolutely need a very deep-dish look on the wheels? Do you want to have different and/ or staggered wheel sizes front to rear? If so, you may have to tub the car, narrow the rear axle, flare the fenders, etc. These procedures are neither inexpensive nor easy. If you are flexible with the look of the wheel, you can likely find a backspacing to fit.

For fitment decisions, it's better to use backspacing than offset because the former is an actual measurement whereas the latter is a calculation based on the theoretical centerline of the wheel (it doesn't account for manufacturing tolerances).

You measure backspacing by laying a straightedge across the rear edge of the wheel/rim and then measuring straight down from the lower edge of the straightedge to the hub/ flange surface of the wheel (where it contacts the rotor or drum). Be sure to keep the ruler or measuring tape perfectly vertical because any tilting or angularity will introduce some inaccuracy.

Extreme backspacing may provide the look you want but it also greatly increases the loading on parts of the wheel and on the wheel bearings. Independent suspensions are more sensitive to extreme backspacings than is a solid axle. Extremes can also increase the "scrub radius" on the front wheels, thus further negatively affecting handling and braking performance. It's best to have relatively neutral backspacing (i.e., the wheel center is close to the center of the rim).

Drum/Rotor Thickness

If you are converting drum brakes to disc brakes (or even from single-piece rotors to two-piece/composite rotors) make sure you consider the fact that the drums and rotors can have different thicknesses and thus affect the final/mounted location of the wheel. Discs are normally thicker than drums, and two-piece rotors (which use an aluminum center/hat) are often thicker than one-piece iron rotors. These push the wheel toward the fender unless any difference has otherwise been compensated for. It's best to mock up the wheel on the car and measure the clearances before mounting and balancing the tires so you can change the backspacing if you need to.

The size and shape of the brakes also matters in terms of internal clearance to the wheel. Radial clearance (to the rim) and lateral clearance (to the spokes) have to be addressed. Multiple-spoke profiles provide greater fitment flexibility but not all wheel manufacturers offer them. Many provide a worksheet for you to take specific measurements to send to them so they can verify if their wheel will fit before you buy it. Many brake manufacturers provide templates that represent the shape of their calipers to mock up inside the wheel to help determine if you have adequate clearance.

Rim Width

You can use a slightly wider rim if you minimize lateral movement of the suspension. In the front this is mainly a function of the suspension geometry and can be affected by moving the control arm mounting points and/or using stiffer bushings (or bearings) instead of soft-rubber OEM parts. In the rear you're basically talking about the leaf-spring bushings and shackles.

Switching to polyurethane or, preferably, Delrin (such as Global West's Del-A-Lum) greatly reduces lateral movement of the axle and thus allows you to use a slightly wider rim and tire because the axle stays put. A coil-spring suspension with a panhard rod is not as effective in this regard because it causes the axle to travel trough an arc, thus actually introducing lateral movement. For coil-spring suspensions a Watt's linkage is the preferred option because it does not introduce lateral movement.

Additional rim width can also be accommodated by "massaging" the fender lip with Eastwood's Fender Rolling Tool for the inner side of the

Wheel and Tire Combinations

The wheelwells on the 1964½–1966 cars are much smaller than those on the 1967–1973 cars and thus can't take nearly as big a tire without modification to the body. With a 17-inch or larger wheel you can get a 235 tire up front if you have the right backspacing and follow other suggested guidelines. At the rear you can go to a 255 with good bushings and a rolled lip on the fender. The later cars can go to at least a 245 in the front and a 275 in the rear without too much trouble, again, if you make the right choices and have no worn-out parts.

Listed below are some general combinations that work on the smaller 1964½–1966 cars under most circumstances. Every car/wheel/tire combination is different so do your homework before you buy, mount, balance, or install your wheels and tires.

- For 14- and 16-inch wheels you should use a 3¾- to 4-inch backspacing and can go up to a 245 tire in the rear with the 16-inch rim but only a 225 with a 15-inch.

- With a 16 x 8 wheel you should use a 4½-inch backspace and can get a 235 (possibly a 245) in the front with a 245 to 255 in the back, if you have the right suspension parts.

- With 17-inch wheels you need a 3¾- to 4-inch backspace for a 7-inch-wide rim or a 4¾- to 5-inch backspace for an 8-inch-wide rim. Maximum tire sizes are about the same as for the 16 x 8 wheels but you should have even less trouble clearing the front suspension/ball joints with the larger 17-inch rims.

- With the 1964½–1966 cars an 8-inch-wide rim is about as wide as you can go without body mods on a 17-inch or larger rim.

- For 1967 and 1968 you can get a 9-inch rim on the back but only an 8-inch on the front, again with 17 inches and up.

- The 1969–1973 cars are basically the same as the 1967 and 1968 cars except that you may have to relocate the rear stabilizer bar. ◼

tire. There's usually not much you can do in the front other than make sure the brake hoses are secured out of the way. In the rear you can generally gain clearance by bending the forward edge of the inner wheel housing because this is generally where the tire hits first.

Make sure you stay within the tire manufacturer's recommended width range when choosing your wheel. Wider is not always better but it is always heavier (for the same wheel design). You want to ensure the tire shape is correct when the vehicle load is on it. Too wide or too narrow a rim distorts the tire, reduces performance, increases wear, and, potentially, is less safe. While this is a bit less critical with radial tires it is very important with bias-ply tires. If information from the manufacturer is not available you can use the resting/static bead width of the tire to get a good approximation of the optimal wheel width.

Lugnuts

Whatever wheels you decide on you need lugnuts to mount them to the hub. With stock wheels the standard OEM-style lugnuts usually suffice. When you put down some serious money for new rims and tires, however, you want to do what you can to make sure they don't get stolen. Locking lugnuts are easy to find and not that expensive but some are better than others.

Instead of using one large locking lug it's better to go with a locking lug on each stud. This makes theft much less likely, they look better, and they don't create an imbalance. These lugs require a special key or socket to remove or install them. The lugs themselves have some form of external pattern that the key/socket matches so a

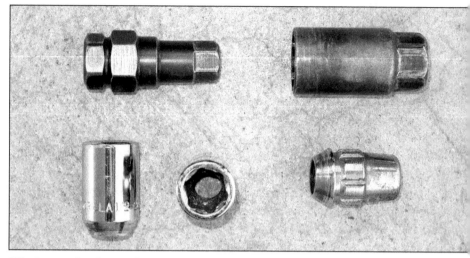

Whatever wheel you choose you want to invest a few more dollars in getting a good set of wheel locks. Gorilla Automotive Products specializes in such products and offers numerous options under their The System series. This photo shows internal and external/splined styles, which require a special tool/socket (shown) for removal. These are offered in many unique patterns so the likelihood of someone else nearby having the same pattern as you is minimized. This approach (either internal or external) is more visually pleasing plus it avoids any potential issues with imbalance while providing even greater protection due to the multiple locks per wheel.

normal socket doesn't work. The best ones are also tapered so locking pliers, for example, slide off.

For race cars you may also need special lugnuts that allow the wheel studs to protrude through them to be legal for some forms of racing. They can also be lighter in weight to provide a small reduction in PMOI. Unless you're racing, they should probably be avoided because they're generally not protected from the elements so they rust and corrode easily.

Tire Categories

Tires are the "rubber" that meets the road. As such, they are responsible for transferring all of the forces generated by the vehicle to the road. Tires are generally divided into categories to indicate their capabilities. The following list is for passenger cars only, in the order of increasing

dry-traction performance potential under "summer" conditions:

* Grand Touring
* High Performance
* Ultra-High Performance
* Max Performance
* Extreme Performance
* Track and Competition DOT

Clearly, I can't cover every category for each of the three types of vehicles so I've made some assumptions most likely to apply to each of the vehicle types. Keep in mind, tires frequently get updated or are superceded by a newer product line so specific suggestions may no longer be available. However, because tire manufacturers generally have only one product per category you should be able to figure out what replaces the particular tire I use as an example.

First, I need to cover a few basics that apply to every tire: the tire size designation, service description, and the Uniform Tire Quality Grading (UTQG) ratings.

Tire Size Designation

Tire sizes are represented by four components; 275/40R18, for example. The "275" refers to the cross-sectional width of the tire (not the tread width), the "40" refers to the aspect ratio (the cross section's height divided by its width), "R" is for radial tires (versus bias ply), and "18" is the wheel diameter for the tire.

Performance tires have relatively wider section widths for better dry traction and lower aspect ratios for improved steering response and handling. The tradeoffs for these generally include a greater tendency to hydroplane (lose traction on a wet surface) and a harsher ride.

Tire Service Description

The service description is a combination of the load rating and the speed rating and is usually expressed with two or three digits and a letter; 88W, for example.

The digits refer to the load rating of the tire, which ranges from 70 to 110 with higher numbers being able to handle a higher load. You must ensure that the combined load rating of your tires exceeds what's needed for the vehicle. This is almost always not an issue with a Mustang but it does become an issue with trucks

when towing something and/or carrying heavy loads.

The letter in the service description refers to the speed rating/limit of the tire. You can go to a source such as tirerack.com to get the full listing of what each letter represents. For our purposes, the most relevant codes are:

- S = 112 mph
- T = 116 mph
- U = 124 mph
- H = 130 mph
- V = 149 mph
- Z = in excess of 149 mph
- W = 168 mph
- Y = 186 mph

If a Y-rated tire, for instance, has been tested to have a rating "in excess of 186 mph," the service description is surrounded by parentheses such as "(88Y)."

Uniform Tire Quality Grading

The UTQG is generated from a federally mandated series of standardized tests and must be shown on the tire sidewall, as must the tire size and service description.

The UTQG is composed of three parts: a treadwear rating, a wet traction rating, and a temperature rating. An example is 300 A A; the "300" is treadwear, the first "A" is wet traction, and the second "A" is temperature.

Treadwear Rating

The treadwear rating is derived from actual on-road testing and is compared to the wear experienced

on a standard test tire. If the treadwear of the test tire was the same as that of the test tire it would score 100. If it lasted twice as long it would get a 200 rating, and so on.

Because there is some room for interpretation in how each tire manufacturer calculates this rating, it is most useful for comparing tires within the same brand. Small differences between brands may not really tell you much but a larger difference can still be used reliably between brands to determine which tire will last longer.

Wet Traction Rating

The wet traction rating is meant to approximate the coefficient of friction of the tire while braking on a wet surface. It really is related more to the compound of rubber used in the tread than anything else. The ratings range from the highest "AA," to "A," then "B," to a low of "C," which signifies the worst wet traction.

Temperature Rating

The temperature test is used to find the maximum speed a tire can be run before heat buildup leads to its failure. The ratings are: "A" (more than 115 mph), "B" (100 to 115 mph), and "C" (85 to 100 mph).

All new tires sold in the United States must be able to get at least a "C" rating. Anyone looking at running the car on a track (or in a high-speed on-road event such as the Silver State Classic) should definitely not use any tire with a rating less than "A."

INTERIOR

The inclusion of a chapter covering the vehicle interior may, at first blush, seem out of place in a book discussing performance upgrades. That is, of course, until you consider the single most important factor in the performance of the vehicle is the performance of the "nut behind the wheel," otherwise known as the driver. No matter how optimized a vehicle may be due to the parts and pieces used to upgrade it, performance isn't realized if the driver is not able to perform optimally and safely.

In this chapter I discuss how keeping the driver safe, stable, comfortable, and informed can allow the driver to consistently perform at a higher level and thus realize more of the vehicle's performance potential. I also include a few examples of things that, while not performance related in the speed/handling sense, can improve vehicle reliability, driver comfort/convenience, and/or provide a more unique performance and custom look.

Safety Considerations

Drivers do not perform at their best if they are concerned for their

A less-costly alternative to fabricating a roll bar is to purchase a pre-made bar such as this one from Autopower. This is their race style for a 1965–1966 fastback. It's made from 1.750 x .120-inch DOM steel and is not intended for use with a rear seat. The horizontal bar provides additional strength as well as a place for securing shoulder harnesses. Versions more suitable for street use omit the diagonal brace and also can be made with a removable horizontal bar so the rear seat can be used.

safety. I don't discuss safety measures needed for a racer car because they vary by sanctioning body. I do, however, describe a few things that can be done to increase safety and possibly provide improved performance.

Roll Bar

A roll bar must meet minimum requirements in terms of material, tube diameter, and wall thickness. There may be further requirements for the number and type of attach-ment points to the vehicle body and frame, the presence of specific bars and braces to better protect the driver (and/or provide for the proper mounting of safety harnesses), and whether or not padding is required on the bars adjacent to the driver.

Generally, the requirements are more stringent for the lower elapsed times (ET) of drag racing and other acceleration-based events. Similarly, this applies to higher speeds in other types of events.

Roll Bar Weight Offsets

If you plan on entering your vehicle in competitive events you may be required to have a minimum amount of safety equipment before you're allowed to compete. The most common of these requirements are a roll bar and/or safety harness. A roll bar adds weight but it can be mostly offset by these and other common adjustments:

- Temporarily remove other items (such as the spare tire, jacks, audio equipment, factory power seats, and even the rear seat) when actually running on the track.
- Permanently substitute lighter-weight materials such as aluminum, fiberglass, or carbon fiber for door panels, dash panels, exterior sheet metal, and add-ons such as spoilers and scoops.
- For more radical/dedicated vehicles that see minimal

use on the street you can also replace the windshield and other factory glass with Lexan to save a substantial amount of weight that's located higher up on the vehicle, thus lowering the center of gravity and improving the handling potential. Lexan, however, should not be used for vehicles stored outside, in direct sun, and/or in very dusty areas.

- Permanently remove factory front seats and substitute lighter-weight, supportive racing seats.
- Remove the rear seats and replace them with lightweight panels from the aftermarket or have them custom-made.
- You can also remove carpets, sound deadening, trim, and other items for an even greater reduction in weight, if you're willing to accept the tradeoffs (noise and heat) of doing so. ■

The main section of the bar goes in with minimal effort if all the seats are removed. Because this car doesn't have a rear seat anymore I just removed the fiberglass Shelby panel I had in its place. At this point you're just finding the proper location for the bar, marking where you need to drill, verifying where the carpet and pad need to be cut, and making sure the bar doesn't interfere with anything.

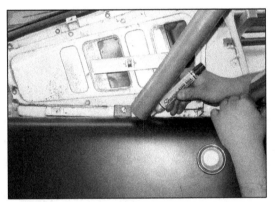

Once the main bar is bolted in place use a section of tubing to mark the area that needs to be cut to make room for the rear support bar on each side. A dark marker is a neat and easy way to do it because the thickness of the tip is just right for the amount of clearance you need around the bar. Use a straightedge to mark where the top will hit. You can temporarily install the rear support bars to act as a template for the drilling of the holes on the wheelwells for their bases.

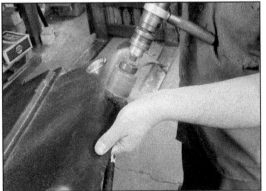

Mark the center of the circle you've made and use the appropriate size hole saw to cut the holes in the panels. It is generally better to do this outside the car not only to keep the shavings from getting all over the interior but also to provide the most accurate center mark and the best bracing for the panel while it's being cut. Be sure to cut the hole by holding the drill at a similar angle to what the bar is in the car. This requires care and slow cutting to avoid problems. Be sure to smooth and paint the finished holes.

Once the rear support bars and/or side panels are loosely put back in place install the wheelwell support plates from the other side. It may be necessary to bend the plates on both sides of the sheet metal to conform to the curvature of the wheelwells. Only three bolts are required, though a fourth can be installed for extra insurance. Then bolt the rear support bars to the main bar, prior to tightening them.

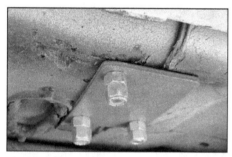

Use double locknuts at each location and save the floor plate bolts for last. They are the easiest to get at and are also the strongest. Don't overtighten them as all it does is warp the plates and/or the sheet metal between them. Because I don't have to worry about rain I didn't need to paint the plates. If that is a concern be sure to prime/paint or otherwise protect the metal support plates before final installation.

Fire Extinguisher

One requirement you can be sure of, even at most of the lower-speed/performance category events, is the need to have a fire extinguisher inside the vehicle. A racing-level,

The finished installation looks relatively clean with the rear tubes going neatly into the side panels and the floor plates covered by the carpet. I installed padding on the bars that pass near the occupant(s). This may not always be required but I decided to do it for the appearance and the extra safety. Zip ties work fine.

An easily accessible fire extinguisher of the proper type (ABC) was mounted on the Shelby panel between the front seats. It's a stable and convenient location when properly bolted down. Note the retainer and removal clip are made of metal rather than plastic. This is much safer and is required by most sanctioning bodies when running in a class where speeds are higher. Nobody wants a fire extinguisher (or anything else, for that matter) flying around in the car, during an accident or not.

dedicated, halon-type fire system may be required for some high-speed/performance categories but in most every other instance a simple handheld unit usually suffices. There may, however, be restrictions on the specific size and/or ratings of the extinguisher, as well as requirements relating to the type and location of its mounting.

For example, the extinguisher may need to be mounted within easy reach of the driver plus the mounting material must be made of metal (versus the more common and less costly plastic) and be securely attached to a rigid surface. The latter requirement ensures the extinguisher does not come loose, or lost, or become a potentially dangerous projectile in the event of a serious impact. In many instances, the need to remove all loose items from the interior of the vehicle and to ensure all allowed items (gauges, displays, GPS, and/or datalogging units, etc.) in the inte-

rior are securely mounted is enforced at tech inspection and often just before you are released to run.

Safety Harness

Another requirement for all but the lowest speeds (including most autocross events) and/or performance levels is the need to install safety harnesses. Factory three-point shoulder/lap belts may be good enough for local and federal authorities but they clearly are not adequate when speeds increase beyond those seen on public highways.

Safety harnesses that meet the requirements of sanctioning bodies and/or are certified to industry standards such as by SFI provide a substantially greater degree of protection than factory belts. They also help stabilize the driver by holding him or her in position under hard cornering, braking, etc. Safety harnesses distribute the forces more evenly over a larger area of the body, thus reducing the pressure at any given point, as well as the likelihood of injury.

Bottom line: Race drivers use safety harnesses to potentially help save their lives in an impact. Factory belts are designed more for convenience and low cost than for safety. Ironically, even though safety harnesses are far superior to factory belts when it comes to their level of protection they may not always be legal for street use; you need to check your local laws.

Drivers of older Mustangs are less likely to be cited for a belt infraction because there were less-stringent requirements at the time the vehicle was manufactured. Fully street-legal, DOT-certified, four-point safety harnesses are available, though they generally don't meet the requirements of most sanctioning bodies.

The criteria usually specified by the sanctioning bodies for safety harnesses are the width and number of the belts, the location of the mounting points, the type of release mechanism, and the level of certification. If you plan on running in specific events check to see what the requirements are before you buy. If you're going to use them only on the street or in events with minimal requirements, criteria such as cost, convenience, and appearance may be higher priorities.

A common requirement for many events is a 3-inch-wide belt and at least four mounting points (two for the lap belts and two for the shoulder belts). In some situations, a three-point mounting system that uses a Y-shaped shoulder belt (shoulder belts have a common mounting point) may be allowed. This is convenient if you still plan on using your back seat but it usually results in a belt geometry that isn't as safe

The installation of the race roll bar with a horizontal bar allows the use of proper shoulder harnesses for safety and to meet the requirements of many sanctioning bodies when racing. The Autopower harnesses are the simple wrap-around style, which offer the most flexibility. These Procar seats already had openings for them. They can also be used with most stock seats because they can be draped over the top of low-back seats, around the sides of some high-backed designs, and even around/under the headrests on seats that have them. Proper shoulder belts are critical for safety and driver stability.

as a proper, four-point mounting strategy.

Whenever safety harnesses are specified there is inevitably also a requirement for a single-point release mechanism. This can be a rotary or latch type, though the specific type is usually not specified.

The rotary type is generally more user-friendly for street-driven vehicles because the latch type requires some instruction prior to use. This is especially true when five- or six-point "anti-submarining" straps are specified.

These lower straps are generally not needed at lower speeds but when they are, they also require some form of pass-through provision in the seat

to function properly. Just draping them over the lower seat cushion really doesn't get the job done and is rarely accepted at tech. They can be inconvenient on the street so it's best to remove the lower belt(s) for street use and reinstall it as needed.

Meeting the requirements for certification and/or legality is simply a matter of comparing the certification level of the safety harnesses to the requirements of the sanctioning bodies and/or your local vehicle codes. As speeds and performance increase so do the requirements for the belts. Most of these additional requirements are only relevant for track use, though they can provide additional protection in street use, when practical.

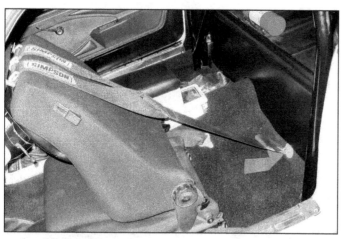

Some vehicles may not lend themselves to the installation of a roll bar or you may simply not want one. In these cases, you can still use shoulder belts but you have to find another location to securely mount them. This is a floor-mount location using eye bolts, locknuts, and mounting plates specially designed for this purpose.

This required using a Y-style shoulder harness (one mounting point for both straps instead of one for each strap) and a less-than-optimal mounting point. Ideally, the shoulder straps should be parallel with the floorpan. This strap is mounted low and the angle of the strap is steep. This is not as safe or effective as the desired mounting method plus it is less likely to be accepted for racing.

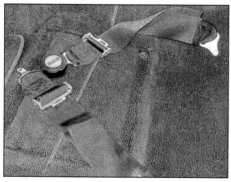

Lap belts can usually be mounted using the factory seat-belt mounts. These are already reinforced to take the high loads and are generally positioned so that the angle of the lap belts is correct. If this is not the case (or if for some reason your car is missing them) you have to get patch panels or use different mounts. Because the belts are different for each side (driver and passenger) the common practice is to have the belt with the latch toward the inside of the car and the other belts closer to the door.

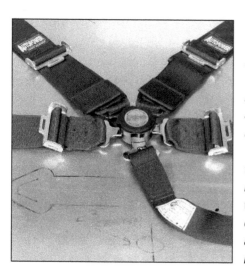

This Autopower safety harness set uses a Pro-Cam rotary latching mechanism. This is generally easier to use (only 1/4 turn to unlock) and less bulky than older latches. They use 3-inch webbing for the four main belts and 2-inch webbing for the crotch belt. They meet SFI spec 16.1 and, because they're made in the United States, it's much easier to have them recertified when needed. This can be after a collision but also when the belts reach a specific age (threads, etc., must be replaced to stay in spec).

Beyond the criteria and specifications already discussed there may be additional requirements for fire resistance (the need for protective coverings, for example), longevity, and/or the use of additional equipment such as a HANS (head and neck system) restraint device. The latter works with the safety harnesses to prevent excessive movement of the head during an impact, thus reducing the likelihood of certain injuries.

Safety harnesses should be checked at specific intervals to

Whenever securing safety harnesses the proper mounts must be used. This example shows how the reinforcement plates are a larger diameter than a standard washer so as to spread the load over a larger area of sheet metal. They are also thicker and made from a specific material. Perhaps more important is the fact that the diameter of the bolthole is precisely matched to the eye bolt so there's minimal play and maximum contact between the plate and the shoulder of the eye bolt (as well as the lock washer on the opposite side). In a collision the forces on these parts are extremely high; proper alignment, engagement and materials are critical to preventing the mounts from failing and/or pulling through. Also, the eye bolt is positioned vertically so the mounting clip is perpendicular to it. You always want the webbing of the harness to be at a right angle to the mount.

ensure they're still compliant with the applicable standards. The belt materials and stitching deteriorate over time so the harnesses may need to be recertified to remain compliant. Many sanctioning bodies require this.

If the harnesses are made in the United States (such as those from Autopower Industries) it's simply a matter of sending them back to the manufacturer where they are disassembled and re-stitched to regain compliance. Tags sewn onto the harnesses indicate this status.

Seats and Pedals

The best roll bars and safety harnesses don't do much to protect you if you're not sitting in a good enough seat. One thing is abundantly clear: Original early Mustang seats are not good enough for any kind of hard driving, let alone racing. Nor were they ever intended to be. Let's face it, they're more about style and form than function. Even as a seat for a cruiser they leave much to be desired.

For the most part, OEMs are more-or-less flat and thus offer virtually no side support while cornering. They're generally covered in shiny, slippery vinyl to match the rest of the interior, and in many cases, their seatbacks lack a sufficient latching mechanism to prevent the seat from moving forward in a collision. Furthermore, the matter of the structural integrity of the seat is an area where factory seats fall far short of what's needed for safety.

The installation of an upgraded seat necessarily starts with the foundation it's mounted on. The aftermarket and motorsports industries have generally settled on a univer-

sal mounting system for racing-style seats. Most seat manufacturers and others offer the appropriate brackets for installation.

Their construction is fairly simple yet they're strong and able to accept many different types of seats.

Fixed-Back Seats

Professional racers almost always use stationary fixed-back seats with integral custom aluminum mounting brackets that bolt directly to the floor. This setup is fine for racing but not comfortable in normal driving because it can't accommodate heavier, reclining seats and/or those with fore/aft sliders.

Reclining Seats

Many owners want seats for use on the street that are also capable of

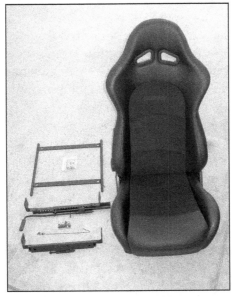

This is a Procar Sportsman Pro model. It is very much like a full-race seat in overall design, yet it reclines (for maximum comfort and support), can be tilted forward (to allow passengers to more easily get into the rear seats), and has a dual sliding mechanism to allow it to be properly positioned in terms of leg room.

meeting the requirements specified by the sanctioning bodies of most amateur-level events. These seats have movable and/or reclining backs as well as the ability to slide forward and back to help properly locate different-size drivers and passengers relative to the pedals, gauges, steering column, steering wheel, etc. There's no shortage of options for this type of seat, especially for Mustangs.

Procar, for example, makes an extra effort to offer seats tailored to them. Some of their seats emphasize the characteristics needed for aggressive driving; others stress comfort and appearance for street and cruise use. All are built with a strong steel frame and have a positive seatback latching mechanism. These seats are lighter, stronger, and safer when compared to most stock seats.

Another option emphasizes function over form. It is the best type to use if you plan on doing a lot of aggressive driving and/or entering a lot of events. The Sportsman Pro, for example, is a modern-looking seat that does not exactly match the original interior of an early Mustang yet it is right at home in one that has been customized to some degree.

This seat has a very fine resolution reclining mechanism, which helps in finding the optimal seatback angle; it's better than seats that have only a few discrete steps. The side and shoulder bolsters are aggressive for better driver stabilization yet not to the point of being uncomfortable on longer drives. The seat also has provisions for the pass-through of shoulder harnesses but not for the lower belt.

With its smooth fiberglass back this is one of the lighter options that still reclines. Numerous color and material combinations are available to suit virtually any need.

If you want comfort with a more classic/vintage look you can opt for the Procar Rally seat. It is very similar to the Elite Lumbar seat except for the lack of a lumbar support and the clearly different styling. The material choices and colors are also a bit more limited but the most common colors for early Mustangs are available. There are multiple patterns (smooth versus fully pleated, etc.) in addition to the slightly more aggressive bolsters, which provides a bit more support compared to the Elite Lumbar seat. They're also lighter than the Elite Lumbar at a mere 28 pounds. (Photo Courtesy Procar)

Cruising Seats

If you want more of a cruising seat and are willing to give up the classic look for greater functionality you should consider a cruising type of seat. The Procar Elite Lumbar, for example, is wider and has less-aggressive bolstering for greater comfort plus it has an adjustable headrest and a manual lumbar adjustment to provide additional support. A headrest is included, again mainly for comfort, but it also adds more safety relative to the low back seats many early Mustangs were originally equipped with. Shoulder harnesses

If you are more concerned with appearance than lateral support, Procar offers their Classic seat. It is styled in a manner much more reminiscent of the original factory seats of early Mustangs yet it has the benefits of superior construction, materials, and functionality. They are more comfortable and offer more support than the factory seats (especially with a cloth covering). This seat is available as a mid-back design with a headrest and a low-back design without one. (Photo Courtesy Procar)

can still be used because they generally straddle the head support and lay on the top of the seat.

These seats feature dual sliders and infinite recline with various color and material combinations including cloth and vinyl. They weigh 32 pounds each.

If you want a more classic look while still retaining somewhat aggressive bolstering you can opt for a seat similar to the Procar Rally series. These have a traditional look and are a bit wider than performance-oriented seats for greater comfort. These seats are available in high-back versions with headrest or low-backs in cloth, vinyl, or leather.

Or you may want a traditional type of seat that emphasizes appearance over function but still performs better than a stock seat due to its strength and reclining mechanism. Bolstering is a bit more aggressive than stock so there should be a slight improvement in driver stability. The

positive latching seatback also adds stability and safety.

An example is the Procar Classic Like the Procar Rally series this seat is available in various colors of vinyl and cloth plus black leather. There are also two seat-back configurations (high or low).

In order to provide a more coordinated appearance for some early Mustangs many manufacturers, such as Procar, offer custom rear seat covers. They are made from the same fabrics, patterns, and colors used in their Rally and Elite series of seats. These perfectly match the front seats and are custom tailored to be a direct fit.

Dead Pedal

Even with a stable, grippy seat and a tight set of safety harnesses there can still be a need for additional support when cornering or stopping hard. An excellent solution in these situations is to install a "dead pedal" to brace yourself against.

Many newer vehicles come with them from the factory, especially

One feature on many newer sports cars that's sorely lacking from early Mustangs is a dead pedal. Aftermarket versions such as this Lokar product can make a significant difference in the driver's ability to remain stable while also being aesthetically pleasing. This custom-billet dead pedal matches the easily installed Lokar pedal set.

The installation of a Lokar pedal set is a vast improvement over the factory pedals in terms of both aesthetics and functionality. The rubber inserts prevent slippage while the adjustability of the throttle pedal allows perfect positioning. The Lokar throttle-pedal assembly is an excellent upgrade for stock linkage. It is adjustable so you can set the throttle pedal at the optimum angle for heel-and-toe operation of the throttle and brake pedal.

sporty cars with manual transmissions. They are normally custom fabricated for race cars and the same can be done for your pony car though it's often easier to find a universal aftermarket product that works. One example is Lokar's direct-fit throttle pedal in a finish that matches the other pedals.

The aluminum Lokar throttle is CNC machined to have a "billet" look to it. It's also designed with Delrin bushings and other features to provide a very smooth response to pedal pressure, thus allowing better modulation of the engine's speed and power.

When used with the Lokar Teflon-lined throttle cables to completely eliminate the hard,

mechanical linkage from the factory you get a buttery-smooth movement that requires no maintenance and lasts indefinitely. The flexibility of a cable linkage is especially valuable when converting to EFI from carburetion.

A cable kit makes the installation of a late-model AOD transmission into your early Mustang quite a bit easier. The throttle-pedal kit also includes additional reinforcement for the pedal mount, further enhancing stability and precision. The Lokar kit parts have a cleaner appearance than the stock pedals. They also have grippy rubber inserts to help prevent your foot from sliding off under heavy pressure.

Tilt Steering Column and Steering Wheel

Performance gains can be realized through proper, stable placement of the driver and by ensuring optimal placement of controls relative to the driver. Pedal placement is not easily changed in an early Mustang so you must use seat travel to find a good position. This leaves the location of the steering wheel as a major issue. The best solution is an adjustable tilt-steering column and an upgraded steering wheel, which provide other benefits as well.

The 1964½–1966 early cars used a single, solid steering shaft that arguably represents the worst-case scenario for this upgrade but many products are available to overcome the challenges.

For example, the Ididit column's design is such that it doesn't look out of place in a Mustang. It is offered in three finishes (bare/paintable steel, chrome, and black powdercoat) and in configurations for vehicles with

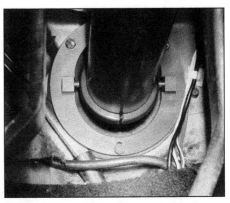

Because I had already installed a Total Control rack-and-pinion steering kit on my car I decided to stay with the lower steering column mount that came with it. For most tilt-column installations, however, you use the lower mount supplied with it. Little force is applied to the lower mount; the upper mount under the dash does most of the work to support the steering column. The lower mount serves more to keep the end of the column properly located to minimize possible binding. It also provides a seal from the elements.

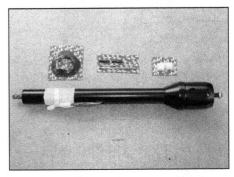

The tilt steering column from Ididit comes with everything you need for installation. Important items to consider are what finish you want (bare, black, or chrome) and what type of shaft connection you need. Their kits generally include the necessary wiring and connectors, new levers and knobs, and a new lower mount and seal. You use the factory underdash mount. Sometimes, other modifications may be needed.

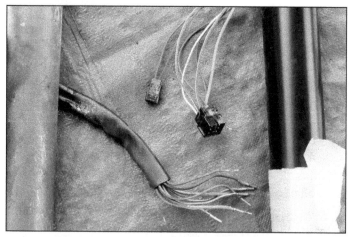

Remove the wires from the original connector with an appropriate terminal removal tool and replace them with the appropriate wires from the Ididit column. There may be variations in the color codes so use a factory wiring diagram. It's usually preferable to retain the factory electrical connectors (whenever possible) to minimize the work involved and for easier reference when using a service manual.

The Grant wheel is smaller in diameter for quicker response yet it doesn't obscure the gauges to any significant degree plus it feels solid when turning. The rim is thicker, padded, and covered with perforated leather (shown) or a similarly grippy synthetic. It also features recesses for your thumbs at the 3:00 and 9:00 positions.

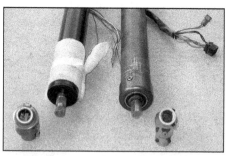

The shaft and coupling on the left are generally used when an aftermarket rack-and-pinion steering conversion has been performed. The coupling connects to a short intermediate shaft, which then connects to the steering rack via yet another coupling. U-joints are the preferred type of coupling for precise feedback but couplings with rubber isolation and even rag joints can be used in some applications.

The Double D connection on the right is commonly used when connecting to a factory steering box. It simply connects to the cut, shortened steering column on one side and the similar factory steering shaft on the other side.

The couplings and U-joints simply slide onto their respective shafts; no lubrication is needed. Take care to ensure the shafts don't protrude too far into the coupling or binding may occur. The final placement of the couplings must ensure there's sufficient engagement of the splines and/or shafts while still allowing free movement/rotation of the steering wheel. Clearance with headers, shift linkages, and other nearby components must all be considered to avoid interference, binding, and/or damage from heat.

stock steering or rack-and-pinion conversions. Ididt made the various knobs and handles on the column mimic the design of those found on the factory column. The column also has a Ford top shaft and turn-signal mechanism so original that Ford and aftermarket steering wheels can be used. There are also provisions for retaining the original factory wiring while adding a desirable four-way flasher capability for emergency use.

The Ididit column also uses the stock underdash coupler along with a special floor mount to simplify installation. The most difficult aspect of the installation usually ends up being the modifications that must be made to the stock steering shaft. Depending on your situation and intended use there are different couplings and U-joints that may be used. Those who have already converted to rack-and-pinion steering usually have the easiest time of it because Ididit offers kits designed to mate up directly to most popular systems. If you install one of these columns you benefit from eight possible tilt positions and self-canceling turn signals.

The factory steering wheels on early Mustangs were large in diameter, thin, hard, and slippery—not ideal characteristics for performance. Grant Products, for example, offers many different wheel styles, diameters, and materials. They also offer the ability to add your own personal touch with unique finishes, horn buttons, etc. Their higher-end Corsa GT wheel is a good upgrade choice. It is a 13¾-inch-diameter leather wheel that includes thumb notches and other features meant to maximize grip.

Gauges

For a daily driver or street-performance car that only sees occasional track use, a bundled package such as the Sunpro Super Tach III Value Pack

For a nostalgic look the classic styling of this Sun Super Tach III is a good choice. This tach is very reasonably priced, has a programmable shift light, is very easy to mount/install, and provides more than sufficient accuracy and RPM range. You can mount the tach in a very visible position, directly in front of the driver (shown), where it is low on the windshield so it doesn't block the view or create a distraction when illuminated at night. Having a shift light makes this all the more possible because the shift light going on can still be seen by peripheral vision, thus reducing the need for a higher mounting spot.

can be a good choice. It is classically styled to be right at home in your early Mustang. It includes a three-gauge panel with a voltmeter, oil pressure gauge, and water/oil temperature gauge. It also has a 10,000-rpm tach with a programmable (and visible) shift light that can be mounted with a hose clamp on the steering column for a classic hot rod look.

Mounting Positions

In situations where the tach requires constant monitoring and/or no shift light is used it is best to mount the tach as high as possible on the dash and in the driver's line of sight. If you have a 1964½–1966 model and don't want to alter the dash pad an attractive solution is to use a Shelby-style center gauge pod. It can hold a tach and another gauge in a highly visible location, which requires minimal diversion of the driver's eyes. There's also room for a toggle switch or two.

In the case of a daily driver where you may only want a few gauges to supplement and/or verify the factory gauges, it's most common to use a small setup similar to this three-gauge set from Sunpro. You can choose which parameters to monitor, what gauge face look you want, and also how rugged and/or accurate you want the gauges to be by choosing from the offerings of the various gauge manufacturers.

The importance of having the tach readily visible is also demonstrated in this Shelby gauge pod for 1965/1966 models. The older-style LED air/fuel gauge is a relatively coarse indicator and thus was put here as well. In this instance

it is being used solely to verify both oxygen sensors are sufficiently active and responsive. This is done by using the toggle switch to go from reading the left bank to the right bank. A more-precise digital and LED air/fuel gauge is mounted on the dash to provide a more-exact, averaged air/fuel ratio as determined from its sampling location in the junction of the X-pipe.

The pod can be attached with Velcro (or similar) or by a more permanent means, which, though invisible, may harm the dash.

Common mounting positions for less-critical gauges that do not require frequent monitoring are under the dash or on the transmission tunnel. How you mount them is more a matter of aesthetics than anything else. A simple screw-on or bolt-on, three-hole, mounting panel is generally sufficient.

Custom Gauge Pods

If you want something more stylish you can turn to custom gauge pods designed for particular vehicles. The most common of these mount to the driver-side A-pillar and have up to four mounting holes. They're usually made of black plastic, which can be painted or covered to match the interior. Another option is to mount the gauges in the location of deleted components (such as the radio or vents) for a less-cluttered appearance while providing capacity for more gauges.

Such options are available from gauge manufacturers and others (such as Mustangs Plus) that specialize in performance parts for early Mustangs. Several manufacturers offer complete dash kits that replace the factory gauges. This provides the additional accuracy, precision, and visibility inherent to most aftermarket gauges plus it provides greater flexibility in the choice of gauges. Many displays feature brighter LED turn signal and high-beam indicators, which last much longer. Some use different colors and/or digital gauges.

Data Acquisition

As you go to more and more track events it becomes appropriate to consider using a system to provide data on various vehicle parameters and assist with tuning for the best performance. Just about any vehicle parameter (RPM, boost, steering angle, throttle percent, wheel travel, etc.) can be sensed, especially when you use newer powertrains with their own electronic controllers. These parameters can also be synchronized with video and GPS inputs to allow subsequent evaluation on a computer to help identify potential areas for improvement. A data-acquisition system can be permanently installed or, in most cases, be largely removable to allow for daily street use of the vehicle.

The best systems allow you to replay, lap by lap, an event by watching a video showing the view of the track (and whatever else you may want to monitor) while also having the data and a graphic showing track position displayed in real time. This provides invaluable data for changing vehicle setups and/or driver style. The data can also be archived for subsequent viewing.

You can compare individual laps by laying them over each other to see where time is gained or lost. Segments of laps can be examined in detail to determine where improvements may be possible. Specific parameters (such as speed and acceleration) can be monitored to see if a given change has had an effect. The data can be synched with video so you can compare subjective observations with objective data. There really is almost no limit to how such datalogging capability can be used to gain a benefit.

Even when used to collect data for relatively simple tests (such as 0-60 acceleration, 60-0 braking, etc.), the improvement in the accuracy, precision, and repeatability of the data can easily justify the cost. Such systems continue to come down in price as features, memory, and the ability to interface with other devices such as video cameras and smartphones rapidly improves. Logging valid, accurate, repeatable data keeps getting easier, less expensive, and more valuable.

Many companies offer complete replacements for the factory instrument panel. This setup from Haneline Products replaces the factory gauges and even uses LEDs for the turn indicators and high-beam light. Variations include different combinations of gauges and/or gauge faces, changes to the number of gauges, insert finish (engine turned as shown here, camera case, woodgrain, etc.), plus completely custom setups where everything is open to your specification.

ELECTRICAL SYSTEM

The electrical system in a first-generation Mustang is one of the areas that needs to be upgraded in a high-performance car. The original systems were very basic with little capacity for extra equipment. This isn't surprising when you consider there was little more than a very simple radio, some lights, a horn, and only some of the bare-bones basics found on modern vehicles. There often were no power locks or windows, no rear defroster, no A/C, no power seats, and certainly no navigation, bluetooth, electronic fuel injection (EFI) or other things that are ubiquitous in newer Mustangs.

Should you decide to add EFI, a high-powered ignition, electric cooling fans, power windows/locks, an upgraded audio system, and so forth you very quickly become aware of the limitations of the stock system. Fortunately, you have numerous ways to add functionality and improve performance. You must take care of the basics in terms of having good grounds, no short or open circuits, etc. The rest of the electrical system (wiring, connectors, terminals, grommets, and so forth) must be in good shape. There's no point in putting in better equipment if the rest

of the vehicle is not up to par. Do a complete assessment of the electrical system and make repairs as indicated by the factory service manual before you make any modifications. This will surely save you trouble later.

High-Output Alternator

Having a more stable voltage level can be an absolute necessity if you convert to EFI. Even with just a higher-power ignition you can see significant performance improve-

ments due to less misfire and a hotter spark (see Chapter 4). Power locks and windows become a more reasonable possibility with a better alternator. This provides added functionality and convenience with a negligible weight gain plus it can also improve personal security.

Modern alternators not only can offer higher total output but they also can offer substantially higher output at idle speed. This is especially critical when you have high-current modifications such as an electric cooling

One example of a cost-effective way to upgrade your original alternator is this PowerStar model made for Painless Performance by Powermaster. It's a direct bolt-in for the factory part yet has much higher output, especially at lower RPM where you need it the most if you add things such as an electric cooling fan. The single-wire design of the PowerStar alternator along with its internal voltage regulator may require some minor adaptations. If you use the single-wire feature (the alternator automatically activates above a given RPM), life is simple: just run a suitable wire from the alternator output to the battery. It also allows you to adjust the output voltage and has a V-belt pulley for compatibility (serpentine is also available).

fan, upgraded headlamps, driving/fog lamps, air conditioning, and/or a high-output audio system. Modern alternators can have better output and be far more reliable, smaller, and lighter for the same or an even higher output.

Many are much easier to install and present a cleaner underhood appearance because they have internal voltage regulators and thus can use fewer wires. Some even allow you to manually adjust the output voltage to improve performance under certain conditions.

Special alternators intended primarily for racing use are available to handle sustained and/or extremely high RPM. These may be appropriate and even necessary but they're not the best choice for a street car in terms of durability and resistance to weather. They tend to not have particularly high output, especially at lower engine RPM. Those intended for endurance races can be an exception but they tend to be pricey. Aftermarket companies (such as Painless Performance, Powermaster Motorsports, and others) have better options available for Mustangs in terms of price, performance, appearance, and so forth.

The PowerStar high-output alternator made by Painless Performance, for example, has very high output (92 amps) at idle and a significantly higher (113 amp) total output. It bolts right in to most first-generation Mustang engine compartments and may only require some minor modification of the wiring harness due to its internal regulator and single-wire configuration. It also has significantly upgraded materials and components so it's well suited for high-performance use yet is still able to handle street use and achieve excellent durability. This model also

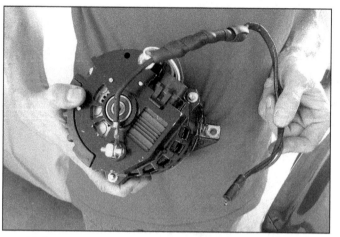

Upgrading the forward lighting is simple, yet tremendously effective. Much higher output headlamps with vastly improved optics/lenses that are direct replacements for the original sealed-beam units are readily available.

Units such as these from Hella look very much like the original lamps yet function much, much better. Due to their generally higher current draw, however, such lamps usually require minor modification of the wiring harness.

These vehicles also features high-output halogen driving lamps instead of the factory fog lamps. These lamps (also by Hella) provide a very narrow beam over a much longer distance to dramatically improve visibility when driving at higher speeds at night. These also require some minor modification to the wiring but they come with a dedicated harness to simplify the task.

has the capability to manually adjust the output voltage. Painless has many color choices, other models with significantly higher total outputs (up to 200 amps!), and v-belt or serpentine drive pulleys.

Headlamps

Upgrading your headlamps is a performance enhancement and a safety improvement as a result of the superior visibility it provides.

The sealed-beam headlamps that came with first-generation Mustangs were state-of-the-art technology in their day but things have improved significantly since then. Modern vehicles now generally rely on removable halogen or xenon/HID bulb "capsules" that are inserted into fixed reflector assemblies that are an integral part of each new vehicle's styling. LED technology has just begun to be utilized for daytime running lights and, at the time this

book was written, have just begun to be used for headlamp applications.

Fortunately, owners of early Mustangs can benefit from this constant evolution of technology as these newer technologies become less expensive, thus allowing the aftermarket to develop products that retrofit to older cars. The prime example of this is the ability to convert the original sealed-beam headlamps on your Mustang to halogen technology. Several aftermarket and OEM suppliers offer simple, direct-replacement products that allow you to remove older lamps and replace them with better-performing lamps.

In most cases, the new lamps even utilize the same type of electrical connectors as the original lamps so there's no need to modify the wiring. However, in cases where the current draw of the new lamps is significantly higher than that of the original lamps it is advisable to

These Hella replacement headlamps install directly in place of the original sealed beam units with no modification other than possibly the installation of relays in the wiring harness if their wattage rating is substantially higher than stock. These lamps provide much more light, which is also of a more natural, whiter color than stock so visibility is further improved. The lens also features a European-style, sharper cutoff to the lighting pattern, which helps to avoid glare for approaching drivers. These lamps use replaceable H4 bulb capsules, which allow you to only replace the bulb.

When installing upgraded higher-output lighting in an older vehicle it is often necessary to upgrade the wiring harness as well because the stock harness can't safely provide enough current for the new, higher-wattage lamps. Fortunately, several companies (such as Painless Performance Products, Mustang Project, and others) offer ready-made kits specifically for this purpose. These usually include relays and a special harness that plugs right into the original factory harness and connects directly to the new lamps (which have the same terminals as the factory lamps). You then run wires directly to the battery and to a good ground. This basically turns the factory wiring circuit into a switching-only circuit because the current for the lamps is now provided directly from the battery over new circuits with upgraded wiring. Even if you don't upgrade your headlamps, installing a relay system like this can greatly improve the performance of your original sealed beams because it ensures greater current and higher voltage at the lamps while also minimizing the effects of corroded terminals, small-diameter wires, etc., that may increase circuit resistance. (Photo Courtesy Painless Performance Products)

modify the factory wiring to incorporate relays to provide better performance and less chance of problems. Several manufacturers offer special harness kits specifically for this.

Halogen lights coupled with improved lens and reflector technology provide greatly improved visibility versus the original sealed-beam headlamps as well as a cooler, bluer light. The latter helps drivers see roadside features such as signs more easily while also giving the older

vehicle a "newer" look. The ability to simply remove and replace the bulb capsule is a further advantage versus having to replace the entire lamp assembly as with a sealed-beam unit.

It's unlikely there will ever be many products for early Mustangs that use xenon/HID technology. This is due primarily to their high cost and the need to have specially shaped reflector assemblies that do not lend themselves to being aesthetically integrated into the styl-

ing of older vehicles. This is of little concern, however, because there are already LED-based solutions available for these cars, which provide an even lower current draw than the xenon/HID lamps (which is less than halogens) without the need for the expensive electronics required by xenon/HID lamps.

These LED headlamps are simple direct-replacement parts just like halogen units yet they draw significantly less current, last even longer (almost

Here is an example of LED lighting modules applied to the instrument panel. The light can be considerably brighter than incandescent bulbs provide while still capable of being dimmed as desired. LED modules should never have to be replaced once they're installed plus they also use less electricity even at much brighter settings.

LED lights provide far greater illumination than typical halogens. These lamps are a direct replacement (notice the wiring pigtail and connector with matching terminals), although they are relatively pricey. That should change over time, however, as LED headlamps become more common. Still, these lamps last about 50 times longer and also draw much less current (4.5-amp high beam, 2.5-amp low beam) compared to conventional lamps. These lamps are DOT approved so they are fully street legal in the United States. (Photo Courtesy Mustang Project)

indefinitely), provide an even whiter (more natural color) light, and are very cost effective once you consider they can use the factory wiring without the need for relays, etc. Although they may not yet have as much maximum light output as the xenon/HID lamp this will surely change with time. They are, after all, available now at a significantly lower cost.

They outperform and last longer than halogens plus they are easier to install than the HIDs; they install just like the original lamps. LED headlamps do, however, have a higher initial cost and a unique appearance, which may not appeal to everyone.

Other LED Upgrades

You can improve safety and visibility even if you decide not to upgrade your alternator through the use of LED technology to replace some of your regular light bulbs.

LED lighting technology offers many advantages, including brighter/whiter light, longer life, lower current draw, better visibility, and unique styling, when compared to regular incandescent lights. In most cases the upgrade to LEDs involve little more than removing the original bulb and replacing it with the appropriate LED module. Some applications require the replacement and/or installation of other components (such as the flasher) but there is no need to install relays or modify the wiring because of their lower current draw. Once the LEDs illuminate there's little doubt something's been changed due to the unique light signature,

greatly increased brightness, different temperature, and even color, if desired. The instrument panel is a prime example of where the almost-infinite life of LEDs is a particular asset because replacing those bulbs is not generally an easy job.

Rear backup lamps, front turn signals, and parking lamps are among the popular upgrades. In addition, the license plate light, side-marker lights, and even hood-mounted turn signal lights can be upgraded.

The single most popular LED upgrade is the taillamps. LED technology provides improved brightness, visibility, longer life, added functionality (such as sequential strobing), and/or a different-color light for a unique look. Furthermore, little attention is given to the very real safety benefit LED taillamps provide due to the quicker response time. Because LEDs are brighter and look different, plus they also light up quicker and have the ability to flash sequentially, they tend to get the attention of a following driver sooner and more completely, thus providing more time to slow down or stop.

The rear backup lamps on these cars are, to say the least, not very effective in illuminating what's behind the car. Higher-output LED modules provide much more light output while using less electricity. They're less affected by deterioration in the wiring plus they last indefinitely. They cost more but they're a one-time purchase and they provide a unique appearance to go along with their greatly improved performance.

Various kits, such as this one made by Mustang Project, include LED lamp modules, new gaskets, and the necessary longer screws needed for proper installation. The LED module is wired into a base that plugs right into the factory bulb socket for very easy installation.

An even simpler way to upgrade your backup lamps is to just install LED replacement "bulb" modules rather than these modules. They won't have quite as much light output or the high-tech look but they are less expensive. (Photo Courtesy Mustang Project)

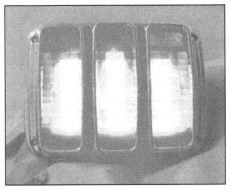

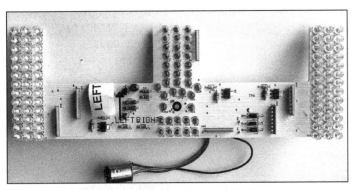

Custom LED strips can be used for a CHMSL (center high mounted stop lamp, or "third brake light") in an older vehicle. This gives your car a more modern/custom appearance plus it can improve safety by making your brake lights more visible (especially in close traffic) and by lighting faster than regular bulbs (giving the driver behind you more time to brake).

If you want to make an even more bold statement at the back of your Mustang there is the option of upgrading to LED taillamps. These LEDs provide all of the normal functions (brake lights, taillights, and turn signals) plus they produce a strobe effect where the individual lamp segments light sequentially when the turn signals are operated. This kit from Mustang Project is about five times brighter than stock bulbs.

This vehicle clearly shows the benefit of adding LED technology to your older car. The LED taillamps are much more visible than would be the case with the stock bulbs plus the added LED CHMSL further enhances safety and visibility while also providing a unique styling element. Because the LEDs last almost indefinitely there is no issue installing them in a location that can't be easily serviced in the future.

SOURCE GUIDE

Abaco Performance
P.O. Box 638
Clinton, IL 61727
877-693-9269
abacoperformance.com

Accusump
232 Branford Rd.
North Branford, CT 06471
203-481-9460
accusump.com

Advanced Clutch Technology
206 E. Ave. K-4
Lancaster, CA 93535
661-940-7555
advancedclutch.com

AEM Performance Electronics
2205 W. 126th St., Unit A
Hawthorne, CA 90250
310-484-2322
aemelectronics.com

Aeromotive Inc.
7805 Barton St.
Lenexa, KS 66214
913-647-7300
aeromotiveinc.com

Air Flow Research
28611 W. Industry Dr.
Valencia, CA 91355
877-892-8844
airflowresearch.com

Agent 47
2221 Rutherford Rd.
Carlsbad, CA 92008
760-496-3809
agentfortyseven.com

American Powertrain
2199 Summerfield Rd.
Cookeville, TN 38501
931-646-4836
americanpowertrain.com

ARP
1863 Eastman Ave.
Ventura, CA 93003
800-826-3045
arp-bolts.com

Astro Performance Warehouse
601 E. Alfred St.
Tavares, FL 32778
866-253-0019
astroperformance.com

Autopower Industries
3424 Pickett St.
San Diego, CA 92110
619-297-3300
autopowerindustries.com

B&M Racing
100 Stony Point Rd., Ste. 125
Santa Rosa, CA 95401
707-544-4761
bmracing.com

Baer Racing
2222 W. Peoria Ave., Ste. B
Phoenix, AZ 85029
602-233-1411
baer.com

Barillo Speed Emporium
10523 Kingston Pike, Ste. E
Knoxville, TN 37922
865-531-1840
barillarospeed.net

Be Cool
310 Woodside Ave.
Essexville, MI 48732
800-691-2667
becool.com

Borgeson Universal
91 Technology Park Dr.
Torrington, CT 06790
860-482-8283
borgeson.com

Bosch Auto Parts
2800 S. 25th Ave.
Broadview, IL 60155
888-715-3616
boschautoparts.com

Bruce Couture's Modern
 Driveline
25308 Arroyo Ct.
Caldwell, ID 83607
208-453-9800
moderndriveline.com

Canton Racing Products
232 Branford Rd.
North Branford, CT 06471
203-481-9460
cantonracingproducts.com

Classic Tube
80 Rotech Dr.
Lancaster, NY 14086
800-882-3711
classictube.com

Coast High Performance
2555 W. 237th St.
Torrance, CA 90505
310-784-1010
coasthigh.com

Cometic Gasket
8090 Auburn Rd.
Concord, OH 44077
800-752-9850
cometic.com

Comp Cams
3406 Democrat Rd.
Memphis, TN 38118
800-999-0853
compcams.com

Crane Cams
1830 Holsonback Dr.
Daytona Beach, FL 32117
866-388-5120
cranecams.com

Currie Enterprises
382 N. Smith
Corona, CA 92880
714-528-6957
currieenterprises.com

Dart Machine
353 Oliver St.
Troy, MI 48084
248-362-1188
dartheads.com

Detroit Speed
185 McKenzie Rd.
Mooresville, NC 28115
704-662-3272
detroitspeed.com

Doug's Headers
440 E. Arrow Hwy.
San Dimas, CA 91773
909-599-5955
pertronix.com

Drake Automotive Group
130 Cassia Way
Henderson, NV 89014
702-853-2060
drakeautomotivegroup.com

Eastwood
263 Shoemaker Rd.
Pottstown, PA 19464
800-343-9353
eastwood.com

Eaton
70 Sir John Rogerson's Quay
Dublin 2, Ireland
800-386-1911
eaton.com

Eddie Motorsports
11479 6th St.
Rancho Cucamonga, CA 91730
888-813-1293
eddiemotorsports.com

Edelbrock
2700 California St.
Torrance, CA 90503
310-781-2222
edelbrock.com

Energy Suspension
1131 Via Callejon
San Clemente, CA 92673
888-913-6374
energysuspension.com

Extrude Hone
8800 Somerset Blvd.
Paramount, CA 90723
562-531-2976
extrudehoneafm.com

Ford Racing Performance Parts
1 American Rd.
Dearborn, MI 48126
800-367-3788
fordracingparts.com

Fuelab
826-A Morton Ct.
Litchfield, IL 62056
217-324-3737
fuelab.com

G-Force Transmissions
150 N. Grant St.
Cleona, PA 17042
717-202-8367
gforcetransmissions.com

Gano Auto Filter Coolant
P.O. Box 1502
Carmel Valley, CA 93924
831-659-1961
ganofilters.com

Gateway Performance
 Suspension
10461 N. Service Rd.
Bourbon, MO 65441
866-805-1878
gatewayperformancesuspension.
com

Genisys
755 Eisenhower Dr.
Owatonna, MN 55060
800-533-6127
genisysotc.com

Global West Suspension
655 S. Lincoln Ave.
San Bernardino, CA 92408
877-470-2975
globalwest.net

Gorilla Automotive Products
2011 E. 49th St.
Los Angeles, CA 90058
323-585-2852
gorilla-auto.com

Grant Products
1770 Evergreen St.
Duarte, CA 91010
800-952-6947
grantproducts.com

Hedman Hedders
12438 Putnam St.
Whittier, CA 90602
562-921-0404
hedman.com

Hella
201 Kelly Dr.
Peachtree City, GA 20369
734-414-0900
hella.com

Hurst
100 Stony Point Rd., Ste. 125
Santa Rosa, CA 95401
707-544-4761
hurst-shifters.com

Ididit
610 S. Maumee St.
Tecumseh, MI 49286
517-424-0577
ididitinc.com

Inland Empire Driveline
4035 E. Guasti Rd., Ste. 301
Ontario, CA 91761
909-390-3030
iedls.com

JBA Exhaust
440 E. Arrow Hwy.
San Dimas, CA 91773
909-599-5955
jbaheaders.com

Jon Kaase Racing Engines
735 W. Winder Industrial Pkwy.
Winder, GA 30680
770-307-0241
jonkaaseracingengines.com

Kenne Bell
10743 Bell Ct.
Rancho Cucamonga, CA 91730
909-941-6646
kennebell.net

Lokar Performance Products
10924 Murdock Dr.
Knoxville, TN 37932
877-469-7440
lokar.com

Lithionics Battery
2449 McMullen Booth Rd.
Clearwater, FL 33759
727-726-4204
lithionicsbattery.com

MagnaFlow Exhaust Products
22961 Arroyo Vista
Rancho Santa Margarita,
 CA 92688
800-824-8664
magnaflow.com

Melling Engine Parts
2620 Saradan Dr.
Jackson, MI 49204
517-787-8172
melling.com

Milodon
2250 Agate Ct.
Simi Valley, CA 93065
805-577-5950
milodon.com

MSD
1350 Pullman Dr.
El Paso, TX 79936
915-855-7123
msdignition.com

Mustangs Plus
2353 N. Wilson Way
Stockton, CA 95205
800-999-4289
mustangsplus.com

Mustang Project
300 Brushy Creek Rd., Ste. 403
Cedar Park, TX 78613
800-631-0507
mustangproject.com

NGK
46929 Magellan Dr.
Wixom, MI 48393
877-473-6767
ngksparkplugs.com

Nitrous Express
5411 Seymour Hwy.
Wichita Falls, TX 76310
888-463-2781
nitrousexpress.com

Odyssey Battery
2366 Bernville Rd.
Reading, PA 19605
800-538-3627
odysseybattery.com

Optima Batteries
5757 N. Green Bay Ave.
Milwaukee, WI 53209
888-867-8462
optimabatteries.com

Painless Performance Products
2501 Ludelle St.
Fort Worth, TX 76105
817-244-6212
painlessperformance.com

PerTronix Performance Products
440 E. Arrow Hwy.
San Dimas, CA 91773
909-599-5955
pertronix.com

Powermaster Performance
1833 Downs Dr.
West Chicago, IL 60185
630-957-4019
powermastermotorsports.com

Powertrain Control Solutions
10511 Old Ridge Rd.
Ashland, VA 23005
804-227-3023
powertraincontrolsolutions.com

Power Brake Services
1701 Fashion Ave.
Long Beach, CA 90813
562-394-8218
powerbrakesonline.com

Probe Industries
2555 W. 237th St.
Torrance, CA 90505
310-784-2977
probeindustries.com

Professional Products
2205 W. El Segundo Blvd.
Hawthorne, CA 90250
323-779-2020
professional-products.com

Pro-M Racing
77 Snow Rd.
West Brookfield, MA 01585
336-644-8668
promracing.com

Quick Fuel Technology
129 Dishman Ln.
Bowling Green, KY 42101
270-793-0900
quickfueltechnology.com

Ridetech
350 S. Charles St.
Jasper, IN 47546
812-481-4787
ridetech.com

Ron Francis Wiring
200 Keystone Rd., Ste. 1
Chester, PA 19013
800-292-1940
ronfrancis.com

Ron Morris Performance
1001 Reno Ave., Ste. 2F
Modesto, CA 95351
209-605-1590
ronmorrisperformance.com

ProCar by Scat Enterprises Inc.
1400 Kingsdale Ave.
Redondo Beach, CA 90278
310-370-5501
procarbyscat.com

Snow Performance
1017-A E. Hwy. 24
Woodland Park, CO 80863
866-365-2762
snowperformance.net

Spal Automotive USA
1731 SE Oralabor Rd.
Ankeny, IA 50021
800-345-0327
spalusa.com

Specialty Wheel
1317 Chestnut St.
Chattanooga, TN 37402
800-959-5800
specialtywheel.com

Speed Bleeder Products
13140 Apakesha Rd.
Newark, IL 60541
888-879-7016
speedbleeder.com

Stainless Steel Brakes
 Corporation
11470 Main St.
Clarence, NY 14031
800-448-7722
ssbrakes.com

SunPro
3000 Apollo Dr.
Brookpark, OH 44142
800-228-7667
sunpro.com

SuperBrightLEDs.com
4400 Earth City Expy.
St. Louis, MO 63045
866-590-3533
superbrightleds.com

Tanks, Inc.
260 Welter Dr. at Hot Rod Lane
Monticello, IA 52310
877-596-3842
tanksinc.com

TCI
151 Industrial Dr.
Ashland, MS 38603
888-776-9824
tciauto.com

The Restomod Shop
2461 N. Wilson Way
Stockton, CA 95205
209-942-3013
therestomodshop.com

Torsen
2 Jet Dr.
Rochester, NY 14624
585-464-5000
torsen.com/home.htm

Total Control Products
8661 Younger Creek Dr.
Sacramento, CA 95828
888-388-0298
totalcontrolproducts.com

Tremec
14700 Helm Ct.
Plymouth, MI 48170
800-401-9866
ttcautomotive.com

Trick Flow Specialties
285 W. Ave.
Tallmadge, OH 44278
888-841-6556
trickflow.com

Truck-Lite
310 E. Elmwood Ave.
Falconer, NY 14733
800-562-5012
truck-lite.com

TwEECer
6311 Holly Canyon Ct.
Katy, TX 77450
832-464-4110
tweecer.com

Vintage Wheel Works
471 W. Imperial Hwy.
LaHabra, CA 90631
714-278-1600
vintagewheelworks.com

Weld Racing
6600 Stadium Dr.
Kansas City, MO 64129
800-788-9353
weldracing.com

ZEX
3418 Democrat Rd.
Memphis, TN 38118
888-817-1008
zex.com

CPSIA information can be obtained
at www.ICGtesting.com
Printed in the USA
LVHW020149070121
675855LV00012B/795